City Centre Redevelopment

City Centre Redevelopment

*A study of British city centre planning
and case studies of five English city centres*

edited by
John Holliday
and with contributions by
NEVILLE BORG Birmingham
TERENCE GREGORY Coventry
W. KONRAD SMIGIELSKI Leicester
FRANCIS J. C. AMOS Liverpool
KENNETH A. GALLEY Newcastle upon Tyne

Charles Knight & Co. Ltd. London 1973

Charles Knight & Co. Ltd.
11/12 Bury Street, London, EC3A 5AP.
Dowgate Works, Douglas Road, Tonbridge, Kent.

ISBN 0 85314 140 1

Filmset and printed in Great Britain by
BAS Printers Limited, Wallop, Hampshire

Contents

Introduction   1

1   BRITISH CITY CENTRE PLANNING by John Holliday   4

2   BIRMINGHAM by Neville Borg   30

3   COVENTRY by Terence Gregory   78

4   LEICESTER by W. Konrad Smigielski   135

5   LIVERPOOL by Francis J. C. Amos   175

6   NEWCASTLE UPON TYNE by Kenneth A. Galley   207

Statistical Appendix   234/5

References   236

Notes on Contributors   239

Index   240

Introduction

THIS book is a record of major changes which have taken place in five
city centres since the war, and particularly during the last ten years.
Whatever the criticisms of post war planning, the achievement is un-
deniable, unique during this century, and likely to stand in the next
century as a monument to the aspirations and values of our society in
the 1960s and 1970s.

The five cities included in the book are sufficiently diverse in their
characters and planning to illustrate differences which arise from traditions, fortunes and personalities, although common social, economic and
technological influences stamp on them the character of the age in which
reconstruction has taken place.

The five have all made special contributions to post war planning in
Great Britain. The inclusion of Coventry needs no explanation; Birmingham has undertaken the most extensive redevelopment of any city centre
not severely damaged during the war; Leicester, Liverpool and Newcastle
upon Tyne are included as three of the few cities which established new
city planning departments in the early 1960s, and brought together
large planning teams to tackle the problems of city planning.

Each chapter on the city centre has been written by the chief officer
responsible for city planning during the period of writing, from 1970
to 1972. These chief officers were preceded by others who made major
contributions to planning; Sir Herbert Manzoni in Birmingham; Sir
Donald Gibson and Arthur Ling in Coventry; Graeme Shankland and
Walter Bor in Liverpool and Wilfred Burns in Newcastle.

Of the five cities, Birmingham is the largest, a provincial centre with
a million people and a heritage of strong industrial activity going back

several centuries. Newcastle-upon-Tyne, with a population of 222,000, is a provincial centre as well as an historic port and heavy industrial area, which has led to some of its present economic problems. The other port, Liverpool, with a population of 606,000 and similar economic problems characteristic of the North, lies in the shadow of Manchester, the provincial centre and Asa Briggs' "shock city" of the industrial revolution. Coventry, a prosperous medieval town partially missed by nineteenth-century industrial activity, has been the fastest growing major British city this century, its population rising from 76,000 in 1901 to 334,000 in 1971, and a city which seized its opportunity after the destruction of the City Centre in 1941. Leicester, with a population of 283,000, has been a relatively prosperous and stable city from medieval to present times, escaping the problems of unemployment, congested conurbations and extensive war damage.

To the planner after the war the problems of four out of the five (Coventry was already set upon a new plan) might have seemed similar; traffic congestion, slum housing mixed with old industries, tawdry corner shops and pubs, and many old buildings unfitted to modern needs. But the speed and way in which the problems were tackled varied according to the traditions of the cities. Birmingham, inheriting Chamberlain's great work of the late nineteenth century, itself stemming from the busy industrial activity of the older Birmingham, began its major redevelopment early, and was well under way in the 1950s. Newcastle upon Tyne, less active and prosperous, with a fine historic centre built in the mid-nineteenth century and with less adventurous leaders after the war, saw no great change until the sixties. The twentieth-century energy of Coventry combined with the blitz, a labour philosophy and far seeing councillors and officers, enabled it to match the activity of Birmingham and add an overall planning conception absent from its larger West Midland neighbour. In the more complacent East Midlands, Leicester, like Newcastle, remained quiet until the sixties. While Birmingham, following London, was seeing the beginning of the boom in office towers in the late 1950s, Liverpool remained in profile a Victorian city until the mid-sixties, although capped by Gilbert Scott's twentieth-century anglican cathedral. In Liverpool a political change was the trigger for its redevelopment.

The introductory chapter attempts to set the scene for post war planning in Britain and to assess change in the five cities and in city centre functions. Although in the public eye the planner is seen as being responsible for the changes which have taken place, his influence is often very limited. The changes in retailing structure, the growth of office employment and the use of the motor car, the forces of speculation; all these are outside his control. His influence may be strong but changes would have taken place in any case, particularly as much of the fabric of our city centres was obsolete. But the post-war planning legislation gave new and unique opportunities for initiating and controlling development and the five studies show the extent to which these were taken.

The book attempts to show some of the underlying forces at work, but contemporary studies are bound to suffer from a lack of historical perspective and a limit on political and personal comment. Nevertheless, I believe that the studies are valuable documents in their own right, and I am grateful to the five busy men who responded to my invitation to provide a record of some of the most important developments which have taken place in post-war British planning. Criticism of planners has been heavy and in retrospect some will be seen to have been valid. But criticism is only valid if it really understands the climate of events at the time and the spirit of the age. We live in a materialistic world where big business and profits often count for more than the finer things in life. History must judge whether the planners, politicians and others involved in the rebuilding were able to raise some of their efforts to the level of art in city building.

J.C.H.

I
British City Centre Planning

Change in cities is the result both of social, economic and technological forces at work in society and of particular local forces and physical factors within the city. The planner must work with both sets of situations, taking his general approach from the theory and practice of the day, and his particular approach from the local situation. Any understanding he has of the reasons for changes taking place, and the possibilities of effecting change, must depend upon a recognition of both external and internal factors. This chapter attempts to provide a framework for the particular changes discussed in later chapters, and in addition looks at the changing functions of city centres.

The nineteenth century saw the growth of the large industrial city under the forces of new production methods, the railways and rapidly expanding populations. Over the century, rates of population increase of over 40% in a decade were common in the cities described in this book. In Birmingham the population increased by nearly 150,000 between 1861 and 1871. In every city, similar-looking houses, railways and factories were developed to meet new demands. This was the physical evidence of social, economic and technological change. But within every city particular factors influenced the new development, so that Liverpool's importance as a port gave rise to spectacular warehousing and office developments, and Newcastle's cramped riverside location, in association with the drive of three men, gave rise to the development of a new city centre.

The general problems and characteristics of the Victorian cities led to general condemnation and legislation and to the application of standard remedies for their improvement. In particular, sanitary and housing

4

legislation which eventually led to twentieth-century planning legislation designed to control land uses and structures in the towns. The nineteenth-century statutory requirement that certain local authorities should appoint engineers and medical officers of health gave rise to particular attitudes towards the development and control of towns and cities, and emphasised the problem areas of roads and slums, an emphasis which continued into the post second world war period and eventually resulted in much criticism. Liverpool in particular developed a strong public housing movement, and Birmingham an expertise in road planning and traffic management. Investment and development in the Victorian city centre was largely left to private enterprise, and problems of multiple land ownership made comprehensive planning difficult but not impossible, as Chamberlain showed in Birmingham.

Change in the interwar period was characterised by the growth in the use of the motor vehicle, the attack on slum housing, the domination of the high streets by the new chain and multiple shops, and by the gradual removal of industries. The changes in retailing resulted in a good deal of rebuilding and in the consolidation of ownerships, so preventing the rebuilding of many of these properties in the post-war period. The clearance of slums was carried out under Housing Acts, and most of the land was redeveloped with public housing. (It was not until the 1944 and 1947 Town and Country Planning Acts that local authorities were able to develop such areas extensively for other uses.) The old relationship of railway and industry began to diminish as the use of motor vehicles and electric power developed. In Coventry many of the early car manu-facturers moved out of the central area to bigger sites at the edges of the city.

The car was beginning to become a problem in city centres, although it was still relatively easy to park in the main shopping streets. But already, in the thirties, Birmingham had an effective if notorious one-way traffic management scheme (the same city had produced one of the only two very early town planning schemes prepared under the 1909 Town Planning Act). Herbert Manzoni as City Engineer was responsible for a great deal of road building, and the acceptance of the importance of this work prevailed after the war, when Birmingham's city centre proposals were largely road proposals.

Three major reports published between 1940 and 1942 set the scene for post-war planning legislation, they were the Barlow (1940), Scott (1942) and Uthwatt (1942) Reports. For the future of central areas the most important was the Uthwatt Report which dealt with the problems of compensation and betterment. The problem of compensating owners whose land or buildings stood in the way of planned change had long inhibited, if not prohibited, planned redevelopment in existing built up areas. The report made proposals which would not only restrict the levels of compensation but would also allow for the collection of better-ment, that is, a sum relating to the increase in the value of land and

property resulting from development. It also proposed that powers should be given to local authorities to acquire compulsorily large areas of mixed uses for redevelopment, and proposals worked out with Coventry after the blitz provided a focus for discussion on what were eventually to become the Comprehensive Development Areas of the Town and Country Planning Act of 1947. Compensation and betterment provisions were also provided for under this Act, together with powers for the full control of all development. This legislation gave local planning authorities great power and enabled the more progressive to acquire large areas for re-development on a grand scale, and without excessive payment of com-pensation. Although much was eventually achieved, really effective central area redevelopment did not take place until some of the provisions restrictive on the market were removed, and private investment was allowed to play a bigger part in the process.

The Uthwatt and Barlow reports and the 1947 Town and Country Planning Act to some extent represent a culmination of informed criticism and political action in response to the ugliness of Victorian cities. They were the result of a perception of part of the inner city as a place of ill-lit streets, of dirty houses without adequate light, water or drainage, and juxtaposed with sooty factories; of decrepit corner shops and public houses all jumbled within and around the central area; all seen as having to be removed and unable to be dealt with by existing legislation.

A number of different values and movements lay behind the attempt to bring about the post-war legislation. The social reformers of the nineteenth century, and the practical philanthropists such as Cadbury, moving out from the edge of Birmingham's centre to the green fields of Bournville, three miles away, combined with the vision of Ebenezer Howard to produce a new housing and town planning movement. But there was also the modern movement in art and architecture which, for planning, culminated in Le Corbusier's passionate pleas between the wars and after, for new cities of glass towers, verdure and segregated vehicular and pedestrian traffic. And there were also the advocates of the apparent merits of medieval and renaissance cities, precursors to the post-war townscape movement. The common values held by these diverse groups were light, air, open spaces, beauty and the creation of fine cities. To achieve these the chaos of Victorian cities had to be re-moved and, as private developers were largely responsible for this chaos, the public had to be entrusted with its replacement and strong legislation made available to local authorities.

In fringe central areas the need to clear slum houses provided an impetus for change and was combined with the apparent need for zoning clearly separate areas of housing, industry, commerce and culture into neat lots. The unquestioned assumption that all this, combined with new roads, would solve the problem was made explicit in the model guide for city centre planning, *The Redevelopment of Central Areas*, published by the Ministry of Town and Country Planning in 1947. A redevelopment plan, it stated, should show "the proposed location and size of the various zones in the central area, the density of building accommodation within them, and provision for the convenient circulation of pedestrian and vehicular traffic". The jumbled mixed uses of the old city were to be redeveloped, block by block, stage by stage into a tidier and simpler looking development, controlled in height and daylighting by the use of the floor space index (or ratio of building floor space to plot area) and by daylight indicators or controls.

The social and economic complexity of the centre was not discussed, the model being perceived in terms of roads, buildings and major land uses. It was an idealised conception, with a faith in the ability of local authorities to achieve change with the new powers given to them, and without any apparent appreciation that the business of city centres was a highly complex social and economic situation. While it is easy to criticise now, the publication marked a big step foward in public planning policy at the time.

The government model of the future city centre provided the basis for official planning work, but its objectives, expressed in dry technical terms, were also expressed in the brighter war-time and post-war consultant plans of Patrick Abercrombie for the blitzed cities of Hull and Plymouth.

Parallel with the Central Area Handbook came another, *The Design and Layout of Roads in Built up Areas*, published by the Ministry of Transport in 1946. This advocated ring roads around town centres but assumed major traffic flows in central streets, with pedestrians using underpasses where possible; it also cited the American example without heeding the warning as clearly as it might.

In the professional journals the ideas initiated by Le Corbusier, especially the towers, continued to be advocated, although in the end it required property developers and a loophole in the legislation (Schedule 3 of the 1947 Act) to bring the tall glass box onto the scene. At the other extreme the townscape movement provided a force for conservation, drawing its inspiration from the irregular and romantic medieval city, sired by early writers and in particular Camillo Sitte (1889), fostered by Thomas Sharp in his cathedral city plans, and exemplified in the work of Gordon Cullen and Kenneth Browne in post-war issues of the *Architectural Review*. These values were held by many architects active in planning, and early sketches of the Coventry precinct show the unmistakable influence of the Piazza San Marco in Venice.

Thus it was in the climate of new powers and new opportunities that the town halls prepared their plans for the rebuilding of their city centres, and the architects and engineers waited to carry out the rebuilding.

THE GOVERNMENT SYSTEM

The Town and Country Planning Act 1947, not only provided powers for planning, it reconstituted the planning authorities, removing virtually all planning powers from the smaller towns and rural districts (about 1,300) and placing them with the 145 county councils and county boroughs in England and Wales, which included all the large cities.* But whereas nearly every county council set up new planning departments with chief officers, Hull alone of the county boroughs did the same. In the other major towns and cities it was generally the city engineer who assumed responsibility for planning but sometimes, as in the case of Coventry, the architect. This meant that in the cities the values and expertise lying behind many plans were those of the engineer committed to improving roads and services. In some cities he was also responsible for slum clearance and rehousing, although others, Liverpool amongst them, had long traditions of excellent public housing for which responsibility lay in other departments.

The absence of chief planners, who might have brought different values to bear on city centre problems, meant that the development plans required under the 1947 Act were, so far as city centres were concerned, mainly zoning and road plans used as policy documents for the day to day control of development, virtually all of which, including changes of use, required planning permission. But it is interesting to note that neither the fact of Abercrombie's plan nor the appointment of a city planning officer were able to effect the proposals for radical change in the blitzed city of Kingston upon Hull where local caution and commercial interests led to redevelopment on the old pattern of roads and uses, as might have occurred in Coventry.

The statutory responsibilities for planning were fulfilled by the local planning authorities but the system was strongly controlled by central government. The post-war legislation had been drawn up in an atmosphere of national urgency and confidence in the ability of new legislation to solve the problems of city centres; in giving the lead, and a good deal of the money, central government made provision for approval by the then Minister of Town and Country Planning for all development plans, and also allowed for his approval of significant individual developments. The Act made provisions for public inquiries to be held whenever landowners objected to proposals or control of their activities, and Ministry Inspectors conducted these quasi-judicial hearings, which led to decisions by the Minister. The Ministry's manual on the Redevelopment of Central Areas was only one of a number of advisory guideline documents, and a constant stream of official circulars were issued by the Ministry to local planning authorities.

The preparation and execution of planning work, therefore, was left to the initiative of cities (and counties), but much was controlled by government, and in city centre redevelopment the control was often financial. Land acquisition and major works required loan and expenditure sanction, and in the post-war period of economic stringency, priority

* The 1972 Local Government Act will terminate the comprehensive planning powers of the big cities, placing them within higher authorities for some major planning activities.

went to war-damaged areas and essential works. City centre improvements (unless in blitzed cities) were not essential, and because of the
state of the market little private development took place. Slum clearance,
however, provided opportunities for some road building, new housing
and open space at the fringes of centres, notably in Birmingham.

A further restraint was the need for building licences to be obtained
(as well as planning permission), a hangover from the war-time control
of scarce resources. Controls, high land values and economic problems
all worked against the redevelopment of city centres in the face of the
more urgent problems of housing and industrial renewal. Only the
blitzed cities made much progress, although Birmingham as usual was
busy with road proposals and the clearance of property on new road
lines and of slums. For the local authorities, grants were available under
the 1947 Act to offset part of the costs of redevelopment, but the return
to market values over the period 1951–55 made land acquisition increasingly expensive. A book published by Nathaniel Lichfield (1956)
on the economics of planned development threw some light on the
financial problems involved, but by and large planners were unable to
harness forces to provide a sound basis for redevelopment, and the
country had not yet moved into the prosperity of the 1960s.

However, recognition of emerging change was there, and the Ministries
of Housing and Local Government and Transport showed a revival of
interest by producing a series of Bulletins in the early 1960s, the first
few of which dealt with town centres. In general, however, legislation
affecting central areas saw no substantial changes.

The growing complexities of local government eventually led in the
1960s to the recognition of the need for more effective organisation to
meet the problems of planning and managing large cities. Streamlined
committee procedures, corporate management and chief executives
began to operate in British cities. This movement is discussed in the
later chapters of the book and has been a significant element in changing
views on the role and function of planning and government in Britain.

FORCES FOR CHANGE

The activity of the post-war years and the enthusiasm for planning had
declined in the fifties. Severe economic problems, continuing control of
building, sluggishness in the land market due to the betterment provisions
which removed the profit from land sales, and some disenchantment
with what had been achieved, all contributed. The Attlee labour government gave way to the conservatives in 1951 and the different philosophy
of the new party contributed to the lack of enthusiasm. Between 1951
and 1954 the government dismantled the financial provisions of the 1947
Act. The attempt to collect betterment was abandoned, and compensation
returned in large measure to free market values. But behind this was a
positive attitude in favour of the private sector which in the event stimulat-

ed activity in central area development. In 1954, building licence controls were ended and the way was now open to builders and speculators to seize opportunities for development. At this time the demand for office space was high, changes were taking place in the structure of the retail trade, both the supermarket and prosperity were round the corner, and car ownership was rising.

The story of the property speculators has been told by Oliver Marriot (1967) and typically one of the first was Joseph Cotton from Birmingham. Most of the operations, however, were in London. Ironically, the fortunes of millions were made possible in part by a loophole in planning law. The third schedule of the Town and Country Planning Act, 1947 allowed for the enlarging of a building by up to 10% of its cubic content. The old offices of the big city centres were massive in construction, and had high ceilings. New construction was light and ceiling heights could be reduced. The 10% increase in volume could therefore result in a very much bigger increase in lettable floor space. Marriot cites the Westminster Trust Victoria Street development which resulted in a floor space index (floor area:plot area) of 7:1 as against the 3·5:1 in the planning authority's zoning rules. The only way of preventing this would have been the payment of many millions in compensation. The loophole was not closed until 1963 and even then not entirely, as an extra 10% on the floor space was still allowed. By this time, however, the buildings were up and the fortunes had been made.

The architects of the buildings were mostly not well known and the architecture was, on the whole, undistinguished. Le Corbusier's dream of glass towers was not accompanied by green spaces and high-level roads. But the technology had arrived and over a short period of years every major city had its share of bulldozers and skyscrapers.

Nearly all the early speculation and building was for offices, and most of it took place in London between 1955 and the early sixties. From then on, much of the interest moved to the provincial cities, and the emphasis was on shops as well as offices.

As the shortage and inadequacy of offices and the growth of office employment provided a market for the new speculative blocks, so the growing prosperity of the late fifties combined with changing retail patterns, and led to growth in shopping development. The office boom was in part made possible by the fact that offices were not located in the most central and expensive sites. In Birmingham, many blocks went up beyond the west side of the centre, in the private Calthorpe Estate. For shops it was essential to have a good central location, but here much of the space was owned and occupied by the chains and multiples which had consolidated between the wars. Opportunities did exist in the blitzed cities, where building licences could be obtained, and early developments by Ravenseft Properties, one of the first in the field, were made in Bristol, Plymouth, Exeter and Coventry. In these cities plans were prepared and land was mostly owned by the local authorities who leased it for development. This combination of public control and private interest was later to form the basis of much development in other city centres. With the removal of building licences, opportunities arose in every city where land was available, and Birmingham was the first major provincial city to redevelop part of its centre for shopping.

During the 1950s planners had been much concerned with the amount of shopping space required in central areas, so that the right areas could be allocated in development plans on land cleared or to be cleared of old housing and industry. A great deal of attention was also paid to detailed location factors within the centres. Coventry, Plymouth and other blitzed cities were involved in discussions with chambers of commerce and trade, and with the estates division of the Ministry of Housing and Local Government (previously the Ministry of Town and Country Planning) as to the siting of major stores, levels of rent and terms of leases.

The absence of buildings other than shops from the Coventry shopping precinct reflects the concern to concentrate shops in the right places. In shopping development, collaboration between local authority and developer was often much closer than it was for offices, for the shops were generally new uses on what had previously been housing, industrial or other land, or they were newly disposed according to new street layouts, and control was therefore much stronger than it was in the case of redeveloped office buildings.

The forces behind the development of shops and offices were two major causes of change in city centres. A third was traffic. Outside the blitzed cities new roads were few in the post-war years. But between 1950 and 1960 the number of vehicles rose from under five million to nearly ten, and concern over traffic congestion and safety for pedestrians grew, not that it was absent before. Pre-war by-passes and road widening schemes were common and *The Design of Roads in Central Areas* clearly expressed the need for new inner roads. The level of car ownership in 1960 had reached the stage seen in the U.S.A. twenty years before, and American cities were visited to study means for solving the problem. The presence of the car and the need to provide for it was rarely questioned, in spite of the warnings of Lewis Mumford, and in the big cities the city engineer was keen to embark on road proposals. An exhibition arranged by the British Road Federation at the Institute of Civil Engineers in London in 1959—"Town Roads for Today and Tomorrow"—showed world examples of city roads and expressways with multi level junctions. Of British cities represented only Birmingham envisaged multi-level junctions, noticeably heavy in design compared with those in some continental cities. In embarking on its national motorway proposals in 1959 the government gave encouragement to the roads lobby and to the production of city schemes. Typical of these were the A1 trunk road roundabouts in Gateshead and Newcastle upon Tyne, at either end of the Tyne bridge. With nothing apparently to lose Gateshead achieved its roundabout in 1959. In Newcastle the consequential threatened demolition of the Royal Arcade, part of Dobson and Grainger's Victorian new city centre bought an early example (the argument began in the early 1950s) of what was to become a rising protest against the car as vandal. But in the late fifties planners were still wanting radical change in the Victorian cities. The car, the office tower, and the supermarket gave them the opportunity, but probably few recognised the nature of the fundamental changes in the economics of property and retailing, and in the scale of decision units which were to have such a dramatic effect on the old centres.

THE FIVE CITY CENTRES

A precise measurement of the extent of change in the five city centres is not possible. Apart from the fact that the definition of central area uses is difficult to keep constant over time, measurements of land use and floor space are subject to differences of interpretation and no sets of measurements are available prior to 1951. The appendix gives figures of land use and floor space change in the centres, which, although not all strictly comparable, give a good idea of general trends. Most notice-able are the increases in office and shopping floor space and in land use for transport, compared with big decreases in warehousing and wholesale markets, industry, residential areas and population. The photographs show more dramatically the physical changes which have taken place, particularly the two air photographs of Birmingham, a city centre very little touched by war damage but almost unrecognisable today from the centre of 1958. The larger scale of building complexes and roads reflect the changes in property ownership, production units, and technological advance in building and in the demands of the car.

In the early 1950s, Coventry apart, the physical form of the city centres was little different from their form between the wars. The 1947 Act required all towns and cities to produce development plans (to include a small scale map) in which the centre was to be identified as a set of land allocations each devoted to a primary land use, whether shopping, commercial, civic or other typical central area use. Often a ring road encompassed the centre, and other major roads bisected the area. The differences in what were known as the "town maps" of the five cities (not reproduced in this book) were unremarkable. The other parts of the development plan were a brief statutory written statement of major proposals and a fairly extensive survey and analysis backing up the pro-posals. Central area problems were identified in the terms discussed earlier in this chapter; the problems were seen as outmoded streets and congested traffic, non-conforming uses, for example industry, which ought to be moved, the need for new civic centres, expanded shopping facilities and other standard remedies. One of the specific matters relating to central areas was the use of the floor space index, or ratio between ground and floor space areas. This was a device to be used to control overbuilding and was to become an important issue in some of the early inquiries into proposed office development.

Legislation also allowed for the preparation of larger scale plans for comprehensive development areas, but except for a brief and unsuccessful attempt through the use of "supplementary town maps" to provide a statutory basis for central area plans, the comprehensive development area procedure provided the only formal large scale document concerned with central areas, and it only covered those parts which were in need of major re-construction. Thus many cities had no clear overall guiding plan for the city centre in the post-war period. Only Coventry of the five cities discussed in this book had a complete plan during the 1950s. To a large extent this situation arose from the fact that major redevelopment was not expected in centres which had not suffered war damage. The comprehensive development areas were mainly on the fringes where large numbers of slum houses were to be cleared. Planners and local authorities simply did not expect the major changes which were to come about elsewhere; the idea of solid Victorian buildings being planned for demolition and replacement appeared unrealistic, so that when the underlying economic forces began to move, some cities were caught unawares. It was the appearance of these forces and of the traffic problem which caused Newcastle, Liverpool and Leicester to appoint city planning officers to prepare central area plans. Birmingham had long had a central area road plan and this remained the main guide to redevelopment in that city. Of the five it still remains the only one without a published comprehensive central area plan. It did, however, possess a momentum deriving from traffic and housing policies which made it active in implementation during the early fifties.

At this time Leicester, Liverpool and Newcastle, along with most other cities which had not suffered extensive central area war damage, were relatively static. It was not until the early 1960s that Liverpool, Newcastle and Leicester seriously faced up to traffic and other central area problems, and the importance of traffic as a motivator for new plans is emphasised in the chapter on Leicester.

Between 1961 and 1965 fully documented central area plans for Newcastle, Leicester and Liverpool had been completed as guides to central area redevelopment. These all required substantial departures from the immediate post war development plans, especially in their proposals for roads. Dominant in all three plans (as in Birmingham and Coventry) were major inner motorway proposals with two-level junctions. In all five cities these formed a ring around the centre and had associated with them multi-level car parks. Within the ring the major land uses were allocated, and more detailed layouts were prepared showing individual buildings and associated spaces in civic design terms, although in Birmingham the latter activity was notably absent from published documents.

Variations in the approaches of the five cities can be seen in the emphasis given to various parts of the plan, in particular design for traffic and pedestrians and civic design, using the term in the sense of concern with architectural form. Birmingham and Coventry have tight inner ring roads, about three-quarters of a mile in diameter, with associated car parks. The other cities (later with their planning), have much larger diameter inner motorways enclosing areas one to two miles across. This difference stems from the time of design and implementation rather than the size of the city, the tight inner ring as a solution to central area traffic problems having lost favour to the wider motorway loops forming part of later more sophisticated city traffic plans. The advances in building construction technique allowed cities such as Newcastle to propose radical multi-level traffic and pedestrian movements for major sectors of the town centre, a solution which would not have been feasible when Coventry and Birmingham began on their road proposals.

Detailed civic design was a feature of all plans except for Birmingham, and policies in relation to high buildings were important. The strength of planning legislation allowed for the effective control and design of major buildings to conform to an overall city centre image designed to accentuate or protect critical points and profiles.

Major uses within the five centres are located roughly where they were before reconstruction, with expansion taking place adjacent on cleared housing and industrial land but with one or two major shifts and the emergence of new areas of importance. The critical factors have been land availability, building age, accessibility and conservation. The dramatic increase in office area in the Calthorpe Estate area of Birmingham was a combination of demand and the availability of large areas of relatively cheap but easily accessible land (the Estate is outside the centre proper but lies against a major road), the opportunism of the estate developers and the readiness of the local planning authority to grant permissions. The expansion of higher education in all the cities has been at the expense of housing and small scale industry and is a major development. New road lines have resulted in changes of land use location and conservation policies have tended to result in centres of activity moving to new parts of the centre.

The techniques used for forecasting land and floor space demands have been very variable. Plans for roads and car parks have been strongly affected by the growing sophistication of land use and transportation study techniques, and by the principles outlined in the Buchanan Report (1963) which made it clear that if forecasts of car ownership were fulfilled (as they have been), it would not be possible to accommodate all car owners wishing to park in the centre. All plans, therefore, assumed restricted car access from the new road systems and paid a good deal of attention to public transport. Probably the most categorical statement was made in the Leicester Traffic Plan, which proposed interchanges between private and public vehicles, a fuller use of buses and taxis and hopeful proposals for a monorail and pedestrian conveyors.

Car parking in Leicester is for 22,500 vehicles as against an estimated 67,000 required for full car access. Car parking figures for the five cities are: Birmingham 25,000; Coventry 10,000; Leicester 22,500; Liverpool 30,000; and Newcastle 17,000. These derive partly from forecasts of increased use and partly from policy limiting car access; there is little relationship to population. In no city did the alternatives to the dominance of the car appear.

Much attention was given to shopping forecasts owing to the need to allocate land at stages when major redevelopment was proposed or under way. An early examination of the problem was made by Wilfred Burns (1959), then in Coventry and later the first City Planning Officer in Newcastle. Later forecasts in Coventry are critically analysed by Friend and Jessup (1969). In considering forecasts which relate to private investment the planner is at some disadvantage in not having at his disposal commercial expertise in market research. The problem of office growth is another difficult area, made more difficult by the controls on office building exercised through the use of office development permits introduced by central government in 1965 to restrict growth in the south east and midlands. The tendency for the market to move in waves of office building often followed by temporary over provision, the opportunities for speculation through withholding lettings until rent levels are at an appropriate high level, and the general difficulty of measuring accurately changing employment in offices have all added to the problems of forecasting.

✱The implementation of plans has been a long struggle between conflicting interests: differences of political attitude, public and private interests, the professional values of engineers, architects and planners, and public reaction to change.

The clue to much redevelopment lay in the joining of public powers and private interests. In the days before redevelopment really got under way there was an assumption that most of the change would relate to public activity; to roads and car parks, public buildings and open spaces. As retailing changed its structure and office building developed, however, it became clear that a great deal of the investment would come from the private sector. In the late 1950s a good deal of activity was directed towards the problem of achieving change. Articles in the professional journals were common; a Society for the Promotion of Urban Renewal (S.P.U.R.) was formed; the newly formed Civic Trust became involved and memoranda were prepared by the professional institutes concerned. A great many ideas were aired for the implementation of plans but gradually there emerged a procedure which became common practice and known as the package deal. Whereas development in the public sector was usually unprofitable—slum clearance, new roads, car parks and open spaces—private development was designed for profit and this stimulus often led to attempts to over-build sites and thus to the local authority rejection of proposals.

But it became clear that private and public interest could be combined, and there emerged the package deal, which combined the interests of both parties and in which compulsory powers necessary for roadworks and other public schemes could be exercised by the local authority and opportunities for redevelopment and profit existed for private developers. Before these deals became common, much effort went into schemes involving public acquisition and development, mostly relating to roads, car parks and slum clearance. Government grants of 75%–100% were available for major classified roads, and subsidies for clearance and development in the comprehensive development areas amounted in general to 50% of the net losses incurred. But there were special subsidies for difficult sites and for high buildings, a major reason for the number of tower blocks of flats which were built. All these schemes required central government loan sanction, and control was exercised. The priority given to housing meant that the earliest schemes were mainly around the fringes of central areas where all five cities were engaged in redevelopment in the fifties. The first major road schemes did not begin to appear until the late fifties when Birmingham's Smallbrook Ringway section of the inner ring road was combined with a major office and shopping re-development to provide an impressive example of what could be done (see p. 62, top). This was followed by redevelopment at the Bull Ring in Birmingham, the old market centre, on the line of the inner ring road and at the edge of the central shopping area. A full account of this scheme is given by Oliver Marriot. It was one of the early package deals in which the local authority stipulated the demands in terms of shops, car park, bus station and other uses, and invited tenders and offers of ground rents, leaving the design and the decisions on shopping space to the developers. Tenders were received at the end of 1959 (Laing were the winners) and the scheme was opened in 1964. It has now been linked with a massive redevelopment at New Street Station to provide one of the largest com-plexes in the country. The Bull Ring, however, ran into serious trouble in the letting of shops, partly due to its location and partly to the complexity of the design which was at five interlocking levels.

St. John's in Liverpool is a later example of a similar type and scale, and the whole process of combined activity between public and private interest has been a major force for development in planning. The problems, however, are extremely complex and partly dependent on political attitudes. In contrast to the major redevelopments is the Leicester market scheme where similar large-scale redevelopment was proposed after acquisition of a number of properties by a development company. As Smigielski describes, in the chapter on Leicester, strong opposition grew from stall-holders and other shopkeepers and the scheme eventually gave way to one of rehabilitation and conservation by the city. Marriot mentions in his book that most of the major shopping redevelopments came from Labour controlled councils who were more concerned with the image of their cities than the interests of conservative small shopkeepers. Certainly the schemes illustrate the differences of political approach and the problems of conflicting interest that lie within a council and which are mentioned by Amos in his chapter on Liverpool. These conflicts can be found in almost every city, although Coventry provides an exception with its clear vision of the future after the blitz; a vision not only of Donald Gibson and his plan but of a labour council which saw the need for public ownership of commercial land and the opportunity for profits from rents to be paid into the public purse. The attitudes are forcefully conveyed in the memoirs of George Hodgkinson (1970), a member of the Council since before the war, and an account of the early work in Coventry is given by Percy Johnson Marshall (1965).

It is difficult superficially to detect the influence of politics on the physical structure of a city, but perhaps the clearest indication is the degree of municipal control of planning, and from this the imposition of an overall concept on the form of the city. Paris and Amsterdam show the effect of early municipal control and influence on their form, and so does the "new town" of Victorian Newcastle. On the other hand Liverpool, before its replanning, showed much less order in its form, and in fact it was less comprehensively planned and controlled than the cities just mentioned. The difference lies in the corporate responsibility exercised, and the interpretation of this responsibility lies with the council and its officers. The officers concerned with the five cities have clearly influenced the form of development. In Birmingham Herbert Manzoni's expert technical advice on roads fitted a city more interested with getting things done than with the finer arts of civic design. In Leicester Konrad Smigielski, a noted designer, has imposed high standards upon an undistinguished central area. Coventry's famous choice between the plans of the city engineer and the city architect, plans revolving round a traditional trafficked centre or a pedestrian precinct, came down on the side of the latter and put Coventry into the international planning scene.

With redevelopment well under way new problems emerged. In the mid-sixties it was becoming apparent that the city centre, in some places at least, had less activity at night. This was put down to the decline in population caused by housing clearance, but it was also a result of changes in scale in property ownership, use and construction.

Whereas before many small properties existed in back streets and on the fringes of centres where flats were to be found above commercial premises, and whereas a number of small scale activities were to be found after shops and offices had closed, the new big ownerships and expensive-to-rent comprehensive redevelopments had pushed these uses elsewhere or eliminated them altogether. Perhaps most of the activity was in the zone of transition at the edge of the central area proper, but this was in process of clearance and redevelopment for new housing or educational purposes where old pubs, clubs, cafes and other untidy and perhaps seedy uses were not thought desirable by planners and city fathers. But cities need cheap inner properties if they are to encourage entrepreneurial activity, and with more sympathy and understanding redevelopment could have allowed for the retention of some older uses.

On the other hand, increasing prosperity and car ownership has changed social habits and there are certainly new activities, for example continental and chinese restaurants. But British provincial cities are not noted for their night life, and well-travelled planners often tend to judge them against cosmopolitan European centres in warmer climates. Certainly resident populations in city centres have declined and many cities have introduced proposals to build tall blocks of flats within central areas; Coventry has two as visual stops at the ends of two areas of the precinct and a tower hall of residence for Lanchester Polytechnic next to the Cathedral, which when proposed required all the skilful persuasion of Arthur Ling, then City Architect and Planning Officer, to convince outraged clerics, local architects and others that this was a good piece of civic design.

Another more recent problem relates to roads and may well affect the implementation of the plans which were started late. Birmingham has just completed its inner ring road and Coventry's is due for completion in 1974. But public opinion has now hardened against major road schemes as the bulldozer has continued to drive its way through built-up areas, and confidence in the value of urban motorways has already diminished in some major North American cities.* It will be interesting to see whether Leicester, which has hardly begun, will complete its major inner motorway scheme; probably much will depend upon levels of compensation offered to property owners, or on other financial factors, as discussed by Amos in Liverpool. It is not, however, just a question of resources; opposition to radical change as such is growing and is more clearly seen in the development of the conservation movement.

Planners had long been concerned, some would say overconcerned, about the preservation of historic buildings; but often they worked in a climate of apathy and against commercial forces which led to the destruction of not only single buildings, but whole streets and sections of historic cities. The setting up of the Civic Trust by Duncan Sandys in 1957 was a recognition of the value of attractive towns, and civic societies came into being all over the country. At about the same time the rebuilding of city centres was getting under way so that ironically the informed public as represented by civic societies now turned against the planners for being destructive. An early sign of what was to come was the opposition in the late 1950s to the demolition of the Royal Arcade in Newcastle, part of Dobson and Grainger's new town, and threatened by a major road proposal. This particular battle between the City

* And recently in Nottingham, England.

Engineer (the City Planning Officer had not then been appointed) and local architects, commercial interests in the Arcade and others, continued until the Arcade was demolished stone by numbered stone in the late 1960s with an intention to re-erect it in the later redevelopment. In the event the stones remained untouched and an exact replica was built into Swan House, a major office block standing over the river bridge approach into the city.

Coventry had little to conserve—a word which replaced preserve—after the blitz, but it is interesting to note that what it had was not all intended for conservation in the early planning stages, when a fine row of Georgian houses near the Cathedral was proposed for demolition by the planners. Sometimes Coventry's attitude has perhaps tended to preservation rather than conservation, as shown by its current proposal for re-erecting medieval buildings at Spon End; in the meantime most of its more valuable buildings connected with the ribbon trade and the early bicycle and car industries have gone. Birmingham is another West Midland city which has been more inclined to rebuild than conserve; but Borg shows that conservation attitudes are now evident in that energetic city in relation to Colmore Row.

Leicester, Liverpool and Newscastle upon Tyne have all faced major conservation problems and come under attack for allowing historic areas and buildings to be demolished. However, while powers for protecting buildings are strong, only money will in the end keep them up, and where owners have allowed them to deteriorate or commercial pressures demand changes of use, their retention is often very difficult. But the use of firm control has been effective. In Liverpool the main Victorian banking street is being conserved, following refusal to allow demolition of old property and its replacement with a tall block. In Leicester similar pressures were resisted in the Market place. In Newcastle, with its heritage of the Victorian New Town, problems of redevelopment have been very difficult and the Council has been strongly criticised for the destruction of Eldon Square, a fine Georgian development. For cities such as Newcastle, the influence of the conservation movement seems certain to result in a shift of new commercial activity away from the historic areas, a trend discussed later in this chapter.

Whatever the judgement on the success or failure of rebuilding the extent cannot be denied. The figures on pages 47 and 85 show the extent of change in Birmingham and Coventry. In Birmingham capital investment in new building in the central area since 1945 has been over £200 million. Capital expenditure on public buildings, roads and other works in Coventry and Birmingham is well over £30 million for each city, in Birmingham the majority being spent on the ring road. A large amount of public money has come from central government and the nature of central grants must have influenced the choice and extent of development; this has been especially significant for major roads.

How much of the change is attributable to planning, and how much might have taken place in any case? To what extent are the centres different from pre-war centres and to what extent is planning responsible for these differences?

There is no doubt that considerable rebuilding would have taken place without new planning legislation. Roads would have been built under highway powers, slums cleared under housing powers, and shops and offices built by private enterprise. The experience of London's office building suggests that major land consolidations and developments would have taken place without the need for public compulsory purchase powers.

But the major redevelopment schemes combining road and building development could not have come about at the scale achieved without the powers of the Town and Country Planning Acts. The gap between redevelopment carried out purely for profit and that carried out to provide for a non-profitable public need would have been too great to allow effective partnerships to form. The powers seen as essential to rebuild our old cities were essential to achieve some objectives, in particular those of making life pleasanter for the pedestrian, removing unwanted uses such as factories, providing open spaces and raising standards of design.

The Coventry solution for catering for the pedestrian could only be possible with a blitzed or new town (although only Stevenage of the first wave new towns proposed and achieved it). At the other extreme Birmingham has been content to build pedestrian subways on a large scale, some quite successfully forming small shopping areas of their own below the main shopping level, others desolate and windy. In the other three cities comprehensive upper level pedestrian ways have been planned, linked to existing or proposed ground levels, and in parts of these cities the 1970s will see the emergence of quite large pedestrian systems above the traffic routes. Planning powers were not always sufficient for these proposals and Liverpool had to secure private powers to reinforce them. The ideal of a traffic-free city centre has certainly led to new systems which we should not have seen but for planning powers.

The removal of unwanted uses has also been dependent to a large extent on comprehensive powers for development areas. Not only a great many small back-yard firms, but also many major industries have been relocated on sites provided by local authorities, and sometimes in new buildings. One of the earliest blocks of flatted factories was built in Birmingham to house industries moved from redevelopment areas. This movement of particular land uses in order to clear large sites for new development also resulted in the movement or closure of pubs, small shops, cheap club premises and other low-rental properties which had, together with cheap industrial premises, provided accommodation for new activities wishing to establish themselves in central areas.

There is no doubt that the major rebuilding has achieved the clearer-cut use zones which were advocated as desirable after the war, but it has also deprived the centre of some of the opportunities and variety that it had before. Certainly the loss of old loved pubs and useful small shops has contributed to the public outcry against major redevelopment and helped on the conservation movement. Some of the change would have taken place in the workings of the private market, but planners must take responsibility for the extent to which this clearing up of the old city has gone. The major redevelopment scheme is much easier to design without accommodating the awkward few old buildings which could provide the historic continuity and character that is now lacking in many areas.

Better design, of course, was one of the major objectives in the new planning, but design was often seen only in terms of new building rather than a more sophisticated form of design which would have included rehabilitated buildings. Here the values of the architect as distinct from the engineer resulted in a wish to build exciting new city forms. There is no doubt that the introduction of architectural values into city centre redevelopment has raised standards in general. Newcastle has been at pains to employ the best architects for its most prominent new buildings, and in general much greater attention to detail within city centres has been a result of the planning movement where architects have been in senior public positions. But perhaps Smigielski, a committed city designer, has achieved a better balance of old and new in Leicester, a city with little architectural heritage from Victorian and earlier days, and so unattractive to some that a nineteenth-century Polish compatriot, Leon Szadurski published a pamphlet in Leicester in 1847 describing the poor appearance of the town and suggesting that the Corporation should borrow £6,500,000 from the Government, build a new town to the south and let the old one fall down (Temple Patterson, 1954). Smigielski's efforts against both developers and architects wishing to demolish excessively and rebuild too monumentally are resulting in a city centre which will grow in attraction.

The image of the city centre as a reflection of the values of city councillors and officers has always presented a mixture of the need to present a centre of obvious commercial prosperity and also of traditional historic values, cultural activities and an appearance reflecting pride in the city. The two things are not easily brought together, especially when it comes to new designs and conservation. Amos mentions the problem in Liverpool, where it is partly a result of commercial interest and caution and partly a lack of sophisticated city values on the part of councillors.

Whether the centres are better or worse than they were before redevelopment depends on what you mean. They may be less picturesque but they also have less disease, dirt and disorder. Some qualities of vitality, interest, character and variety have gone, especially those deriving from those who have lived and worked and owned property in the centre. The big commercial planning and construction units which have come in their place are cleaner, lighter and safer. Planning policies have prevented British city centres from going the way of many North American centres; are they therefore any less vital? I think not, but both types mirror the values of their respective societies.

CURRENT CHANGES AND THE FUTURE

The forces which have resulted in so much reconstruction during the last decade are changing and new responses to the problems of city centres have arisen. The very extent of change has caused the car and the bulldozer to come under attack not only in the centre itself but in its fringe housing areas where rehabilitation rather than slum clearance is now the main objective. The growing conservation movement is concerned with this housing, as well as with the historic parts of the centre. These changes also reflect a wider political awareness, with people much less ready to accept change and wanting to be involved in the process of decision for change; a process long fostered by planners in attempts at public participation and culminating in the Skeffington Report (1969); a document which does not explicitly recognise underlying political changes.

The shopping revolution continues, and as the battle of the out-of-town centre and the hypermarket grows its effect on the city centre will be examined in detail by a great many planners and developers.

Planners are less sure than they were in 1947 and 1957 what the answers are, or whether there are any answers. The canons of free moving traffic, safety for pedestrians and the urban aesthetic perhaps now look a little too simple. In their place is slowly emerging a recognition of the social and economic complexity of cities and of our ignorance about how to manage them. Economists, sociologists and others are beginning to get involved in a problem which they have neglected and left to the planners for too long. But it may be that the extent of reconstruction will soon reduce some of the attention which has been given to city centres since the war.

Although Buchanan made it very clear that cities would have to choose between cars, historic centres and other desirable things, it is only from our own experience—it seems that evidence from across the Atlantic is not strong enough to provide a political movement at home—that a political movement against the car and road is growing. The forces behind it come from those whose homes or environment are destroyed, from those who object to the demolition of historic buildings, and from those who deplore the loss of variety from the centre caused by the motorways and big business and of whom Jane Jacobs (1962) is the best exponent.

There seems to be little doubt that the inner expressway has seen its peak. Official exploration of the problem has moved through the range of monorails, new underground rail systems, small cars (Ministry of Transport 1967), minibuses and special bus routes and various never-

stop tube and tracked public vehicle systems. But public transport—
not fully considered by Buchanan—has continued to lose money and
passengers in almost every city. However, there has been some achievement. Only buses are now allowed in main streets in a few towns and
Liverpool's underground rail loop is due for completion in the mid-
seventies. The political response to the problem is interesting. With an
eye on the car-owning public and central commercial interests there
has been a steadfast refusal to make statements about restricting the car
until recently, although a process of restriction has been taking place,
for example through central area parking policies. But as Plowden
(1971) has fully explained, there has never been any adequate policy
in relation to the motor car. Manufacturers produce vehicles without
any responsibility for roads and car parks, and road policy and finance
is not related to motor vehicle production. The role of the engineer in
the Ministry of Transport and some cities has not helped. Public reaction
is now shifting political opinion. Once faced, the problem will be to
develop more efficient public transport systems and the Leicester park-
and-ride proposals are one possibility; that city has an exceptionally
successful municipal bus service. One of the problems in the past has been
to think too much in terms of physical change of the road system. But
better management of our road space, with the use not only of buses but
also of improved taxi services, could cater for larger public movements.
Other solutions could come from more research and development on
new transport systems.

Opportunities have been missed in the reconstruction process. The
old pattern of small private ownerships against street frontages is giving
way to a new pattern of large private and public ownerships at various
levels. This would have allowed a reconsideration of the transport
function, as it has allowed a redesign of pedestrian ways. The Coventry
proposal to link ring road to roof-top and other car parks direct indicated
what could be done with traditional systems. Newcastle has moved ahead
with a more complex development. If such proposals and development
had been sponsored by Government and industry in relation to alternative
new transport forms some of the problems we still face might have seemed
less insuperable. Essentially what is needed in a high value central area
is less use of space by large private vehicles. Methods of taxing private
vehicles for the use of central streets have been researched by Smeed
(1964) and are certainly feasible. But their applications might tend
only to favour the rich and they would not solve the essential problem of
public transport.

It is difficult to avoid the conclusion that the car lobby, the fear of
public reaction, and lack of thought, research and development prevent
effective political decision-taking which could almost certainly result in
great improvements to public transport systems.

Two movements are likely to impede and slow down the large scale
development of new city expressways. In city centres the movement for

conservation, and at their fringes and elsewhere the opposition of residents where their houses are affected. But links to major urban and national networks must be built.

Conservation or the concept of retention with change, which has superceded preservation, a more static concept, has a long history. In this country the preservation movement in towns was based primarily on government action relating to ancient monuments and buildings of historic and architectural interest. All planning authorities were required to take note of individually listed buildings in drawing up plans. But the inadequacy of this policy in protecting historic centres led to the Civic Amenities Act, 1967, which enabled planning authorities to designate conservation areas which could include whole centres and could strengthen control over redevelopment. Britain has now reached a situation where the value of its historic towns is recognised by central government and to some extent by local government. Civic pride in Britain has never matched the civic pride encountered in parts of the Continent which derived from old city republics (as in Italy) or state capitals (Germany), a pride which has led to the retention of many historic areas, or after the war to their rebuilding in the same architectural style. Similar feelings relating to a city's history and its effect on public attitudes is fully documented in a recent book on Paris by Anthony Sutcliffe (1971). Sutcliffe shows how the persistent influence of Haussman's grand boulevard plans was carried through into this century by the Paris Council, in the face of growing opposition by a public concerned at seeing historic Paris disappearing under new road constructions; and how the resultant conservation of areas such as the Marais has led to a shift in the centre of commercial activity.

Conservation policies now determined in this country will be a major factor in the location of new functions in central areas, and will become literally a barrier to radical physical change in some areas. The centre of Newcastle, having been moved north from the congested riverside when Dobson and Grainger's new centre was built, is now seeing most redevelopment concentrated even further north, beyond the Victorian centre, where new public and educational buildings as well as new commercial areas provide a major focus.

A similar situation is apparent in housing. The clearing of the worst slums and the problems of local communities, including the destruction of their houses to accommodate new roads, have combined with government policy for the rehabilitation of old houses to slow down the major comprehensive redevelopment of housing areas. This will mean that at the edges of reconstructed city centres there will remain many nineteenth-century houses, and where these are large and often distinguished, as in Newcastle, they are likely to provide accommodation for students and small households who prefer to be near their places of work.

Since the mid-1960s planning authorities have been concerned with the depopulation of central areas, recognising the need to retain population if local services, cafes, clubs and similar uses are to survive. Although the townscape movement has long advocated the retention of such uses and of the architecturally undistinguished but lively and interesting corners of city centres, it has failed to recognise the economic basis required to support its proposals; and all the trends to comprehensive large scale ownership and redevelopment work against the townscape movement.

The market in housing seems likely to favour a situation where more small dwellings will be provided in and near central areas. The small entrepreneur with his workshop, cafe, club or other enterprise may find life more difficult unless local authorities take a more sympathetic view of his needs, which are for centrally-placed cheap properties. Traditionally, cheap has often meant untidy, but it is in the nature of many new activities to be untidy, and certainly they cannot afford expensive new properties.

The conservation movement, having been applied to architecture and housing now needs to be more widely interpreted in relation to the whole city so that a greater understanding of the complex of activities is reflected in a more sensitive design approach. Design in city centres has not been well based, if good design stems from a basis of understanding of the true function of the artefact. The atmosphere and form of sociability of the centre is the result of a synthesis of social, economic and physical factors to give the true aesthetic which the townscape movement has been searching for.

Continuing changes in retail structure are a major cause of decline in variety in city centres as supermarkets take over from the small shop. The pressures for surburban and out-of-town centres mount, although no statement of policy at government level, or general encouragement at local level, has yet appeared. The problem is one of maintaining variety and prosperity in the old central areas and at the same time accommodating the demands of supermarkets and hypermarkets for large sites and car parks. In the absence of a clear policy of encouragement to the out-of-centre movements, planners are feeling their way on the basis of individual applications. Early applications at Haydock Park, Watford and Bath went to appeal and were refused by the Minister of Housing and Local Government. The evidence presented by the Department of Town and Country Planning at the University of Manchester (1964) at the Haydock appeal is a milestone in the development of transportation land use models in this country.

The difficulty for policy formulation in this area is the usual one where private competition is involved. There is insufficient knowledge and information for planners to assess likely future investment and expenditure patterns with sufficient accuracy to ensure that, for example, the old centre will not suffer seriously if new out-of-centre developments are encouraged. But on the other hand encouragement of investment and expenditure in the old centre can be disastrous for conservation policies. The conservation study for York prepared by Lord Esher (1970) with a technical appendix by Nathaniel Lichfield on economic problems is perhaps the best available study of the problem. Planners need both a better understanding of economic change in centres and more determined attitudes to conservation. A great many buildings which contribute to the social value of centres are being lost in the name of economic reality and through a lack of appreciation of the necessary qualities which make a city worth living in.

The evidence suggest that conservation policies are incompatible with the redevelopment of shopping centres and that where there is conflict a split in the shopping function is necessary. Both Oxford and Cambridge have dispatched major new shopping developments from their historic centres and the pressures for new countryside hypermarkets indicates that retailing interests are anxious to pursue policies which allow the car owner the free access which will never more be available in the old city centres. There will be a gradual change of function in city centre shops as surburban centres remove much of the day to day convenience trade. The problem is fully discussed by Peter Hall (1968) who concludes on evidence from Europe and the U.S.A. that Britain's old centres will retain their strong shopping attraction. This may well be so, but success depends upon a clearer understanding of the interactions between transport and retailing and explicit policies which make clear the varying levels of shopping function which different centres are to perform.

Recognising the continuing attractions of both the car and historic centres, and having seen the conflict at work and at least partly resolved in Cambridge, the lesson seems to point to the need to allow surburban and out-of-town centres to develop. Whatever their location, they will never serve so specialised a market as the town centre, and it should not be difficult to encourage the development of more specialised shopping functions in the old centres, particularly with the growth of office, educational and residential developments in central areas. Statistics from Birmingham (not included in this book) show the growth of professional and managerial employment in central offices, and as consumers change so will shopping functions. It should be possible for planners and retailers to come together to consider the possibilities for both conserving central variety and prosperity and providing out-of-town centres.

The principle of controlling shop types, already conceded in respect of the middle class undesirables such as fish and chips, might well be extended to differentiate supermarkets from boutiques, and cash-and-carry from antiques. Not easy, but possible.

The same problem occurs with offices. Their massive growth has been a major cause of redevelopment. But the market itself has differentiated office functions, so that routine activities (and sometimes prestige activities as well) have been housed away from the major city centres. Peter Cowan (1969) has investigated the process of office growth and change, and as understanding of commercial change develops it would appear that more sophisticated controls by planners could be operated. After all, today's land use controls were devised 25 years ago when our perception of the city centre was in terms of broad categories of buildings and land use. Offices are no more all the same than are apes; they need different environments and controls, and we should by now have learned that controls operated by private forces are inadequate to protect our public city centres. The variety of control does not match the variety of activity; in theoretical terms the law of requisite variety provides an explanatory basis for changing planning practice.

The scale of ownership and production in retailing and office development, in transportation, education and other major uses, has been matched by the scale of construction technology in the development of monolithic complexes of roads, car parks, shops and offices designed and executed as single schemes. Opportunities to build towers, high level streets, bridges and underground car parks have been taken. The fusing of public and private resources and the assembly of large land areas has broken down the conventional street and frontage pattern. But these major changes can be questioned on their fitness for the future. A building is a shell for human activities. The tradition of building in brick, stone and concrete, allied with private land ownership, is a tradition of permanence. But activities (and therefore the shelters they need) change, and permanence is a constraint. The development of less permanent and more flexible structures has been neglected by most builders and architects, except where cheap and flexible structures have been demanded by their clients, as in factory, storage and, more recently, some office and shopping developments. In general the new city centre structures are inflexible and they are not always inspiring. The public's imagination is not caught by the rebuilding of our cities; often it is repelled. There is room for innovation in building forms and interiors. Climate control, already in some new town centres and parts of old cities, especially in colder countries than ours, could provide an answer, but we shall probably have to wait for some decades unless more intensive research goes into architectural and building problems.

The function of a city centre can be looked at in many ways. This book is mainly concerned with the evolution of planning thought and action in a period of rapid change, but the extent to which central area functions can be understood by this kind of examination is limited. What are the major economic forces at work, what are society's requirements for the future, and what can planners do to anticipate and meet these requirements?

The economic force of larger production and decision-making units has resulted in the greater scale of ownerships, developments and activities. Land demand in central areas has resulted in changing uses to meet social needs. The age-old central function of wholesale markets has been or is being removed in many centres; similarly manufacturing premises are disappearing, although certain specialised trades remain. The residential function has almost disappeared. In place of these have come the offices, and in the five cities studied, education is a major newcomer. The mass

movement of goods to and from industry and markets has given way to
the mass movement of people to and from shops and offices. The effects
of telecommunication and motor transport have been to ease the movement out of non-essential uses, but not radically to change some basic
functions. Government, business, banking, retailing and entertaining
remain. On the whole, planners have followed and encouraged much of
this change. In the process they have been party to changes which some
sections of the public now deplore, and which some planners themselves
now deplore. But physical change takes time, and once proposals are
initiated it is difficult to stop the process, so that there is inevitably a lag
between new ideas and their achievement. The new social demands
gaining ground, in relation to roads, housing and conservation, for example,
are finding expression in changing planning policies. But such policies
are often in conflict with economic forces. The financing of shops and
houses may not fit easily into new perceptions of what is required. The
planner often works against private economic interests—the forces of
the market—and in the process changes the nature of the market through
public intervention. His powers of statutory control over development
enable him to do this. By identifying new social needs he can begin to
exercise control to bring about the desired change. His function is to
ensure that change is to the advantage of the community as a whole.

As understanding of cities grows, controls need to become more
sophisticated. At present the planner works with controls devised for
the most part in the 1940s. They are too crude, a point not recognised
by the Planning Advisory Group (1965), although the group's recommendation led to major changes in development plans.

The planning control function is now extending through all departments of city councils; it is no longer confined to town planning; corporate
management is resulting in the identification of problems which require
co-ordinated attacks from across a wide range of departments acting
through central policy boards or committees.

Physical planning objectives will be objectives more clearly related
to social and economic objectives, and after local government reform the
day of the big city setting objectives and pursuing them on its own
account will be past. Birmingham, Coventry, Liverpool and Newcastle
will all be district authorities within metropolitan counties. Major
decisions about their centres will rest with higher authorities. There will
be opportunities to consider central area functions more objectively and
without the same conflicts between local commercial advantage and
social function, but at the same time local tradition and pride may result
in some loss of enterprise.

In the evidence of change in city centres there is nothing to suggest
that they are losing their vitality or power to attract. Nothing is replacing
them as the nodal point for human interaction. Sheer density of people
continues to be of vital importance. This is not to deny Webber's non-
space urban realm (Webber, 1964), but to confirm that Mumford's

city as a cultural force continues. Its attraction for the young and active provides it with continuing energy. The overall function of the centre remains as the intelligence centre for society. What it has lost is much routine service and production which does not contribute to advancement. What it has gained is an increase in new contributors to society's evolution and wealth, in particular government, business and education.

The interaction of land and transportation networks are resulting in the emergence of new centres of activity which would previously have been located in city centres. But sometimes their development is sporadic, and clear concepts of the future function of these areas and old centres have not emerged. Policies on public transport remain weak in comparison to the forces exercised by the private car. We need new visions of our centres as radical as Coventry's if the social values of city centres are to grow at the expense of private profit values. In the end these can only come from political acceptance, but the signs suggest that this acceptance may be coming. An intensive research and development programme in public transport and building, combined with a clearer recognition of the required variety of activities, could lead to centres which provide greater opportunities for people than ever before.

2
Birmingham

A book such as this, intended to teach by example, rather than by precept, should attempt to establish the degree to which the material that is to be discussed is typical of British provincial cities. It is not to be assumed that British experience is of universal application in the urban planning field, but it may be useful for comparative purposes, both here and in other countries, if differences and similarities are identified. Even though general problem situations and propounded long-term solutions may be broadly similar, differences of method—stemming from historical background and from the influence of personalities at critical times—may affect the success and the total costs (of all kinds) involved in producing solutions. The word "solution" is perhaps misleading because it implies final success; "new situations" would be a more accurate way of implying the continuous interplay of supply and demand in corporate life.

A tendency to argue from the particular to the general is a constant temptation to those engaged in the local government of a modern city. This is not surprising, because an atmosphere of rapid and continuous change demands the application of energy and judgment to immediate problems—many of which may appear, misleadingly, to be unique. On the other hand, an uncritical assumption, on the part of an author, that problems and progress in the centre of the city of Birmingham had been of the same nature, and of the same order of priority for solution, as in other big provincial cities in Britain, might be dangerous and, if it turned out to be wrong, would certainly detract from whatever value the work might otherwise have.

The general question is whether Birmingham, and other English provincial cities which grew so rapidly during and after the Industrial

Revolution, are cities of a different kind, in terms of their most important groups of functions, from the city of classic reference in planning literature. Are the central district functions more—or less—important than in the traditional city concept? Is employment so disproportionate in volume, compared with other activities, that the nature and the needs of the city centre are fundamentally different? Does the great volume of traffic, carrying commuters and the daytime flows of shoppers, of business people and other visitors, produce a level of operation that submerges cultural and recreational activities.

We may say of Birmingham that it is embedded in a conurbation: that is, an aggregation of substantial towns ("county boroughs", in the British definition—i.e., local authorities having no interposing level of government between them and the central government). Although they draw from the national Treasury substantial sums of money as grants towards many of the functions that they carry out, in effect as agents of national policy, yet, because they contribute an important proportion of these expenditures from local taxation, and because they have a specific right (subject to conditions) to claim grants once they have made a decision to carry out particular schemes or to provide certain services, they are very powerful, decisive units of local government, with short lines of internal communication and characteristics of decision-making that are by governmental standards very rapid. This kind of authority, which has set the pace for a hundred years, is to be extirpated by the legislation that was before Parliament in the Autumn of 1971.

The city was described as "sui generis" by the Local Government Boundaries Commission some few years ago (1961); probably it is true to say that the city *is* unique in some respects; in its size, in a land-locked situation and possibly until recently in its range of interlocking employment; noted, too, for its adherence over a long period to a system of administration based on the "Chamberlain tradition" of municipal government. This applied to the affairs of a great and growing industrial community certain business principles involving specialisation. Responsibility for the development and maintenance of economic and social development was placed on a single, powerful local government unit. The provision and maintenance of highways, of water supply, of drainage, of power; control of public health inspection and education, was seen, a century ago, as the means of providing the essential mechanism that would enable the resources of private enterprise to operate for the production of enormous commercial benefits—some part of which would flow back to a continuing community, in order to supply new services and to modernise others.

HISTORY AND GROWTH

Twenty-five years ago, the central district of the city was small in relation to the total populations served; however, it supported high-class retail

CITY CENTRE OF BIRMINGHAM 1943
STREET PATTERN, PRINCIPAL BUILDINGS
AND PROPOSED INNER RING ROAD

1 TOWN HALL
2 COUNCIL HOUSE
3 LIBRARY
4 MIDLAND INSTITUTE
5 GENERAL POST OFFICE
6 COUNCIL HOUSE EXTENSION
7 THEATRE ROYAL
8 CHAMBER OF COMMERCE
9 BIRMINGHAM CATHEDRAL
10 MARKET HALL
11 NEW STREET STATION
12 SNOW HILL STATION
13 ST. CHADS CATHEDRAL
14 GENERAL HOSPITAL
15 VICTORIA LAW COURTS
16 CENTRAL HALL
17 ST. MARTINS CHURCH

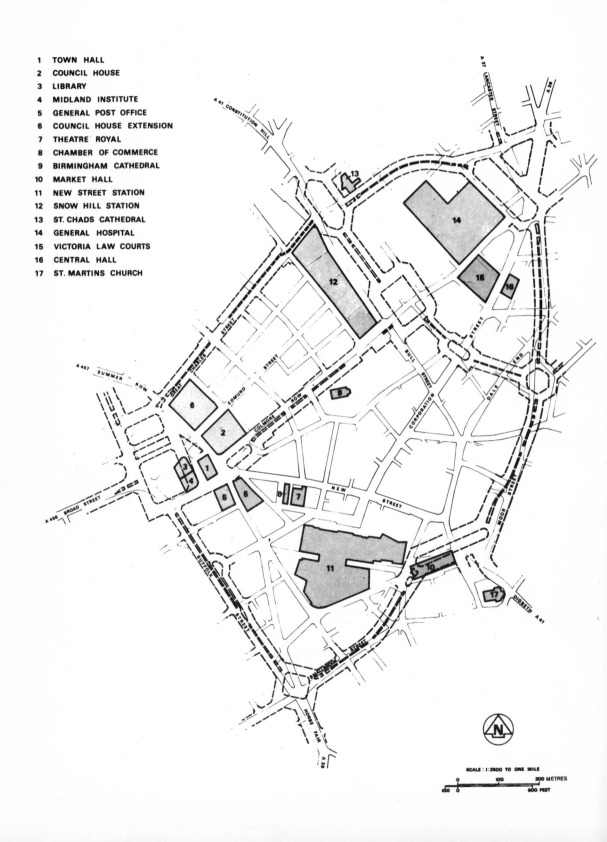

SCALE : 1:2500 TO ONE MILE

shops of some regional importance, and two main and several smaller
railway stations. It was served by two very large bus undertakings, one
owned by the city and the other, providing regional services, owned by
a company; it had one of the finest provincial museums and art galleries;
a Public Library, unique in some of its departments; certain amateur
cultural groups; a particular interest in a famous local live theatre, and
an intellectually strong, if numerically small interest in music. The city
itself had an airport, a water supply drawn from the mountains of
Wales, eighty miles away, and schools which supplied a fair proportion
of undergraduates to the national universities; it had an active political
life, in which competition for seats on the City Council was always
strong.

On p. 32 can be seen the locations of some important buildings carried
out between the years 1830 and 1891. These include, in order, Town
Hall (1832–39), Council House, Library and Midland Institute, main
Post Office buildings, Council House Extension, Theatre Royal, Chamber
of Commerce building (formerly an hotel, now removed to Edgbaston),
the Market Hall in the Bull Ring (burned out in an air raid in 1940,
and demolished during redevelopment after the war), and the two
stations.

Apart from the small extent of the main retail shopping area, and the
limited number of major departmental stores, the conclusion is that, on
the whole, although there were differences of emphasis, the city centre
of Birmingham was similar, in essential functions at that time, to those
of other large provincial cities having a regional importance. The small-
ness of the shopping area in the central district was attributed to the
relatively short distance from London, the capital, about one hundred
and twenty miles to the south; the larger shopping centres of other cities
were ascribed mainly to a greater immunity from that competition. In
addition, there was a more generalised impression that the socio-economic
characteristics of the population played a distinctive, if hitherto un-
measured, part in restraining the size of the shopping centre. It had been
remarked that, although there were fewer overt signs of numerous large
personal fortunes than in the other industrial cities, the peaks of general
prosperity over the years had been higher and more sustained, and the
troughs had been less pronounced than in most other towns (in particular,
during the depression of the late twenties and mid thirties). This situation
was taken also to conduce to an absence of "prestige" shops, but to a
comfortable, if more modest, level of central shopping than in other big
cities. That there were other influences on this condition did not become
clearly apparent for some years; these will be mentioned later.

There was one other feature—abstract rather than material—that
may well be held as characteristically important, that is the absence of

Opposite: 1. Proposed inner Ring Road, 1943, showing important buildings.

developed formality of planning for the city centre in the years immediately following the 1939–45 war; that is interesting in a city that was amongst the first to embrace the very earliest planning legislation. As in earlier periods, enormous attention was paid to identifying and defining what might be regarded as the key planning schemes, to securing the legislative approvals and local powers; above all, to securing enough land to give plenty of elbow room for future flexibility. This was a difference, not of physical scale or of function, but of approach. It was (and still is) held that, in any era, there is a very limited number of essential problems whose solution will allow scope for a large number of subsidiary agencies to develop their interlocking interests.

This approach to urban planning springs probably from a history of need to deal with a sequence of problems, increasing in size and gravity as the city's population grew sixfold in a century. Growth of population was accompanied by rapid changes in technology (that is to say, by increases in power consumption and in consequential levels of physical and social activity). Consciousness of a history of social problems solved, and of a maintained local prosperity, was likely to commend to the City Council the virtues of the methods by which these successes had been gained. Clearly, in the post-war situation, the need to seek the solution of "problems" was bound to favour planning that concentrated first on successful function and very little on the control of more obvious matters such as building form.

Some few years ago one publication commented on Birmingham's "resistance" to planning. This was a misconception about what a city, in a particular situation, could regard as the most important aspects of planning.

Before the Borough of Birmingham was incorporated in 1838, under the Municipal Corporations Act of 1835, Birmingham and various townships such as Duddeston, Bordesley, Deritend, and Edgbaston were close neighbours, and have since combined to become the city that is now the largest component authority of the Midlands conurbation. In 1838, their total population was about 180,000 (it was, in 1946, more than one million). Each had a shopping centre—in a "High Street", or its equivalent. Birmingham, which then contained practically no buildings of substantial civic importance, and none that had housed an ancient and continuing corporate authority, became within the next fifty years the seat of extraordinary industrial, social and political activity and, having received a centre of local government implanted almost in its heart, gradually changed character, as much of its area became the central district of the new and growing city.

Towards the end of the nineteenth century, comment reflected some sense of the inadequacy of the city centre, in relation to the growth of a

Opposite: 2. Central Area functions, 1834.

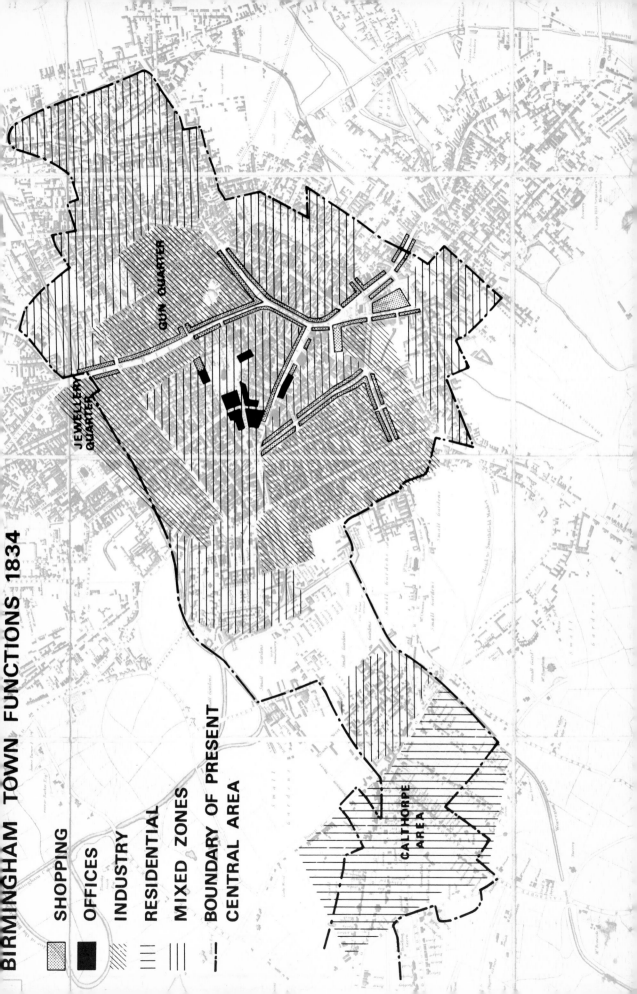

BIRMINGHAM TOWN FUNCTIONS 1834

SHOPPING

OFFICES

INDUSTRY

RESIDENTIAL

MIXED ZONES

BOUNDARY OF PRESENT
CENTRAL AREA

JEWELLERY QUARTER

GUN QUARTER

CALTHORPE AREA

town that was so rapid as to be remarkable even by Victorian standards.
Published material available to the present-day commentator does not
seem to show that many people at that time, including most political
leaders, had an apprehension that, in the middle of the twentieth century,
the functions of a city centre would form the basis of stressful arguments
about traffic problems, "commuter peaks" and the antipathy between
pedestrian shoppers and arterial road traffic. Nor is there any hint, during
that centripetal era (when the agricultural working population in
England was, for a time, diminishing at about eight per cent annually)
of the centrifugal reaction that was to come.

National legislation in Britain, during the nineteenth century, imposed
public duties on corporate bodies for the cure or prevention of insanitary
conditions and of the worst social conditions. These Acts of Parliament
hastened the development of Birmingham's city centre (others also) by
creating the need for a substantial seat of local government. Such a place,
in which political leaders spent more and more of their time, accelerated
a consciousness of the function of the city centre as a showpiece and as
an area of activity, expressing the local virtues and making a statement of
solidity in support of the shop window that was the commercial centre.
In the relatively simple business context of the era, "commerce" and
"industry", although they may have been distinguished for certain social
purposes, were lumped together in considerations of trade, growth and
prosperity.

Most factories were sited near the town centre. A visit to order, or to
buy some product in bulk, would almost certainly involve a simultaneous
visit to the commercial centre for some other transaction. Shopkeepers
knew that, for a certain range of commodities, the town centre was the
only centre. They could expand the range of supply by stocking more
expensive wares, including domestic equipment or commodities that had
been newly-developed or invented; they knew, or sensed, that as far
ahead as they could see the main factors in the growth of a family business,
apart from personal decisions or crises, were likely to be those arising
from peaks and troughs in the prosperity of the surrounding community.

Until quite recently, in historical terms, this town had been less important than several of its near neighbours; it was not to be expected
that the local civic community, developing in domestic peace, should set
about the design of a town centre—still less of a city centre (since most
of them could have had no apprehension of the speed at which it would
grow)—of a kind modelled on any formal precedent. Individual buildings
of importance were commissioned, but there was no obvious inducement
to lay out anything approximating to earlier networks of routes for military
control, or systems of fortifications, including wall and moat, such as
helped to solve the later problems of many Continental cities. It was a
matter of domestic, piecemeal development, according to the proper
local standards of the times, with little apprehension of the intensity of
activity that was to arise from continuous increase in the availability of

energy for production and for transport.

THE EMERGENCE OF THE MODERN CITY CENTRE

The central area, as it is defined on page 42 for the purpose of the statistical appendix, hardly existed as an entity in 1946. The old city centre, not yet so precisely defined as it was to be later for the purposes of traffic and employment surveys and by the location of an Inner Ring Road route, was connected by Broad Street with a nucleus of future development further to the west ("Five Ways"). Five Ways lies within and at the extreme eastern edge of the Calthorpe Estate. This, an area of 1,560 acres (631 hectares) is in the Edgbaston area of the city, and had been developed principally to a low residential density during the second half of the nineteenth century. Some elements of business use existed at Five Ways, which was the junction of five major roads at a point on what was to be defined, during the twentieth-century expansion, as the Middle Ring Road. The general condition in and around the centre had been reached as a result of a series of phases of varying economic activity and municipal decision.

The old city centre itself had begun to assume shape with the construction of the Town Hall (modelled by Hansom on the Roman temple of Castor and Pollux) followed, during the next fifty years, by the construction of the municipal offices (the Council House) and its extension in the early 1900s, laying out of substantial highways, including Joseph Chamberlain's scheme for Corporation Street; Victoria Square, and others. Examination of the phases of physical development in the centre shows that they were related both to immediate ideas of prestige and to the needs that were foreseen to arise from an increase in population. However, the more abstruse considerations arising from movements of population, transportation problems, and secondary growths of employment appear (quite naturally) to have been little appreciated.

During the next seventy years, there were circumferential rings of "byelaw" building, based on the city's development of the highways and of essential services (this was to be the case in the 1950s and the 1960s also).

Poor transport, and the continued existence of substantial populations in a belt around the city centre that, during the nineteenth century, had been the city itself, meant that the first establishment of secondary and other advanced schools was in or near the city centre (the old High School of the Edward VI foundation and the Mason Medical College— which became the nucleus of the city's first University—were already in the centre). Two of them were moved out to suburban areas when it became clear that the demand for accommodation would be great, and must necessarily be met in locations that would suit a population occupying an area of more than eighty squares miles.

The history of development and renewal in the centre is one of movement and renewal of undertakings started during a phase of expansion, but found to be inconvenient and therefore removed (sometimes before the project had even been completed). Some examples are the first municipal houses built in 1892, provided for the rehousing of people disturbed from slums cleared from the area through which Corporation Street was driven. This area, just east of the centre, later became part of the Campus of the University of Aston in Birmingham (the city's second university), and the buildings were demolished in 1971, having just about completed their economic life. An interesting case was that of the Municipal Technical College, which was opened in 1895 in Suffolk Street, near a tramway terminus and quite near the central railway station. Preserved designs show that what was built was merely one quarter of what had been projected as a complete college. Although one street had been closed to enable the construction of the first phase of the scheme, the expansion of secondary education, under the national Education Acts, provided much of the curriculum that the original Municipal Technical College had set out to meet, and it was overtaken by a project for a Central Technical College. This was launched in the early 1930s, and land was acquired at the northern end of the city centre, near to the General Hospital and the Law Courts. After the war, the new Central College was started; it was upgraded to a College of Advanced Technology in the process of cadetship by which some of the new universities were developed, and within a very short time, the massive block which, before the war, would have seemed the limit of accommodation of that kind near the city centre, became merely one element, already dated in appearance, of the new University, which is to occupy an area of about thirty acres and which is already well under development.

By 1950, the City Corporation owned 113 acres (45 hectares) of the total acreage of 695 (280 hectares) within the central area. In 1971, the total ownership had increased to 230 acres, of which 44 had been used for additional highways. By 1966, there had been some reversal of the city's earlier policy of retention of freeholds, whose original benefit had been foreseen as the ability to draw additional and modernised ground rents, as and when the long-term leases, established by the Chamberlain policies, came to an end. In the mid-1960s, the capital debt per head of population of the city had increased to about £200. Interest rates were high, and seemed likely to remain high for a period ahead. The City Council changed its policy so that its sites were disposed of either freehold or leasehold, according to the wishes of the purchaser; this resulted in approval being given to the sale of the freehold of over 6 acres (2·4 hectares), by the end of 1970.

The period between the two wars was not one of great physical activity in the central area. Some modernisation took place in the road network, electric tramways were supplemented by a rapidly growing fleet of motor-buses, and there was a tentative movement westwards along Broad Street, where certain shops of some quality, new to that area, created a link between the old city centre and the subsidiary centre to the west— which began to be spoken of sometimes as "the Kensington of Birmingham". Much of the city's activity during these years was spent in developing the new areas within the extended boundaries, so as to rehouse large numbers of families liberated from old slum areas, and in the provision of the services consequentially demanded; amongst these, road building, water and power were important. The growth of industrial zones external to the city centre and the establishment of many schools in these areas, as well as the characteristic activity of old suburban centres within the city, all tended to reduce the rate of growth of passenger traffic to the city centre, which nevertheless continued to grow in total.

By the beginning of the war, there was a policy, established in principle but not defined in its extent, that recognised successful management of the City would be impossible unless existing conditions in and near the city centre could be modernised. High amongst the proponents of the necessity of redevelopment in order to defeat the obsolescence inevitable in an industrial and commercial city, were Alderman M. L. Lancaster and the City Engineer (H. J. Manzoni), who was appointed in 1935. He followed H. H. Humphries, who had himself introduced certain new concepts (for instance, the Erdington Bypass which, in spite of certain design criticisms, made with hindsight, on the score of a limited re-development of the immediate environment, established in this area a precedent which still forms part of the planning for redevelopment of other local centres within the enlarged city).

During the late thirties, it must have become clear to leaders in policy amongst members of the City Council that the easiest times, in terms of city development, were over. In the future there was to be a much more complex task of renewal and of the proper allocation of existing land areas for purposes appropriate to the needs of the next generation; a strong policy was established for provision of transport to serve a city centre which, it was foreseen, would continue to grow in influence and activity when the new wide-ranging developments on the outskirts of the city should have become stabilised, and begun to contribute their quota of economic benefit.

The traffic situation in the 1930s, although difficult, and complicated from time to time by winter fogs (before smokeless zones had effect), showed as yet only the beginning of the enormous growth of private car and goods vehicle traffic that was to occur from 1947 onwards. The state of large areas of slum housing, not yet cleared, was as bad as had been that of many areas already dealt with. Only a fall in average family size counteracted a little the increasing physical deterioration of the houses, which was soon to be accelerated by bombing and wartime stringencies. Nevertheless, there was an indication of the growing importance ascribed to large-scale modernisation. A scheme of redevelopment for the Duddes-ton area was put out for discussion, and debates took place with groups

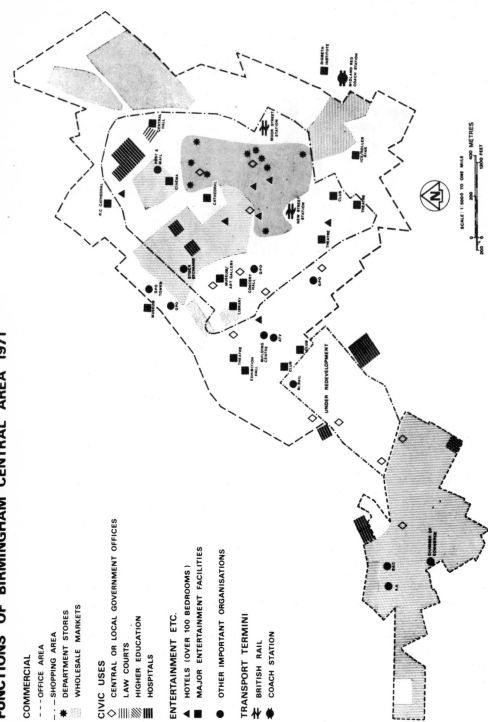

FUNCTIONS OF BIRMINGHAM CENTRAL AREA 1971

COMMERCIAL
- - - OFFICE AREA
- - - SHOPPING AREA
* DEPARTMENT STORES
WHOLESALE MARKETS

CIVIC USES
◇ CENTRAL OR LOCAL GOVERNMENT OFFICES
LAW COURTS
HIGHER EDUCATION
HOSPITALS

ENTERTAINMENT ETC.
▲ HOTELS (OVER 100 BEDROOMS)
■ MAJOR ENTERTAINMENT FACILITIES
● OTHER IMPORTANT ORGANISATIONS

TRANSPORT TERMINI
BRITISH RAIL
COACH STATION

SCALE : 1 : 5000 TO ONE MILE

and with individuals; the city began to practise what, in recent years, has become called "participation", although on a fairly limited scale. When the war came, this scheme had to be suspended, but during the next few years, in the certainty that post-war activity would involve intensive redevelopment, compulsory purchase (i.e., expropriation on a legal scale of compensation) and the infraction of many individual interests, the city took into consultation informal groups which, although restricted in scope, were nevertheless forerunners in a process which has been carried on ever since. The earliest consultation, it might be argued, was of limited extent, in that opinion was taken only from locally defined communities, or groups who might have been supposed to have particular expertise or interests.

At the end of the last war, the City Council, in spite of its preoccupations about bombing, civil defence and other wartime trials, had prepared and discussed certain schemes which it proceeded to launch with what an earlier historian referred to, in another context, as "characteristic energy". Largely in an effort to solve some of the difficulties which Birmingham had experienced before the outbreak of war in 1939, when they were seeking to carry out slum clearance and redevelop Duddeston and Nechells as an area of comprehensive development, the Town and Country Planning Act, 1944 (the "Blitz and Blight Act") was passed by Parliament, and Birmingham (one of the very few authorities to take advantage of it before much of it was repealed in 1947) obtained the necessary Vesting Order in June 1947. This resulted in the granting of powers for the wholesale acquisition of about one thousand acres of slum property, their rapid vesting in the Corporation, their maintenance during a temporary period, and ultimate clearance for redevelopment.

While schemes for five redevelopment areas were being prepared under the 1944 Act, the Corporation were also preparing for the submission of a Private Bill in the Parliamentary session 1945–46; this subsequently received the Royal Assent on the 31st July, 1946. It conferred the necessary powers for the compulsory acquisition of costly sites in the city centre, and for the construction thereon of an Inner Ring Road.

PHYSICAL GROWTH AND DEVELOPMENT OF FUNCTIONS

It is not easy to maintain a constant definition of the "city centre"; the area now so defined, lying within the new Inner Ring Road, contained at one time almost the whole of Birmingham. A map dated about 1834 (see p. 35) shows very little building outside the limits of what is, at present, a business area. The population at that time was under 200,000 and the outward growth, continuous as it was for one hundred years, makes it impracticable to summarise a continuous study of any fixed

Opposite: 3. Central Area functions, 1971.

area defined, for any long period, as the city centre. Growth and change of functions during the last twenty years have now established a much larger central area, whose general influence and range of functions approximate to those of the established city centre. Employment and transportation studies begin to point to a high level of activity within the whole area contained by the Middle Ring Road.

For present purposes, it is necessary to stabilise definition, and the following is a reasonable statement of functions: the "central area" will be defined as the area comprising the old city centre, plus some peripheral sub-areas, and the Broad Street sub-area, plus a principal business zone within the Calthorpe Estate. Reference to p. 35 will show that this boundary reflects the growth westward of the influence of the city centre, and the establishment of what was defined as the "Conurbation Centre" by the Central Government Departments for the purpose of analysis of National Census information in 1961. (The old city centre comprises seven sub-areas, defined for the purposes of employment and transportation survey.)

The establishment of the nucleus of a municipal centre of government in the 1870s, and the development of Corporation Street which, by redevelopment of slum areas, created a substantial addition to the commercial centre of the city, may be taken as establishing a datum against which future city centre growth can be compared. It was at that time that the central business district took form, and attracted the growing functions of commerce, administration and education required for the expanding city. For the next sixty years, development of the city centre involved the gradual displacement of residential and industrial uses by those of principal business, administration, and service employment, as well as those of recreation.

THE GENERAL ORGANISATION AND ADMINISTRATIVE PRACTICE OF THE AUTHORITY

The history of municipal development, of political activity, and organisation in Birmingham has been dealt with definitively by Asa Briggs (1952).

In the knowledge of the existence of that work, it would clearly be frivolous here to pretend to an exposition of the evolution of political management principles in the city. Apart from the danger of superficiality in a brief recital of events and changes, it is difficult, if not impossible, to set out any clear functional relationship between cause and effect, problem and policy, plan and achievement; many decisions were no doubt related to political situations at the national level. Nevertheless, at the risk of appearing to demonstrate a series of over-simplified connections, the development of practice in Birmingham can be summarised as the achievement of all-party agreement on a succession of measures that enhanced the self-sufficient power of the city, whilst conceding to the majority political party the responsibility of method and timing by which that growing influence was wielded.

In 1838, the number of elected members was 65; committees were formed first in 1839. By 1879, the date when the first major council offices were built in the centre of the city, the size of the Council was still 65, but by that date there existed 16 committees with specialised deliberative functions and delegated powers. The decisions to carry out the Chamberlain scheme and Corporation Street construction scheme of city centre expansion, with associated rehousing elsewhere, were taken by City Council on the recommendation of the Improvement Committee (set up in 1875).

By 1914—that is, after one of the earlier boundary extensions, the number of Committees had grown to 21, formed from a Council of 120 members; there were 22 Chief Officers of departments having specialised duties. After the 1914–18 war, there were substantial activities in housing, slum clearance, and later in highways and main drainage works. By 1938, the committee and departmental structure had grown to 34, the Council consisted of 136 members, and Chief Officers in charge of departments numbered 25.

The present phase of consultation and participation by the public in the planning process is, in effect, the re-establishment in large cities of the process which took place automatically in years gone by, when every new proposal was known to a small population and was of immediate potential local concern. In Birmingham, because of the authority achieved by the energetic and powerful City Council and its committees, there was a substantial period during the last thirty years of the nineteenth century and the first thirty years of the present century, when activities were almost all evidently necessary to provide for an expanding or moving population. They produced physical improvements and imposed relatively little disturbance on unwilling communities. It was not until the onset of schemes for comprehensive redevelopment, broached just before 1939 and developed during the war, that it became clear that consultation would be necessary, if only because new schemes would have an effect for the first time on very substantial populations or business communities having interests in the maintenance of the existing local conditions. Consultative procedure at that time involved small numbers by invitation and was limited, in the sense that it was achieved with small groups or influential individuals.

The period since 1945 has seen, together with a growth of redevelopment activity (costing £47 million in 25 years, out of a total of £101 million invested by the Public Works Committee alone), the widening of certain services having a direct social content. Several of the 27 committees and many of the 150 council members had to develop interlocking policies and procedures during this period; the need to explain schemes to local residents produced a practice of local Ward meetings, developed on those first arranged by the Public Works Committee to explain particular projects on a non-party basis.

D

Consultative practice, although developing throughout a period of twenty-five years, has not yet been codified by statute, as it will be required for plan-making under the 1968 Planning Act.* Hitherto considering itself as vested with the corporate responsibility to make decisions and to execute them for general public good, the City Council, and those committees having delegated functions, have made the final decisions about major planning proposals. It might have been said—as it has been recently—that merely to explain to the general public the chosen decision, and to justify it on balance, by informal or formal procedure, did not constitute public participation. Nevertheless, at the time of writing (1971), it has not yet been finally laid down in Regulations that are to be made under the 1968 Act, that the public discussion of *alternatives* is either a required or desirable step. As against the merits of general argument, there is the probability that a prolonged discussion about a variety of ways of achieving a particular object can merely spread the area and duration of "blight", uncertainty and distress, and that the duty of the local government is to govern and to press for the prime objects of its policy, once these have been established on the basis of technical advice and formed opinion.

Writing at a time of local government reorganisation, late in the twentieth century, it is not difficult to distinguish those characteristics of local government in large towns and cities which have, in some cases, promoted rapid growth and, in others, have helped to impose a slow rate of change.

Adverse criticisms of the efficacy of local government in Great Britain, or in England at any rate, have seemed, in the main, to spring from painfully lengthy arguments between warring neighbours—who may have disagreed over boundary changes, or on a major local planning issue, or about the proper apportionment of costs for some common scheme. Probably, much of the gradual accretion of reputed inefficiency (which is arguable—but that is another subject) stems from the comparison of levels of performance between different types of authority— "performance", in the sense of speedy achievement of particular political or physical ends. The approach of different local authorities to the solution of problems, as they saw the need, seems to have varied not only with what might be taken to be the character of local traditional feeling but, more definitely, with the type of authority itself. Distinction of "type" refers to organisational form—which governs the administrative processes; this, in turn, combined with a particular degree of certainty that the necessary resources of political support, of money, or of manpower are available, determines the speed with which decisions can be taken.

---

* For this and subsequent references to the Town and Country Planning Act, 1968, it should be noted that many of its provisions are now included within the Town and Country Planning Act, 1971.

It is axiomatic that, in a struggle between two organisations, given resources that are equal in size and in quality, the one with the most rapid decisive process and the superior system of communications will win the day: so it must have appeared to observers of local government in Britain during the last hundred years. The single-level, all-purpose authorities (i.e. the large county boroughs, many of which were also recently-created cities) used the great powers that had been given to them to attack social problems. Smaller local authority units were dependent, for initiative to deal with many of their problems, on other levels above them, either the county or the central government. County Councils, although having wide statutory powers, could only apply these after persuasion, often long and difficult, of their second-tier constituent districts. In many cases, they did not have financial resources equal to those of the big urban areas.

By 1945, Birmingham had become an experienced, modern city, with single-chamber government, and resources roughly commensurate with the size of its problems. Financially, the Council could rely on a high yield of local property-taxation (the "rates") plus substantial grants from the central government towards the cost of various functions. Administratively, it had developed efficient departments that were expected to initiate and control large capital projects and annual maintenance programmes. Organisationally, the Council practised devolution of much responsibility to committee level.

In the first half of this century, the Corporation, although looking to central government for consents and grants in certain fields, nevertheless developed the sense that initiative at local government level was generally both politically welcome and productive of financial approval, and came to know that, in a pinch, they would be able to deal with most situations, so long as they observed the fundamental requirement that nothing can be done by a local authority without a specific legal power to do so. It became clear that execution of a range of functions, involving a multitude of administrative steps and counter-checks, would soon immobilise the Council, formed of unpaid part-time members, if it were to act both as a single-chamber local forum and a detailed decision-making body.

Expansion of boundaries, expansion of functions and of the prosperity of the town centre, all led to an expansion of problems. It seemed to the City Council over the years eminently sensible to deal with its affairs by a system as close to business management as seemed compatible with control by a municipal assembly. Nothing in the world was more natural to the business community of Birmingham than a strong system

Overleaf: Left: 4. City Centre from the West, 1958: 1. Town Hall; 2. St. Phillip's Cathedral; 3. St. Martin's Church; 4. New Street Station.
Right: 5. City Centre from the South West, 1971.

of delegation, from the City Council to committees, of the statutory functions and powers without which those functions cannot be exercised. Of more than twenty committees the Public Works Committee became one of the most influential because of the wide range of its responsibilities and the consequential oversight of many interlocking programmes or functions. These include the duties of the Council for town planning, providing and maintaining highways, for drainage, control of building regulations, car parking and traffic management.

One well-known aphorism is the statement that responsibility is never given, but is always taken. This, whilst not absolutely true, is sufficiently accurate to make the level of activity of successful personalities in city government surprising, if at all, only in the consistency of application by the large number of people who commit themselves to local politics. Successive chairmen of committees and other prominent members have identified themselves with particular problems and programmes. The example of Joseph Chamberlain was still regarded with respect seventy years later, not only because, in a commercial sense, his judgment had been proved right, but because it was clear that what was done in the way of organisation and management, within the programmes that he took a great part in stimulating, was done efficiently. Chairmanship of committees, particularly of the Public Works Committee, has always been associated with a responsibility for fostering new concepts and choosing new projects.

PUBLIC OPINION: GOAD OR MIASMA?

What proportion of the city's population may have a conscious view of the city centre as a physical or social entity is a matter of conjecture. It became commonplace in the 1960s that most comment about local government activity in the redevelopment of the city centre was adverse, much of it concerned with day-to-day grumbles about dirt and inconvenience, but a high proportion relating to change; it is probably a fair deduction that change in itself is almost automatically unwelcome to a high proportion of people. The loss of familiar conditions, even when, in some respects, they are far from perfect, always excites some resistance.

It is interesting, however, to compare the difference of attitudes towards schemes of slum clearance and comprehensive residential redevelopment, on the one hand, with those towards city centre redevelopment on the other. In the first case, not many of the local people affected by the city's redevelopment schemes, in the inner ring around the centre, grumbled about them as a concept or as a social process; the excellence of motive and the existence of a planning thesis seemed to be accepted. They grumbled about what they regarded as inefficiency in everyday practical matters; some were dissatisfied with the available choice of housing, or the cost of moving, or—most often—about dirt and nuisance whilst demolition was going on. There was comment on costs, on the form of housing, on aesthetics, and effects on the community's spirit of neighbourliness. Abstract, critical comment came mainly from professionals of various kinds: planners, and others working in some social context; it was about theory in relation to the concept of wholesale rehousing or the resultant mass housing production, or about the break-up of a local social spirit which, although existing in some cases only because of shared conditions of some adversity, nevertheless was to be regretted when it was disrupted.

The pattern of critical comment about the redevelopment of the city centre was different. Certainly, there were complaints from local sources in this case also, about what were regarded as matters of practical inefficiency: these came often from central business interests, or from members of the City Council; occasionally from visitors or Members of Parliament. However, comment or question about theoretical justification, or about the form, speed, scale and necessity for what was being done in the city centre, came from a whole range of people, most of them local, who objected to (or sometimes supported) a particular process or some elements of the overall scheme. The fact that much of this criticism was—and continues to be—"abstract" in content, if colloquial in form, seems to indicate that there is a considerable but probably unmeasurable degree of interest in the future of the city centre.

This interest may be constructive, in the sense that the critic is concerned about the success of a scheme, or at least that existing conditions should not be worsened, but also possibly because many of those now speaking or writing experienced the atmosphere of the city centre as children or as adults, under conditions in which it was removed from work-a-day life. It was the place where some form of recreation of a greater intensity, or education on a higher level, was enjoyed. It was the place where the more occasional and larger and therefore more important and exciting purchases were made. It was the place where, during visits for these kinds of purposes, children had perhaps a little more to spend on signal pleasures than they normally had. The shops were bigger and brighter, the range was greater; the staffs in many of the shops had something of an "air"; the Bull Ring was, at times, a wild and romantic place, the Art Gallery was another world. Not many experiences are necessary, at an impressionable age, to form an image which, although it may be physically inaccurate, nevertheless stamps affection on the familiar. Stability, rather than efficiency of function, is the criterion by which a provincial city centre is judged in the affections of the local majority; ironically enough, a different—and silent—judgment may be offered by the same people on a lack of modernisation of retail shopping conditions by the transfer of their custom to more convenient places.

Recognition of a problem by the public, or by their elected representatives and officers, is not always followed immediately by specific proposals for its solution. Perhaps one ought to add to the earlier comment about the apparent reason for impressions of the inefficiency of local government a slowness in making apparently necessary decisions. The reasons for this phenomenon, when it occurs, include the deferment of projects because of a change in political power, a difference in degree of readiness by central and local government, at a particular moment, to contribute their respective proportions of money, and the local unpopularity of compulsory acquisition of property and disturbance. However, an increasing tendency towards deferment of decision almost certainly has its source in matters other than these.

In the city of one hundred years ago, there were demands for "improvement". These, in many cases, went no deeper than the substitution of a better type of paving for an old one, a main drainage system that did not flood and did not leak, and traffic arrangements that could be solved by road widening or by elementary but resourceful redevelopment, such as moving the street market to another spot. The establishment of a reliable water supply was the most taxing problem.

Apart from certain formal town plans of an earlier age, usually undertaken under patronage, the first generally influential movement in industrial England reflected a reaction towards rural domesticity—the garden suburb or model village. These attempts to unite modern building and sanitary standards with rural charm, established the concept that governed planning thought for nearly half a century. The object of town planning became, in effect, to produce compatible neighbours, reflecting what the sanitary reformers had done some years before, and to bring about urban "improvement". It was possible for Birmingham to carry out the Corporation Street redevelopment in the town centre because it was recognisably related to slum clearance and rehousing; the first municipal houses, built for this purpose, provided the key to unlock all policy difficulties; rehousing was understandable by everybody. The implications of the larger purpose were accepted as a bonus.

The difference in decisive speed between the "confident Victorians" in local government and their present heirs is due to the fact that the decisions they had to make were, relatively speaking, child's play; if they had the money for the obvious solution, there was rarely any other significant complication in policy consideration, and seldom any pressure for careful weighing of the economic and social aspects of different possibilities. The function of planning expanded, during the first half of the twentieth century, to comprehend not only design for amenity but the relationships between land-use and other activities and the concept of socio-economic evaluation. The wide differences in effective speed of decision in the "case-histories" that follow seem to suggest that it is those with a supporting element of current, arguable, social effect that achieve a relatively rapid policy decision, whereas the apparently "single-purpose" scheme, aimed at the achievement of efficiency in a single technical or economic field, is subject to the greatest degree of counter-argument and delay.

THE INNER RING ROAD

It was before 1920 that the City Council were first asked to consider an Inner Ring Road; to have carried it out at that time—or within ten years afterwards—would have been a most extraordinary feat. Motor vehicles were few and far between, horses and pedestrians still debated priority at street junctions, and it would have been a bold and powerful man, or body of men, who could have prevailed upon the City Council, during a period of depression and hardship after the first World War, to undertake very heavy expenditure in order to provide for a traffic problem whose scale could not then have been foreseen. In 1917, before the first World War could have been safely considered won, the City Engineer and the Public Works Committee set the City Council on a course that was to produce a major highway improvement programme. Neville Chamberlain persuaded them to establish the first Municipal Bank, ostensibly to assist in saving, as a resistance to inflation, but with what other municipal motives may be guessed. This planning for the future, in discouraging times, was repeated quite remarkably twenty-five years later during the second and even more threatening war.

In the years after 1917, there were no immediate social needs that would have been cured by an Inner Ring Road; true to traditional lines of thought, the City Council put other and more obvious things first—housing, unemployment relief works, main drainage to cure flooding that was both a danger to health and an obvious nuisance.

It is recorded that the first proposal to construct an Inner Ring Road was made after the return of a delegation of City Councillors, accompanied by the City Engineer (H. E. Stilgoe), from Germany and Austria in 1910. The idea of a "ring" or loop seems to have developed from impressions of Vienna, as did also proposals to provide wider streets, offering not only high traffic capacity but amenity also.

In 1917/18, the Public Works Committee recommended to the City Council that widening lines should be laid down on arterial routes, in order to produce ultimate widths of 110 ft. and 120 ft. (33·4 metres and 36·5 metres). The intention was that the setting-back should be imposed at a time of rebuilding, so as to reduce the cost of compensation. Although neither a specific location nor a width was proposed for the Inner Ring Road, a first draft route was suggested, roughly circular, having a diameter of about one mile.

From the early twenties, traffic congestion grew; physical conditions in the city centre became gradually more difficult until, in the thirties, the difficulties of circulation ranked as the greatest single source of criticism of the city centre. The relationships between work and daily travel were becoming apparent, because expansion of the city boundaries to accommodate thousands of families rehoused from near the centre, natural increase, and immigration in years of worse depression elsewhere in the United Kingdom, had created the demand for transport, public transport in particular, for work journeys.

In the middle thirties, the Public Works Committee approved one-way schemes, by successive City Engineers (H. H. Humphries and H. J. Manzoni)—early examples of traffic engineering based on economy in the use of existing resources enabling city centre traffic congestion to be reduced. These sufficed until temporary relief from traffic, during the war of 1939–45, produced a breathing space, in which, as invariably happens, enforced abstention from peaceful, constructive, if irregular advance, produced a pent-up pressure of thought, argument and energy which, when released after the war, was to convince the local electorate, the members of the City Council, and both Houses of Parliament, that Birmingham's central traffic problem justified the granting of legal powers to the City. Again, a few recognised the larger implications of the immediate purpose, although they were stated simply enough by H. J. Manzoni, who had succeeded H. H. Humphries in 1935.

By 1939, when the second great war broke out, no dual carriageways had been provided in the immediate approaches to the city centre, nor had any positive steps been made towards the definition of an Inner Ring Road. The policy of acquiring highway improvement land had been followed energetically in outer areas because, naturally enough, it was most easily available where development on agricultural or suburban land had never before taken place, and where costs were relatively low. One or two major widenings to single carriageways of streets within the centre had been carried out, to improvement lines which were rapidly to prove inadequate.

In retrospect, it is possible to say that it was fortunate that more of a moderate standard had not been done by the beginning of the war, because the delay imposed on the growth of civilian motor traffic by six years of other preoccupations, and by a period of resource rationing for some years afterwards, meant that when production of cars for the domestic market became possible, it went ahead at a rate which began to give some indication of the size of the problem that was to develop; moreover, the prototype problem, across the Atlantic, was available for inspection in a more developed form.

In spite of unfavourable conditions, the one-way street system operated well. In at least one street, motor vehicles ran against the direction of the fixed-rail trams. This situation which, it is fair to guess, would not have been permitted to the motor omnibus, is in line with current thinking about priority for public transport, even by motor bus, in cities at the present time.

Although aerial bombing in 1940/41 produced some clearance on the general line that was finally selected for the Inner Ring Road, the effect was not nearly so profound in its influence, either on location or on the date of redevelopment, as was the case in other cities that were severely bombed. Birmingham had received, after London, the greatest weight of

aerial bombs on a single town in the whole of the United Kingdom—
a fact retailed with gloomy local pride—but the size of the city and of
the surrounding conurbation, with large and scattered industrial zones,
had acted to distribute attack over a proliferation of targets. There may
have been other factors, such as the absence of large waterways and other
target aids; at any rate, the concentration of damage was less than in
Coventry or Plymouth, or in many Continental cities.

The scheme approved by the City Council in 1943 established the
Inner Ring Road line approximately as it had been suggested in 1917,
but with some additions, including the widening of Colmore Row and
the introduction of a cross-connection from north to south, on the line
of Snow Hill/Lower Priory (see p. 32). General widths proposed
were 110 ft., with the exception of Colmore Row, which was to be 80 ft.
The area of land to be acquired was about 66 acres, in addition to the
14 acres already owned by the city on line (26·6 hectares and 5·6 hectares).
The estimated cost of property acquisition, including all compensation,
was put at about £12 million (including the value of property already
in Corporation ownership), and of construction, about £2½ million—£21
million and £13¼ million respectively, by 1971, allowing for increased
standards of design, and increased prices.

In July 1944, the main design of a scheme was approved. It was a
single level, geometric layout, but this lay within an area having wide
limits of deviation, the scope of which, in the end, was to prove the most
important single component to have been included in the Parliamentary
Bill. There was some opposition to the whole idea in the City Council,
and an amendment was proposed that the scheme should be referred
back "on planning grounds" and that additional opinions of town
planning experts be obtained; it was approved, however, provided that
the progress of the Inner Ring Road should not "impair, delay or obstruct
the provision of houses whilst the need for houses remains urgent and
acute".

1942 was the date that would have been saturation date for the city
centre road system, but for the effects of war in reducing civilian production and consumption. In that year, the City Council set up an ad
hoc committee—the Advisory (Traffic) Planning Panel, in order to
consider the expected post-war traffic problems in the city centre. This
Panel (Chairman—Alderman H. E. Goodby) comprised members of
the Public Works Committee and others of the City Council, the Chamber
of Commerce and the local Architectural Associations; it considered
evidence from officers of the Corporation, from transport undertakings,
from the Chamber of Trade and other bodies.

In its first year, the Advisory Panel recommended that a north-south
tunnel would be most effective for the purpose of diversion of through
traffic from the city centre. This recognised the importance of the A.38
route, on which volumes of traffic flowed to and through the city centre,
and which was to play a large part in all sub-regional planning con-

siderations after 1945. (The A.38 was a Class I Route, redefined as a Principal Route in 1967, linking Bristol and Derby. It carries heavy traffic flows and is a candidate for "corridor" growth in current planning studies.)

However, in 1944 they issued a report which recommended the construction of an Inner Ring Road, so called to distinguish it from the Outer Ring Road which was already established as a planning concept. With the report of the Planning Panel, there was included the City Engineer's estimate that the cost, including acquisition of property, would probably be about £15 million. The Town Clerk (Sir Frank Wiltshire) was in favour of seeking Parliamentary powers so as to achieve maximum relief from detailed step-by-step approvals from the various Ministries when the work came to be carried out.

In 1943, the Public Works Committee recommended to the City Council that the rapid completion of an Inner Ring Road was vital to the future of the city centre, having in mind the dual purpose of traffic improvement and city centre extension; perhaps they were guided also, either by instinct or by some unrecorded argument (traffic studies being as yet in their infancy in Britain), to a realisation that many of the vehicles approaching the city centre would not be "through" traffic, and that, in the future, a distributor would be essential.

A record of deliberations and policy decisions is almost always misleadingly undramatic: formal steps in the process of achieving full Council approval to go to Parliament, and to undertake an operation of major surgery on the city centre were few. Debates are summed up in unemotional summaries which do not reveal what must have been a very wide range of uncertainty, reluctance, uncritical confidence or, in a minority, some sober apprehension not only of the cost in money, disturbance and discomfort that would be entailed by this plan, but also of the perceived alternative, namely, that of complete traffic seizure within a small, old-fashioned city centre. This would have had results that, in the short term, would have hamstrung the economy of a large part of the West Midlands Region as a whole, and affected the working efficiency of tens of thousands of people. The long-term disadvantages to the area of a functional failure of the central business district were clear perhaps to relatively few, who had begun to perceive the essential relationship between land-use, traffic and the local economy, and who sensed, if they could not calculate, that the day of importance to shopkeepers of "the carriage trade" was past.

On the recommendation of the Town Clerk and the City Engineer, in January 1945, the Public Works Committee approved that Parliamentary powers should be sought, and the necessary Town's Meeting was arranged to discuss the Bill. There was only one objection—from a local property owners' association—and this was on the score that too much property was being acquired. In December, 1945, the Town's Meeting approved the Bill: about two thousand people attended, on behalf of one million (many of whom, admittedly, were on military service), and the Bill went for successive consideration by both Houses of Parliament. The Commons made no significant change, but the Lords required certain amendments, the major effect of which was to enable property owners and occupiers to retain possession of their property until such time as it was required for demolition, prior to the commencement of roadworks. This was achieved by a form of "option" which imposed time limits for the giving of notice and the commencement of the work.

The outline scheme for the Inner Ring Road, submitted to Parliament, was almost exactly as is shown on p. 32. The Bill was approved, with some amendment, and became the Birmingham Corporation Act, 1946, conferring on the City Council particular powers for acquisition and construction, and relieving them of some of the general statutory or procedural steps that are usually necessary to achieve successive levels of approval from the Government, for the carrying out of a major scheme that qualifies for central grant. Shortly afterwards, the Public Works Department was asked by a developer to define the required ground-floor level of a certain new building on the future Inner Ring Road. This and similar incidents had the effect of concentrating minds wonderfully, to adapt Dr. Johnson, and on the 1st January, 1947, a special Section was set up as an off-shoot of the Highways department—then called the City Surveyor's Drawing Office (this department later became the Highways and Survey Department—since renamed the Highways and Transportation Division). The new Inner Ring Road Section was re-named the Special Works Section in February 1956, with specialist duties extending, at times, to matters other than the Inner Ring Road. (This small section was at the centre of activity not only in the development of the concept of the Inner Ring Road, but of other city centre activities stemming from it. It was led by J. L. Macmorran, whose applied thought, over a quarter of a century, gave reality to many abstract concepts and prudently suppressed others.)

The scheme for the enlargement of the city centre by the construction of the Inner Ring Road—implicit in the Corporation's approach to the scheme—was explicit in the wording of the preamble to the Act, which was:

> "An Act to provide for the improvement of the central area of the City of Birmingham by the construction of an Inner Ring Road and other works . . ."

Twenty years later, this wording was to prove very significant in relation to the claim by the City Council on the Government of the day for a grant towards the cost of the scheme. There was no question of doubt in the city's mind at that time about the permanent continuity of function of the city centre—it had been; it was; and it would be—although note was being taken of centrifugal tendencies in American cities. It is fair to say that this process, although feared, was judged to be unlikely in Britain, because of the relative tightness of the planning code, springing mainly from the limited supply of land. At that time, however, the probabilities of competition between local planning authorities, to provide shopping centres within their respective Development Plans, were not so clear.

The central Treasury maintained its emergency controls over all public capital expenditure, despite the powers of the local Act to proceed without most normal controls, but in 1950, after a deputation from the City had visited the Treasury, the argument was accepted by the Government that, whereas expenditure on construction would have been inflationary at that time, the purchase of property would not have that effect (one can only assume that, somewhere in the recesses of Government, the wish was father to the thought, and that some generous civil servant must have introduced the word "relatively"!), and the authority was given for the acquisition of property in advance of constructional work. As property was acquired it was demolished, and by 1956 most of the sites in Smallbrook Street, some of which had been badly damaged by bombing during the war, were cleared.

The next hurdle to be cleared was the approval of the Ministry of Transport to the payment of financial grant (notionally 75%). This was authorised in 1956 for part of Smallbrook Ringway (see p. 62, top); the Public Works Committee authorised the invitation of tenders, the lowest was accepted, and on the 8th March, 1957, the work was inaugurated by the then Minister of Transport, Mr Harold Watkinson—now Lord Watkinson—who detonated a demolition charge which cleared some remaining remnants of a wall. Excess of enthusiasm had prevailed over the textbook, and there were some narrow escapes from flying debris; however, this was to prove symptomatic of the energy that carried the whole scheme to completion almost exactly fourteen years later.

During the period of development of design and construction, those who were politically or professionally concerned with the project were conscious mainly of an unremitting stream of problems covering the choice of commercial developers, major redesign in the light of revised traffic forecasts, daily problems of construction and traffic handling, and progress of sections of the scheme through City Council procedure. They were less conscious, on the whole, of the fringe effects of puzzlement, irritation, and sometimes positive dislike of elements of the scheme, that were displayed by individuals or groups of the public. Especially in the earlier years of the construction period, the public generally took a great interest and some pride in the progress of the scheme; it was only as the pace of the work increased and obstruction to traffic flow occurred in several parts of the city centre simultaneously, that criticism developed.

On reflection, it is probably fair to say that the greatest strain on fortitude and determination during this long period was upon elected members. Some, relatively few of them, in positions of specific responsibility, had much the same sense of physical and financial preoccupation as had the professional staffs; in other, political, respects no doubt they had even livelier apprehensions at times. The majority of Members, however, were the vehicles for many complaints, and the apologists for a temporary state of affairs which, to outward appearance, caused only upheaval and traffic difficulties. It was not possible for them to speak from detailed knowledge of programmes and proposals; they could only have had some degree of faith in a corporate decision, first taken some years before many of them had had anything to do with it.

On the 7th April, 1971, the Inner Ring Road was opened by the Queen as fully operational. Traffic flowed on three miles of circumferential road (one and a half miles of it including a central expressway from north to south, in tunnel or on flyover), and within a few days, marked reductions in traffic volumes in the centre of the city were evident. From first to last, from the first glimmerings of the thought to the consummation of the deed, sixty years had elapsed. The change that this and other developments wrought on the city centre are shown from the air photographs on pp. 46 and 47.

One or two case histories follow which have a much shorter life cycle; perhaps they had also other differences.

THE COLMORE ROW DECISION

By what seemed a common consent of opinion and of events, there was, during the summer of 1971, a pause in the constant roll forward of road construction and of private redevelopment in the City centre; a temporary relief from disturbance and demolition before the final elements of central highway improvement in Victoria Square and in one or two other places were begun. Buildings on a well-known site, Galloway's Corner, had been demolished in 1970 by a confirmatory decision of the Public Works Committee, after they had reconsidered their original decision at the request of the City Council.

The history of the most recent decision on Colmore Row, the remaining link in the network—which had not been included in the original design of the Ring Road scheme, but had been added to the Parliamentary proposals, reflects a change of emphasis and an apprehension that there is enough traffic capacity in the central highway network as it exists, following the completion of the Inner Ring Road. The small area surrounding Waterloo Street, Bennetts Hill and Colmore Row was one of the few remaining in the city that had any distinction of cohesive style and architectural or historic interest. Of the buildings that were now offices, some had been private dwellinghouses up to about 1855; others, mainly in Colmore Row, had been purpose-built in the nineteenth and the early twentieth century—one of them, designed by Lethaby (see p. 75), was the first functionally modern design in the city centre in its departure from the limiting influence of current handcrafts.

In 1879, Colmore Row became the name of a thoroughfare which, in whole or in part, had been called by seven other names during the previous one hundred and fifty years, being variously a "lane" or "street" at different times. The final naming followed the building of the civic offices (the "Council House") completed in that year on land bought by the Corporation, in what was then Ann Street, twenty years earlier. The space in front of the Council House was later named Victoria Square: it was neither square nor impressive in size, and suffered in its proportions, in later years, some damage from the loss of Christ Church which stood on a site at the corner of what became Colmore Row and New Street, and which had been presented by W. P. Inge in 1803. The church had been "designed for the accommodation of the lower classes", and all seats were free. Money was subscribed by a number of people, including (according to Gills' History) the King—but slowly—and the church was not opened until 1813. It was demolished in 1897, and offices and shops, known latterly as "Galloways Corner", were built at about the turn of the century.

In 1943, the Advisory (Traffic) Planning Panel, which had been set up in 1942, received a recommendation from the City Surveyor that Colmore Row should be widened to 80 ft. (24.3m.) but in the ultimate scheme recommended by the Public Works Committee to the City Council, it was shown as 120 ft. (36.5 m.) wide.

In 1952, the Minister of Housing and Local Government issued a schedule under the provisions of section 30 of the Town and Country Planning Act, 1947, listing buildings of special architectural or historic interest; this included properties in Bennetts Hill and Waterloo Street: others in those streets were included on a supplemental list—not giving the same degree of statutory protection against change or demolition. None of the buildings on the south side of Colmore Row (to be affected by widening) was included.

During the next two years, there were two events which seemed to be fairly conclusive for the future of Colmore Row. Firstly, a strip of land, approximately fifty feet wide on the Colmore Row frontage of St. Philip's Churchyard, was acquired by the Corporation under their new powers, from the Ecclesiastical Commissioners, who took advantage of the Notice to Treat to request purchase, although the Corporation said they were in "no hurry" to acquire at that time. Secondly, the Inge Estate said that they had heavy death duties to meet, and asked the City Council if they would purchase the freehold interest in the area on the south side of Colmore Row, which was scheduled under the 1946 Act, and this was agreed.

Part of the discussion before the Parliamentary Committee, about the ultimate traffic situation in the City centre, had developed from evidence that probably the whole of the enlarged City centre would be limited to pedestrian traffic, with the exception of the Ring Road and two cross chords (Colmore Row and an enlarged route along Snow Hill and the

Upper and Lower Priories); on these, as on the whole Ring, it was predicted public transport would run.

It was stated that the widening of Colmore Row would probably be one of the last sections to be constructed. It was concluded that—public service vehicles becoming restricted to the Ring Road, including the two new chords—passengers would be brought sufficiently near to shops and offices: the criterion suggested was that they should not have to walk farther than three hundred yards from a bus stop. The intention was to provide dual carriageways (or two-way flow, at any rate) in Colmore Row.

The original outline design of the Inner Ring Road had included single-level junctions with the arterials, and had been prepared before the development of any national motorway programme. During the years of developing standards of design of the Ring Road junctions, there had been severe difficulties in developing a balanced network. Successive sketch designs for the connection between what was then Congreve Street, Victoria Square, Colmore Row and Paradise Street, ran into trouble, and it was some time before the design of what is now called Paradise Circus containing the new City Library building, the School of Music and a bus station produced a reasonable solution. Part of the difficulty arose from the need to provide some continuity of feeling and function between the old civic centre and the newer extensions, existing and proposed, to the westward. Continuous interdepartmental discussions, following definition of the expressway function of part of the Inner Ring Road, eventually produced the present scheme, which was capable of handling, in addition to all its other functions, a situation based on two-way flow in Victoria Square, springing in turn from the dual carriageway concept of Colmore Row.

In preparation for the approaching prospect that Colmore Row would develop into a central "Boulevard", the City Council accepted, in principle, a Public Works Committee proposal, in 1959, for the provision of a major open space on the south side of Colmore Row, to occupy the whole area between St. Philip's Churchyard and Victoria Square. There was some discussion, at that time, about the possibility of retaining the buildings in Waterloo Street (the oldest of all those affected), the rear of which would have been exposed to the new wide boulevard, but the attraction of the proposal for the first great open space in the city centre was enough to convince the Council that they should forego the prospect of any commercial development on the areas of land that would remain after Colmore Row had been widened.

However, when the time approached for the demolition of buildings in Colmore Row, there was a change of heart, attributable to a number of factors: the financial climate was less genial, and the activity of the Victorian Society, the Civic Society, and other conservation interests, was becoming stronger and more positively directed to preservation of many buildings which, comparatively recently, had been thought of

E

little account.

In 1968 and 1969, procedures moved in a normal kind of way towards the necessary stages of approval of clearance and construction in Victoria Square and Colmore Row. There were, however, slight, but perceptible, signs of a "slowing-down" in what had, up till then, been a consistently decisive sequence of commitment to a complex, physically difficult and costly programme. Authority was given for the preparation of a layout for Victoria Square, "having regard to the traffic requirements", but this stage was to be limited to the Old Square plus "Galloway's Corner" (and no other properties, owners of which were to be advised that they would not be disturbed before the end of 1971; notices, however, were to be served to enable roadworks to be carried out in 1974).

When the Public Works Committee reported to the City Council in December 1969, for approval, an amendment was moved in Council, and approved, referring back this item of the Public Works Department's business. Under the system of majority party government, this procedure, although in normal use as a method of political criticism, seldom achieves the desired end of reference back of an item. The motion, in this case however, was proposed by a member of the majority party (Councillor J. C. Silk), who said that he and others thought that the Inner Ring Road, then seen to be approaching completion, might well perform its essential but reduced traffic function without any requirement for the widening of Colmore Row—which he would deplore, because this was a street which had retained a particular character, where there were buildings of architectural and historic value, and where, in any case, the cost would not be justified. His main plea was for the conservation of the area, and there was sufficient support for the reference back—which was judicially worded to ask the Public Works Committee to consider the advisability of varying their plans for Colmore Row and "Galloway's Corner", in order to preserve the buildings.

That Committee were in little doubt about Galloway's Corner, and confirmed the intention to demolish the buildings there because—whatever the ultimate design for Colmore Row—a traffic improvement was needed in Victoria Square. (For many years there had been a "scissors" crossing, controlled by traffic signals, which were reputed to be temporary, although they had been there since 1952.) They also intended to take advantage of the need for the improved traffic scheme to provide a dramatically better setting, in an enlarged Victoria Square, for the buildings that would remain, including the Council House and the Town Hall. In taking this decision back to the City Council, the Public Works Committee said they would consider and report again on Colmore Row.

In order to go more deeply into the question, they asked for additional reports from Chief Officers; they visited the buildings, some of which were void in expectation of demolition, and called for more information. The arguments were strong on both sides of the case: on the one hand, heavy cost, further disturbance and nuisance, and the loss of listed buildings; on the other, physical deficiences of the buildings, an assurance of traffic capacity, and the creation of a central open space—narrow and elongated, certainly—but running along the highest ridge of the city centre and comprehending St. Philip's (now the pro-Cathedral) and its grounds in the east, and the Town Hall, the Council House and Victoria Square on the west. In the ensuing twelve months, the Committee held five meetings on this subject, and the Chairman invited public comment on the question. Fewer than a dozen responses were made, and these mainly from conservationist interests.

In the month of January 1970, the central government "listed", as of architectural or historical interest, further buildings in the area, including, for the first time, some on the south side of Colmore Row itself.

In the end, the Committee decided to recommend to the City Council that it was not now practicable to demonstrate a traffic need for a major widening of Colmore Row, and that the possibilities of the rehabilitation of the properties be considered: this was approved in Council. The headlines in the *Birmingham Mail* on 12th February, 1971, read "Colmore Row saved as City concedes open spaces battle". During the latter part of these deliberations, Galloway's Corner had been demolished, and the site was turfed over in the spring of 1971, while a revised scheme for Victoria Square was being developed. The quiet summer had come to pass and, on sunny days, many people sunned themselves on the new grass which had cost a few hundred pounds sterling, as a temporary treatment for a site that had cost nearly a million pounds and much mental tribulation! Clearly, this was the beginning of a new era.

ASTON UNIVERSITY

The history has been mentioned briefly on page 38. The first section of a Municipal Technical College (which was never completed) housed also, for many years, a secondary school that became a grammar school. In the middle 1930s, land was acquired, at Gosta Green, near the north end of Corporation Street extension, for a major Technical College, and foundation work started in 1938; it was suspended during the war of 1939–45. As soon as resources were available after the war, the scheme was revived and a building programme was established, based on the original designs, a process which was criticised on the grounds that the design should have been modernised. Some changes were made, under the influence of the first City Architect (A. G. Sheppard Fidler) and the construction was resumed of what remained, in essence, a rectangular

Overleaf: Left: Top: 6. Smallbrook Ringway.
Bottom: 7. Paradise Circus, including Central Library complex and Town Hall.
Right: Top: 8. Central Area and principal road network, 1971.
Bottom: 9. Extent of post war redevelopment.

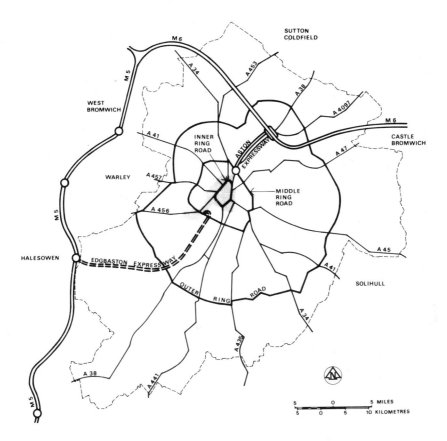

BIRMINGHAM CENTRAL AREA

Extent of Post War Redevelopment

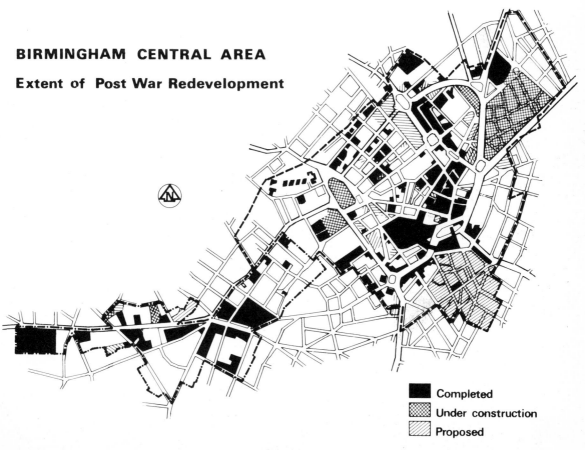

■ Completed

▨ Under construction

▨ Proposed

design, with substantial areas of teaching space served by continuous corridors at each level.

In the report of the Percy Committee in 1945, the idea had first emerged of the establishment of Colleges of Advanced Technology, and the concept developed rapidly during the early 1950s so that the idea soon became familiar and acceptable to the informed public. These Colleges were to be defined as being capable of providing further technical education up to Degree standard. In November 1955, the new College building at Gosta Green was inaugurated by the Queen, and was to house part of the work of a College of Technology. Following the Robbins Report of 1963, the Colleges of Advanced Technology were accepted as suitable for development to University status, with all the implications of transfer to the ambit of the University Grants Committee. This happened in 1964, the local education authorities having relinquished in 1962 the Colleges of Technology, as they then were, which became autonomous bodies in receipt of direct grant from the Government; this was the penultimate step in their development.

In January 1956, there had been appointed a new Principal of the Technical College in Suffolk Street (Peter Venables). He took post in May 1956, in a situation which had developed, in February of that year, from the publication of the White Paper on Technical Education, which announced Government recognition of the concept of Colleges of Advanced Technology. In September 1956, the new College of Technology at Gosta Green was designated as a College of Advanced Technology, and proceeded to shed some of the old Technical School work in two stages, in the two following years.

In April 1966, the new College had been transformed into a University and had received its charter; the University Grants Committee was soon approving the financial requirements for its first years, and was considering the area of land that would be required for its development. We can see, therefore, that in a total period of not much more than ten years, an important but relatively small Technical School had developed into a second University within a city which, about fifty years before, had already established one such under the general, if indirect, aegis of the Chamberlains and others who were responsible for policy in local government in those times.

Such a project certainly never existed as part of the city's Development Plan in the early 1950s. How did it all come about? The answer is that a small number of people, led by the new Principal and two successive Chairmen of Governors (J. J. Gracie and Joseph Hunt) read the signs aright about the needs of the times. Certainly, they were not alone in this, but there were fewer who would have agreed, at that time, that it was better to build upon a nucleus already forming, that is the new Technical College, than to find a new site for a university in a town or in an area offering fewer and less costly difficulties over land. Still fewer would have agreed, in spite of some successful examples elsewhere, that the place for such a University was in the central area of a city such as Birmingham. Nevertheless, by persuasion; by force of personalities; and by a tactical sense that was able to convince local and central government, this end was achieved. In 1971, the university was in possession of most of the 38 acres that had been rezoned as an amendment to the Development Plan (and towards which the city had made generous grants of land), the number of undergraduate and post-graduate students had reached 3,400, the staff numbered 1,065, and new teaching and residential building was being pushed forward.

As planning authority, the city had encouraged this metamorphosis from first to last. Such a story might be taken, variously, as an indictment of the lack of imagination of earlier planning, or an adverse judgment on the consistency of planning control, or a simple recognition of a familiar situation—that is, a project containing both the recognisable, politically sympathetic, need for improved facilities (for higher education in this case) and the potential for longer-term replacement for some of the obsolescent elements in the city's economy and influence.

ASTON EXPRESSWAY

In the middle 1950s, the central government, through the then Ministry of Transport, was settling the location of the highly important Midlands link in the network of national motorways. These had been planned to take the form of an elongated "H", with a motorway running from north to south, on the west and east sides of the country respectively, and with a connecting link somewhere in the Midlands (an area which, as a matter of historical interest, had seen the link between the upper and middle level canal systems in the eighteenth century, and the first regional railway links in the nineteenth century). Consideration of motorway experience in other countries led the Ministry of Transport to compare the relative advantages of locating the Midlands link through open country, so as to reduce its cost, or of finding a route through the densely urban areas of generation and destination, thus avoiding the cost of long expressway connections from the motorway to the urban centres. Rapid consultation with the authorities in the West Midlands conurbation, initially with Birmingham, produced a decision to locate the cross link between the two main legs of the motorway system through the built-up area of the conurbation, including eight miles in Birmingham, instead of through more open country to the north.

This decision, contributed to by the city, imposed a sudden and remarkable change on the local authority's own major highway priorities. Such was the effect on preconceived ideas and on certain decisions already made that resistance, rather than support for the new concept, would not have been at all surprising. In fact, within a period of fourteen months, the city gave formal approval to the central government's plans, and changed its programme of priorities so as to include a completely

new expressway connection from the north (p. 63, top). The location of
a route through this densely built-up area would have presented great
difficulty for the policy-makers if there had been no basic planning for
that area of a kind such as did, in fact, exist. It existed because, in 1946,
the city, acting under the short-lived 1944 Planning Act, had acquired
large areas of slums in a compact ring around the central area, and since
1950, had been demolishing and redeveloping comprehensively, with the
assistance of planning grants from the government, an area containing
30,000 houses and thousands of other buildings. The policies and techniques were continually extended to take in and deal with additional slum
areas, in order to meet the stated policy of clearing entirely the backlog
of slums. A favourable route for the new expressway connection to the
national motorway link was found, parallel in general direction to the
Lichfield Road (part of the A.38 already referred to) and passing through
an area already approved for clearance and redevelopment. The amount
of additional disturbance to provide for the road was absolutely minimal,
because the same area was due for complete clearance in any case.

Changes to the zoning layout of this relatively small area provided
extra open space between the road and the locally historic Aston Hall
and its park. A rapid engineering analysis preferred elevation to tunnelling
for the most difficult part of the new expressway, which was approved
and virtually completed at a total cost of about £11 million in a period
of three years. Here is an interesting example of planning initiative (in
this case by the central government) attracting to itself a subsidiary but
strongly supporting activity (on the part of a local government agency),
which was possible because of the ability to change tactical direction
whilst maintaining strategic purpose, the only requirement being that
there should indeed be a situation of active pursuit of strategic ends by
the application of strong and controlled resources.

DECISIVE INTUITION—OR "METHOD"?

The general form of the (U.K.) 1968 Planning Act seems to imply that
there is now general acceptance of the proposition that there should be
concentration of major resources on those projects which are demonstrably
capable of yielding rapid return, whether social, financial or political,
and which, therefore, are capable of attracting to themselves supporting
activities in public or private sectors. The concept of structure planning
was adopted in legislation following the work of a consultative group;
apart from rejecting those elements of former procedure which were
found to be too detailed, the purpose was to sponsor initiative and,
accepting the inability of the local planning authority to plan positively
for private initiative, to use investment in the public sector to "prime
the pump" in a selective way. It is fair to say that the merit of such a
process is supported by successful examples of rapid and decisive action
of the kind undertaken in Birmingham under the system of delegation

of powers to Committees, and the "loose-rein" guidance of Chief Officers by the Town Clerk.

It remains to be seen whether the current national emphasis on greater formalisation of management functions and central administrative control will enable the larger strategic intent to operate.

It is doubtful whether formal analysis of past planning histories, involving analysis, diagnosis, prognosis and implementation is often accurate. In the absence of the spoken word, it is impossible to construct, after a series of events, a sequence of diagrams which accurately represents all the processes that took place. In a highly political situation, which sees an annual peak of competitive activity and a less frequent but more intense surge of activity and argument, at periods when there appears to be the prospect of a change of political power, it is illusory to expect the same view to be taken of the case for or against a particular proposal, by different political groups or personages. There are matters of high policy—and there are those merely of local improvement, where questions of priority, involving delay or acceleration, may be all that is in doubt, or where identifiable party politics may have nothing to do with the argument or the decision.

One such case can be described briefly: this is the development of the argument about forming pedestrian precincts in the central area of Birmingham. During the construction of the Inner Ring Road, which involved building pedestrian subways and bridges, and somewhat unusual measures, at times, for maintaining traffic, there had been comments about subordination of pedestrians to vehicular traffic. A common question was "Why can't they put the traffic underground and let the pedestrians have the normal levels?" (This usually ignored questions of practicality and cost.) Towards the end of the period of construction of the Inner Ring Road, however, there was an increase in interest in the argument, which was taken up by the Junior Chamber of Commerce, the Chamber of Trade (i.e., the retail shopkeepers), by certain individuals and by a local newspaper—the *Birmingham Evening Mail*, which, as one of its social activities, sponsored a discussion group called the "Housewives Circle". This newspaper, and its contemporary the *Birmingham Post* (both under the same general management) undertook energetic reportage and encouraged discussion, but without coming down in favour of a particular principle.

In 1963, the Public Works Committee formally established an element of planning policy by resolving that the private car would not be completely excluded from the city centre, and that public transport in the form of bus services would be maintained to the main areas of retail shopping and business. The question of pedestrian shopping areas was not a new one to the Public Works Committee and its officers; in fact, discussions with an advisory group of local businessmen had taken place in the years 1964, 1965 and 1966 on this and other problems relating to the city centre. Opinion at that time amongst the business community

was very mixed: a group of shopkeepers had told the then Chairman of
the Committee that anything in the form of pedestrian shopping precincts
would be anathema; that nevertheless the success of shopping depended
upon convenient car parking—which was the duty of the taxing authority
to supply; that the cost of parking should not be high; and that the
shopkeepers would not consider it fair if they had to make a contribution
towards its cost. Some business interests, however, believed in pedestrianisation; the range of opinion amongst councillors was wide and was, as
yet, unformed in detail amongst officers. The only firm statement had
been to the effect that the control and decrease of conflicting traffic
streams in the city centre would be a first priority when the Inner Ring
Road had achieved its object of eliminating the through traffic. It is
true that prophetic statements were said to have been made by the
city's officers at the time of the Parliamentary Bill in 1946, to the effect
that all traffic would disappear from the city centre, which would be
served by buses, but this could not be described as the establishment of a
planning policy.

In practical terms, the matter was one of maintaining confidence in a
shopping centre that had always had its difficulties and was now under
a new attack (the growth of out-of-town hypermarkets), and which had
had a period of considerable physical inconvenience. In November 1970,
a scheme for a very modest pedestrian area was put to the Public Works
Committee; this would have involved taking the buses out of Union
Street, eliminating all private cars in certain roads, and excluding
also all goods service vehicles between the hours of 10.00 a.m. and
6.00 p.m. The Public Works Committee took opinion from a number
of groups with established interests and invited public response, which
was minimal. The result was such a range of objection from specific
interests, and such an absence of supporting public comment, that the
Committee regarded the case as very much in doubt. The scheme was
of a kind which, they felt, must have the positive support of influential
and weighty sections of the public, because it could be recognised that
there was the possibility of difficulty and hardship for some particular
shopkeepers if the predictions of general benefit were wrong. The
Chamber of Trade pressed for the scheme, as did some individual stores.
Those who deemed themselves likely to lose trade by the removal of bus
stops, resisted the scheme very strongly, as did those whose servicing
arrangements would have suffered badly. On balance, the Committee
decided not to go forward with the scheme after offering, as a possibility,
a trial on Saturdays only. This was the only proposal that met with a
wholesale reaction, which was one of rejection. The Committee instructed
the Chief Officer to seek for another scheme based on deflection of traffic,
rather than coercion, taking as an example a small traffic regulation
section which had had the effect of reserving almost entirely one particular
short route in the city centre for buses.

During 1971, the City of Leeds brought into operation a scheme that they had had in preparation when Birmingham began its own, and which was now available for inspection. A visit by the Public Works Committee and officers in September 1971 demonstrated several things. Firstly, that the absolute control in pedestrian streets of every element of traffic by regulation was not necessary so long as "through" traffic could be eliminated; in other words, relatively small exceptions could be made in favour of established rights of access which do not require a sledge hammer to crack a nut. Secondly, that the immediate resurfacing and landscaping of certain streets as pedestrian areas by right, had a very strong moral effect on those goods services or other vehicles that were permitted to enter; their speeds and their conduct were very cautious. Thirdly, that the shopkeepers fronting onto the new pedestrian ways all reported good results. The visitors from Birmingham reported favourable impressions when they returned home. In November 1971, a new scheme was put before the Committee containing somewhat similar elements to the first; apprehensions by officers about the need for strict traffic regulations gave way to confidence in more flexible methods, some additional lengths of highway were marked out for pedestrian treatment, and the scheme was accepted by the Public Works Committee, whose antennae had told them that those sections of the public directly affected were now ready to agree, and that those elements (always the most numerous) who had no particular feeling of responsibility for a decision would accept what the Council decided, reserving only the right to criticise inefficiency in execution. The local newspapers now expressed positive approval. Here was a situation where, at the first time of asking a year earlier, it might have appeared that there was sufficient vocal support and sufficient reasoned argument to carry the proposals forward, but they failed to gain support. Twelve months later, the climate was such that there was almost universal support for what had formerly been highly suspect. How to present such a sequence in terms of formal symbols? It would be possible to do so either as having been a deliberate, preliminary consultative exercise to be repeated later, with the deletion of certain "expendable" elements, or as a genuinely considered proposal, which failed to succeed for reasons which were later corrected to some extent. It was, indeed, the latter—but whether the scheme could have succeeded in 1970, however constructed, is incapable of demonstration.

One can say only that the first decision may have been due to one or more reasons: either the political sense of the Committee told them a breathing space was needed, after a period of intense physical change in the city centre; or they had been insufficiently prepared by professional advice—perhaps excusably, during a period when there was intense concentration on other matters—or that the particular situation of vulnerability of the city centre, in a new and more widely competitive shopping climate, required the demonstration of larger scale examples in operation than it had been possible to study in Norwich, Oxford and elsewhere, up to that time.

During this time, the question of the ultimate traffic design in Victoria Square had to hang fire, to some extent. It would have been possible, indeed it was the intention, to design a scheme so that, in emergency or in future circumstances as yet impossible to foresee, traffic should not be completely disorganised by emergencies but could be reversed through the Square, in the event of a need for change in the one-way system.

Decisions about pedestrianisation that might affect traffic flows, particularly bus flows in New Street and Colmore Row, were clearly highly critical to the design of the Victoria Square system, and during the remainder of 1971, which thus produced a breathing space, there was a kind of simmering process going on which was likely to begin to produce fresh movement towards the end of that year. During the three or four years preceding 1971, doubts about the future viability of city centre shopping in general, and that of Birmingham in particular, had begun to come to the surface. Whilst most commentators and critics agreed that there were strong competitive tendencies, for instance, the more rapid development of shopping centres by smaller local authorities nearby, and the prospect of out-of-town shopping centres and "hyper-markets" near trunk road or motorway junctions, there was an inclination, on the whole, to say that the disruption and activity in the city centre had produced a situation which had irreversibly driven away or dis-couraged a certain proportion of trade. A small but highly critical school of thought blamed the lack of central car parking: another wing of opinion blamed the presence of vehicles of any kind. It was clear that here there was a situation where various forces were at work which, on the whole, might well prove inimical to the further expansion and success of the city centre but which, nevertheless, were not wholly understood.

A remarkable range of opinion or advice was available. One visit to a responsible and well-informed advisory trade body produced the comment that what shoppers really liked was narrow streets, fairly well packed with traffic moving at a safe and slow speed, in two directions, so that there was both an atmosphere of activity and a certain reduction of danger to shoppers, who could skip from one side of the road to the other. This kind of comment, from highly experienced traders, might well create a momentary despair on the part of those who were seeking some long-term stable technical solution.

One profoundly important fact emerged under persistent examination; this was that most of the national "multiples" found a lower ratio of sales as between their city centre stores and the branches in the suburbs than in other cities. This was evidence of competition within the city which might delay central growth, but might also postpone the effect of out-of-town hypermarkets in neighbouring local authority areas.

There was, during 1970 and 1971, a perceptible lull, almost as though the city was asking an audible question. The new shopping centre, built by a consortium, including British Rail, over New Street Station (see p. 47, ④), was almost unoccupied by the second year after physical completion. Some shops were still unlet on the eastern side of Corporation Street, in the pedestrian ways which formed the spines of the new construction there. Staff agencies (private employment exchanges mainly for temporary office posts) moved into small shops in the centre of town. There was some return of the small trader, moving back into compartmented shops formed within the carcasses of what had once been large stores. These, on the whole, were modern clothing shops.

The question at this time is whether retail shopping will contract or remain stable, or whether it may be able to expand slightly in the centre of the city. Powerful forces are at work against it: it might seem to be defying the waves, to attempt to restrict the mobility that the car confers upon the activity of shopping, as upon so many others. Nevertheless, it is clear that if retail shopping disappeared from the centre, there would be a devastating void in the city's heart. As we see from the statistical appendix, the central business district is an area of high employment. The workers are also shoppers, to some extent; they get pleasure and re-creation from the ability to stroll and see shops. If the shops go, there will be a tendency for some work places to go with them, or near them, and the dismantling of the city centre will have begun. Will it then be possible to retain interest in those somewhat fewer social, recreational, and cultural centres that remain, or that have been renewed?

THE PRESENT STATE OF THE CENTRAL AREA

Investment
Capital investment committed in new building in the Central Area since 1945 has been more than £200 million. Most of this investment has come from private sources, has been channelled into commercial develop-ment, and was initiated in response to the city's own capital investment in the modernisation of the functional networks.

Local authority capital investment itself has been high. Pressures for redevelopment in the middle ring of comprehensive redevelopment areas, with their high complement of unfit dwellings and obsolescent factories was great, and priority was given to investment in those areas. In the Central Area, resources were concentrated on the provision of services and in improving roads; of the £32 million spent in the 22 years between 1946/47 and 1968/69, 87% was allotted to roads and most of this was devoted to the Inner Ring Road Scheme. The annual rate of local authority investment increased substantially over the period, 70% being undertaken in the 10 years up to 1969.

Uses
The Central Area is the focus for retailing, office activity and administra-tion for the city's population, but it is much more than this, having functions which serve a much wider population. In public administration, it houses the regional offices of several central government departments

and the Regional Hospital Board. The Central Area also supports regional offices of the major clearing banks and of the Bank of England, and a Stock Exchange.

A study of changes in land-use and floor space in the post-war period seems to indicate a great specialisation of activities and an intensification of the functions of a regional centre. The area of residential land-use has fallen to less than half in the past twenty years. Terraces of nineteenth-century houses, many of them unfit for habitation, have been cleared in the outer parts of the Central Area to make way for other uses. During the same period, however, there has been some offsetting introduction of new municipal multi-storey housing, with little difficulty in lettings. Routine manufacturing and warehousing have both shown a marked reduction: in 1950, a quarter of the land in the Central Area was in industrial use; now the proportion is only one eighth.

Office accommodation has been the major growth element. Clearly, close mutual location is important to functional inter-relationships in service employment, and for a firm's centrality in relation to its clients. This does not emerge clearly from the land-use statistics partly because the 1950 figure includes other uses, but the figures show that the office floor space has increased by about three-quarters from 540,000 square metres to 938,000 square metres in 1968. Most of this growth has occurred through physical expansion outside the old city centre core where, traditionally, the area between Colmore Row and Great Charles Street held the main concentration of offices. Wartime bombing produced a need for temporary accommodation, and the large Victorian houses in the Hagley Road area of Edgbaston—where some medical consultants and specialists had already established themselves—were conveniently situated, and suitable for conversion. After the 1947 Planning Act, this area was allocated for principal business purposes in the City's Development Plan, which also embodied the private plan of the Calthorpe Estate Company, who hold the freehold interests of almost all the land in this area. The Calthorpe Principal Business Area is linked to the city centre core by principal business zoning on the south side of Broad Street, which was programmed for redevelopment. The office floor space in these two areas has increased from 17,700 sq. m. in 1950 to 243,000 sq. m. in 1968.

Controls on office development in the city were imposed by the central government in 1965, and operated until the end of 1970, during which period there were few approvals for new office development. Since the relaxation of control at the end of 1970, there has been a burst of energy in this field, in which the period of enforced restraint seems to have accentuated the normal cyclical pattern of office development, where, because of the considerable time lag between the initial discussions on a new scheme and its occupation, a period of scarcity tends to be followed by a period of surplus.

Although there has been extensive redevelopment of the major shopping zone in the Central Area, the increase in retailing floor space has been only a little more than 30%, and an increase in shopping frontage from 11,600 m. to 15,000 m., much of it in the form of internal arcades or malls. There are, of course, other major shopping centres within the West Midlands that compete with the city centre, and within the city itself there are several district shopping centres which are developing, becoming more attractive, and competing in all but the most specialised sections of retailing.

The large increase in floor space attributed to "Transport" usage is, at first sight, somewhat misleading, because it includes off-street car parking. It does, however, illustrate the provision that has had to be made, at present standards, to accommodate the private car. The greatest increase has been in the peripheral zones immediately outside the Inner Ring Road where multi-storey parks have been built.

Employment

The most convenient and comprehensive source of employment data are the returns of the National Census of Population. The Conurbation Centre, as defined for census purposes, coincides almost exactly with the Central Area as chosen for this analysis, and statistics have been published for the 1961 and 1966 Censuses: these were based on a 10% sample, however, and may be subject to errors of bias.

Subject to this caution, in 1961 about 121,000 (18·5%) of the city's work-force of 655,000 worked in the Central Area: by 1966, the total in the city had dropped slightly to 646,600, but proportionally the work-force in the Central Area showed a greater fall; the figure of 109,000 representing only 16·8% of the city's total. This is surprising because of the greater intensity of the new development, but reflects a trend which appears to be common to the other major conurbation centres in Britain, as discussed by Ray Thomas (1968).

The 1966 figures show a heavy concentration (82%) of central area employment in service employment, as defined in the Standard Industrial Classification. Amongst these, the distributive trades, professional, scientific and miscellaneous services, and transport and communications employ the largest numbers. What is more, the proportions so employed are increasing, particularly in professional and scientific services; insurance, banking, finance and miscellaneous services. More than 60% of the total city employment in insurance, banking and finance, and over 52% in public administration occur in the Central Area. Comparing the 1961 figures, there appears to be a slight reduction in centralisation in these services, but it would probably be inaccurate to state a firm trend on the figures so far available.

Traffic

Mode of travel to work was a topic introduced for the first time into the census in 1966; no comparable information from earlier dates is available for direct comparison.

Journey to work at peak hour is, at present, the critical element of the "load factor" (a design consideration that applies to design of highway network capacity, as to other dynamic supply problems). In 1966, only 3,000 of the workers who worked in the Central Area also lived there; of the remaining 106,000, 71,000 lived within the city. Therefore, almost one third of the persons working in the Central Area resided outside Birmingham, and over 30% of these were in Solihull and Sutton Coldfield.

There was a heavy dependence on bus transport (60% of trips) for those travelling into the area to work, and remarkably few people came in by train (7% of trips). Trips by car formed 25% of the total. There is a significant variation in the mode of travel depending on the place of residence, reflecting predominantly the ease of access by different methods of transport but also the relative levels of car ownership associated with the type of residential area. Travellers from both Solihull and Sutton Coldfield were heavy users of train and private car, whereas the workers living in Birmingham itself, and most of those coming in from Warley and West Bromwich, used buses.

Traffic counts taken on the radial roads approaching the line of the Inner Ring Road give some measure of the increase in road traffic to and from the city centre in the morning peak period over the last 10–13 years: the total increase in the volume of road traffic has been almost 50%. The number of motor cycles and buses in the flows has fallen, and although a change in definition makes direct comparison difficult for private cars alone, the volume of cars and goods vehicle traffic has gone up by over 70%. A substantial element (38%) of the total was traffic passing through the city centre, but no doubt the destination of some of this was other parts of the central area.

Rateable Value and Ownership
Increases in rateable values since 1945 reflect both the effect of re-valuations and the extent of new development. The proportion of total land value for local tax purposes, attributable to commercial properties, has been maintained despite the various changes in the basis of valuation. Industrial premises have increased their share of the city's total rateable value from 5% over the 20 year period from 1947 to 1967. The rateable value of properties in the central area increased from £1·9 million to £9·3 million during the same period; nevertheless, this area's share of the city's total rateable value dropped from 24·5% to 18·1%.

This was a period also, of course, of much major activity in other parts of the city, which resulted in the development of virtually the whole of the land remaining available for housing within the city boundaries, and the redevelopment of an area of over 1,000 acres in the middle ring (around the Central Area) which had contained over 30,000 dwellings and a population of about 106,000, together with a considerable amount of industry and other mixed uses.

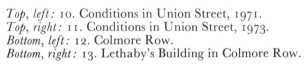

Top, left: 10. Conditions in Union Street, 1971.
Top, right: 11. Conditions in Union Street, 1973.
Bottom, left: 12. Colmore Row.
Bottom, right: 13. Lethaby's Building in Colmore Row.

The total range of activity within the city centre and the larger central area was the result of public and private investment. The former, carried out at a rapid pace, attracted the latter and comprised not only the transport facilities, including the main railway station, the new grade-separated highways, re-drainage and massive works by the Statutory Undertakers, but the city's own Civic Centre development. The Civic Centre plan was to develop westwards from the old Council House to comprise the new library, etc., in Paradise Circus, and was developed successfully under three separate architects, the first of whom, A. G. Sheppard-Fidler was appointed in 1952; the second, the late J. R. Sheridan-Shedden who most unfortunately died soon after appointment, and J. A. Maudsley appointed in 1966. Under them, the concept of the thesis underlying the provision of a Civic Centre, developed as a freely flexible concept eschewing the original, more monumental ideas.

SUMMARY

The forces acting for change in the period after 1945 were the need for expansion of service employment, reflecting the gradual change-over from manufacturing industry, and the requirements for a modern environment in which the business activities necessary for a high material standard of living could function, plus a requirement for some expansion of local government function which was necessary to provide and modernise the supporting services, without which private business could not have carried out rapid development on the scale that was achieved in the city.

What was done by a variety of people and organisations is plain to see. The speed at which it has been achieved may legitimately be described as remarkable within the context of government process, and this relative success may surely be said to be great—without claiming absolute success in every detailed respect.

The results are a product of a system so loose in its central control as almost to be called a Code of Practice, under which political initiative, in certain directions, was combined with official energy and inspiration. Men and companies with a keen instinct for the opportunity in which to take decisive action (for example, Jack Cotton, Laings, the Birmingham Co-operative Society) were able to do so because a powerful authority followed the advice of a few men. Amongst these was one whose intuitive grasp of the relationship between social need and political solution enabled very great material advances to be generated, if not as a by-product, at least as a secondary objective; this was Sir Herbert Manzoni.

At about the time this book will be published, the whole structure of local government in England and Wales will be changing. Whether the same executive energy will ever be brought to bear again, along short paths, to the achievement of planning goals, cannot be said. Certainly the great industrial cities of Britain, Birmingham amongst them, will not exercise the same direct governmental influence as they have done in the past.

3
Coventry

Coventry is one of the oldest settlements in the Midlands. Following the destruction of a nunnery by the Danes in 1016, a Benedictine Priory was founded in 1043 by the Saxon Earl Leofric and his wife Lady Godiva, and some remains of it are still evident. The legend of the ride of Godiva naked through the City in order to lessen the burden of taxes is now internationally known, and her statue in Broadgate is a tourist "must".

Common rights of pasture outside the town walls appear to have evolved from the use of Godiva's lands, and the freemen's resistance to loss of their rights was a major factor in constraining expansion of the town until the late nineteenth century. But this ensured the survival of open areas close to the centre, which today include Greyfriars Green and Top Green.

The priory and later monastic settlements attracted trade, cultural and social activities, and because the city was situated at the crossing of the major trade routes of the country it emerged as a market and industrial centre, becoming one of the chief English wool trading and cloth-making centres of the Middle Ages. Merchant Guilds developed and Coventry was then ranked as the fourth wealthiest town in England (after London, York and Bristol). The Guildhall of St. Mary was built in 1340, and it has been a focus of the life of Coventry ever since, being the cornerstone of the gradual development of a civic area.

The fourteenth century was a period of great growth, and the title of City was authorised in 1363. The construction of town walls was author-ised—a physical constraint which influenced urban development for some centuries. Only small portions of the three miles of wall, and two of the twelve gates, at Cook Street and Swanswell, now remain. In 1451 the status of County was granted to Coventry and surrounding districts, and this wider influence continued until 1842 when the districts were removed from city jurisdiction. A reduced city area was defined, corresponding to the then built up central area, Hillfields and Spon End.

That thriving medieval city is still evident from St. Michael's spire (the third highest in England after Salisbury and Norwich), Holy Trinity Church and Christchurch; the basis of the traditional description of the "City of the Three Spires". The Church of the Guild of St. John, vaulted undercrofts of merchants' houses, timber framed almshouses, Bonds and Fords Hospitals and domestic buildings in Spon Street, are remaining fragments of the "burghers' city" that was a characteristic medieval centre. It was sited around a small hill, and the street pattern reflected the convergence of radial trade routes through the town gates to a focal point near Broadgate. The burghers' houses fronted onto the streets, with large garden plots behind them. The textile industry remained dominant but declining until the eighteenth century and Coventry then became the ribbon-making centre of the kingdom until, in about 1860, foreign competition forced a rapid decline. Watch- and clock-making also prospered in the eighteenth and nineteenth centuries, but foreign competition killed these too.

During this period there was infilling of the former town gardens with industrial workshops as the encircling commons checked the ordered growth of the town. New building in the old town was also becoming a threat to public health, so from 1857 until 1927 various Awards and Acts gradually extinguished the freemen's commoning rights with compensation. Thus land was slowly made available for recreational or development purposes.

Improvements to communications fostered further growth. The Coventry Canal was completed in 1769, with a terminal overlooking the City Centre just outside the city wall. This encouraged industrial development to the north. Turnpike Trusts and tollgates were introduced and in 1812 Hertford Street was built to relieve traffic congestion in Greyfriars Lane, which had been a main city approach from the south. In 1838 a railway station was built on the London and Birmingham line to the south of the town wall, improving accessibility from the national lines of communication.

Meanwhile some 20 miles to the north-west Birmingham had expanded rapidly on the basis of coal and iron reserves; and the industrial revolution of metal-based industries gathered a momentum which firmly established Birmingham as the West Midlands' regional commercial centre. When physical restrictions on expansion were eventually removed in Coventry in the late nineteenth century the city assumed a sub-regional role.

James Starley began making sewing machines about 1860, and later developed bicycle manufacture; Coventry became the home of the cycle industry, but at the turn of the nineteenth century this work began to move out of the city. Motor cycles were introduced, the Daimler car factory dated from 1896, and the car industry became established. There are records of some 20 motor manufacturers established near the central area by 1914. Names later well-known were Humber, Lea Francis, Maudslay, Rover, Rudge, Siddeley, Standard and Triumph. A phenomenal expansion was based on new sources of power, mobility, local skills and ability for innovation. An international reputation evolved for quality and mass production of vehicles, engines, machine tools and electronic equipment. Coventry's exceptional export achievements made a major contribution to the national economy and the balance of payments. The rate of change is shown by the growth in area of the city and its population:

Year	Population	Area (ha.)
1520	6,601	—
1801	16,034	—
1842	—	601—loss of county status
1890	—	1230
1899	—	1678—county borough status
1901	69,978	—
1911	106,349	—
1921	128,157	—
1928	—	5211
1931	167,043	—
1932	—	7756
1941	193,070	— (bombing of city)
1951	258,242	—
1961	305,060	—
1965	—	8160
1971	334,839	—

The town centre road framework changed little over a hundred years. The medieval "through-city" routes remained, based on east–west links

Opposite: 1. Coventry City Centre Location Plan. For many centuries Broadgate had been the focus of radial through-routes. Queen Victoria Road (1887) and Corporation Street (1931) were early by-passes, while Greyfriars Road, New Union Street and Fairfax Street were linked with existing roads to complete the post-war Inner Circulatory road. West of Broadgate the pedestrian shopping area is a major redevelopment. On this map the three asterisks represent the spires which dominated the traditional central scene. Greyfriars Green and Swanswell Pool were the significant open spaces. The Coventry Canal Basin is in the north, and the main line railway passes south of the centre. A new Ring Road has been superimposed upon the old street pattern.

from Leicester and London through Earl Street and Broadgate towards
Holyhead Road and Birmingham. The routes from south to north passed
through Hertford Street and Broadgate towards Tamworth and Nuneaton.
Through coach traffic led initially to demolition of the town gates.
Tramways from 1882, buses from 1914, and a pre-war car ownership of
nearly double the national average brought increasing congestion to
the narrow central shopping streets and the need for a new road pattern
became increasingly evident. A by-pass immediately round the town
centre on the south-west, from Greyfriars Green to Holyhead Road was
built by 1887 as Queen Victoria Road; this served Leamington, Warwick
and Birmingham traffic.

In 1925 Ernest Ford, then City Engineer, suggested that a series of
outer, middle and inner ring roads should be adopted to divert through
traffic at varying distances from the city centre. A six mile long southern
outer by-pass (A45) to take London and Birmingham traffic was eventually
completed by 1939 at a distance of some three miles from the centre.
It seems that his inner ring road alignment would have included Queen
Victoria Road, Corporation Street and Trinity Street.

In 1931 Corporation Street was constructed to by-pass the Smithford
Street shopping centre on the north-west, with a view to creating new
shopping frontages, but it also helped traffic from the Birmingham
direction towards Tamworth, Nuneaton and north eastern industrial
Coventry. In 1937 Trinity Street was constructed to improve the link
from Broadgate to the north; it created further shopping frontages, but
consolidated the "cross-roads" traffic in the heart of the city.

Slum clearance of the congested areas of decayed timber-framed
buildings had made the building of Corporation and Trinity Streets
possible, and added to a gift of parts of the city wall by Sir Alfred Herbert
in 1931, formed a new small park, Lady Herbert's Garden. Together
with Swanswell Pool, Greyfriars Green and areas near the Cathedral
Church of St. Michael and Priory Row, these were the only amenity
spaces of the densely developed town centre in 1938. The rapid expansion
of the city required extensive municipal services, and a new Council
House was built by 1917 adjoining St. Mary's Hall. In 1934 the Council
began to consider the need for a civic centre with art gallery, museum,
library, college and civic hall. It was already evident that extensive reconstruction of the central area would be necessary if it was to service
the phenomenal city growth properly.

In 1937 the Labour Party took control of the City Council for the
first time. It set up a Policy Advisory Committee to spearhead new
policies, and consider priorities for a five year capital development
programme. Leading personalities included Aldermen Halliwell, Stringer
and Hodgkinson. In 1938 the Council resolved to appoint a first City
Architect—responsible for designing buildings and supervising their
erection, closely collaborating with the City Engineer who was the
responsible officer for town planning schemes. The first City Architect

was Donald (now Sir Donald) Gibson, an architect-planner; and the then City Engineer was Ernest Ford, an engineer-planner. In 1939 the architects prepared a model of their redevelopment ideas for 40 acres around the old Cathedral. Ernest Ford studied highway improvement. But in 1939 war intervened, and in 1940 many of Coventry's houses, schools, central shops and public buildings were totally destroyed. Redevelopment, which had been desirable, became an absolute necessity.

INITIAL APPEARANCE OF FORCES FOR CHANGE. PERCEPTION OF CITY CENTRE
PROBLEMS OF POLITICIANS, PLANNERS AND OTHERS

Coventry is believed to have expanded more rapidly than any other town in Great Britain in the first half of this century. For much of the period between the wars, 1919 to 1939, the population rose at a rate some seven times that of the country as a whole, not taking into account boundary extensions. The rapid development of the engineering industry, with attractive wage rates, caused high migration into the city, reaching over 9,500 persons in 1937. War-time "shadow-factories" and, later, trade in export industries, continued the trend significantly until the 1960s.

The effects of this migration were to increase the proportion of young workers and to decrease the proportion of old people relative to the national average, with a high annual flow of people both into and out of the city. Native Coventrians were subject to rapid change, the city was described as "cosmopolitan" (and by 1966 over 10 per cent of the population had been born outside the United Kingdom). A relatively high birth rate (even though it declined from the mid-1960s) resulted in the more recent growth being predominantly due to natural increase. Before 1914 Coventry was described as an artisan town, and this characteristic is still evident. In 1966 some 55 per cent of adult males were skilled workers, 22 per cent semi-skilled and only 7 per cent unskilled. At the same time the proportion of professional, technical and administrative classes living within the city area was below the national average.

The implications of rapid expansion and the local social structure indicated the need to increase the attractiveness of Coventry as a social, cultural, educational and civic centre. Growth had outstripped services, the inadequacies already evident by 1939 were increased by losses due to the air raids and the rapid post-war expansion of city development. It was clear that increased diversity of employment would be beneficial and compatible with a more positive role as a sub-regional centre.

Before 1939 the City Council had recognised the need for comprehensive central reconstruction, but there were legal and financial problems about how this could be initiated. The town centre was generally a patchwork of small freehold interests, although an area of the former Cheylesmore Park formed a major private ownership with small leasehold plots. Commercial pressures on the central sites along the medieval street

Air Views of Coventry Central Area

Above: 2. circa 1938, looking ENE (origin unknown).
A densely developed City Centre, the white dash
lines showing the cross routes. The three spires
are: A – Holy Trinity; B – St. Michael; J – Christchurch.
Also in the picture: 1 – Broadgate; 2 – Coventry Theatre;
3 – Corporation Street; 4 – Spon Street; 5 – GEC factory;
6 – Greyfriars Green.

Below: 3. August 1969, looking NE (P W & L Thompson Ltd
copyright photograph). The traditional cross routes
have now been severed by redeveloped pedestrian areas, and
the Inner Circulatory and Inner Ring roads. There is
controlled development of the lighter coloured high
buildings. Lettered and numbered items are as in the
1938 view.

pattern had resulted in piecemeal growth and speculation due to the lack of effective planning controls. The high value of these sites had made the cost of comprehensive development before 1939 almost prohibitive, except where slum clearance and Local Act powers had allowed limited road development. The Town and Country Planning Act, 1932 did not include financial incentives to promote positive redevelopment, and in any case Coventry City Centre was an "excluded area" and lacked an approved plan. Whilst there was a willingness by the Council to buy limited central area land, there was an inability to promote large-scale acquisition to assemble sites suitable for comprehensive redevelopment in the face of private interests.

The earlier physical constraints on development outside the town centre had caused a high density of mixed uses within it; workshops and factories intermixed with business uses, offices and shops scattered in larger properties which were originally houses. Redevelopment would need to permit acquisition or resiting of many activities elsewhere, in order to allow the centre of the city to develop in a planned manner to the size required for the efficient service of Coventry and the sub-region. Clearly in general it would be preferable socially and financially to relocate businesses, rather than to close them down with compensation, loss of service and employment; but to do this, development land would be necessary in the city centre and elsewhere.

Increasing commercial pressure was now changing the scale of development; a large new bank (classical style) and a pseudo-Tudor office building began to alter the pre-war character of Broadgate. This was the central place, the city crossroads, and hub of the radial road system. Buses, trams, commercial and car traffic brought increasing congestion in narrow and often original medieval roads. Through traffic was causing nuisance and danger and amenity areas for pedestrians were lacking.

Air raid damage itself added to the problems. An expanding city could not wait for implementation of new overall redevelopment plans; new temporary buildings and caravans rapidly appeared, and ruins were adapted; commercial uses spread along radial routes to link to existing inner centres and brought to them a temporary function in support of the deficient centre.

Many central area facilities were scattered in temporary accommodation. The possibility of commercial exploitation of bombed sites was of concern. Immediate post-war accommodation needs included shops, offices, a library, colleges of art and technology, swimming baths, police headquarters, courts, an art gallery and museum and civic offices, together with the rebuilding of the Cathedral. For an ancient city Coventry retained comparatively few historic buildings. The pressures of rapid expansion in the late nineteenth and twentieth centuries, decay of the timber-framed town houses, slum clearance before 1939, and subsequent war damage all took their toll. The three spires remained as historic symbols, but otherwise retention of the city's diminishing ancient heritage would be increasingly at risk with the needs of large scale reconstruction and difficulties of finding finance and suitable uses to retain them.

By 1939 there was public interest in central area redevelopment and the local newspaper sponsored a competition relating to it. The elected representatives' concern to reflect community pressures and values was already evident. The period 1937 to 1967 was one of Labour Party control of the City Council, a period of as great a challenge as any in the City's history, a period adequate to define and realise political ideals. Alderman George Hodgkinson was an original member of the City Redevelopment Committee of 1941, following the devastation of air attack. Hodgkinson (1970) stated his reconstruction aims as adherence to a master plan comprehensively developed, provision for pedestrian and vehicle separation, a public share in the equity of development, and planning for people by participation. He believed that town planning had to do with people and their environment, and that ways and means should be devised to enable them to share in the planning process. These political aims were to achieve a functionally efficient city, a town safe for the enjoyment of all ages, with a stake for the community in the appreciating development values of the central area.

Local commercial activity prior to 1939 reflected a decline in the number of independent shops and multiple traders were increasingly evident. The artisan social structure probably also contributed to a lack of adequate demand for a variety of specialised or quality shops. This was complemented by accessibility to the services offered in London, Leamington and Birmingham. If Coventry was to satisfy a full sub-regional role as a shopping centre it would need to encourage an attractive diversity of shops. This would also apply to offices, where central area rateable values were remarkably low compared with towns of like size. Coventry was midway between the established regional commercial centres of Birmingham and Leicester, and rapid but late industrial and residential expansion had not been matched in services. The pre-war deficiency in central area shopping and office accommodation, intensified by war damage, largely prevented the decay often found on the fringe of town centres, but this could pose the problem of later overshopping following reinstatement of the central area.

The area around Broadgate formed the nucleus of the traditional shopping centre. Access for goods and pedestrians was becoming increasingly difficult. Development had consisted of corridor shopping streets with a covered market and city arcade, but these became war casualties. The sector to the west of the northern road axis through Broadgate and astride Smithford Street, including the major stores, was almost entirely demolished by the bombing. Smaller businesses remained on the fringes in the cheaper properties, often converted residential premises.

Before the opportunity for rebuilding arose, as a result of the bombing, there had already been local professional activity in response to environmental conditions. The Civic Guild (or Civic Society) in 1937 produced four plans for a civic centre—on Greyfriars Green and on sites near to the Council House. They were exhibited publicly and included ideas to create a Civic Square, to extend the Cathedral Close and to introduce surface car parks. These reflected a perception of the needs to provide additional civic services, amenity spaces and off-street car-parking.

In 1938 Ernest Ford, the City Engineer, stated his aims to make the city work, and to make it noble. He later stressed the need for areas where pedestrians could move about freely and safely and was concerned about the problem of motor traffic and pedestrians mixing in shopping streets. The new City Architect's Department under Donald Gibson started work in January 1939, and set up a team under Percy Johnson-Marshall to consider a civic buildings scheme. A large model for public display purposes was produced in out-of-office hours as an "ideas scheme" to promote an awareness of the possibilities of radical change. The Civic Guild principles of a large Cathedral Close and Civic Square to the north and east of the old Cathedral were adopted, but civic buildings were now linked in continuity to frame spaces, rather than being single plot developments. An awareness of the need for increased scale of development was evident.

A large green park was proposed, to be sited between Trinity Street, Pool Meadow and Cox Street—a parkway setting for Cathedral, Holy Trinity and Civic Buildings on a grand scale. This was indeed a brave assertion at a time when the area was a mixture of historical buildings, shops, offices, houses and large factories, and when legal and financial powers were minimal. But it was evidence of the urge for change, for the need to define areas for different primary uses, a civic design concern for buildings linked with spaces and for the introduction of major pedestrian areas.

In June 1939 a public exhibition was held, "Coventry of Tomorrow", sponsored by the local Association of Architects, Surveyors and Technical Assistants (generally the staff of the City Architect's Department), the National Association of Local Government Officers and the City Guild. Town planning lectures were arranged for the public, specialist organisations and schools in a positive campaign to inform the citizens by illustrated talks of needs and opportunities. It was becoming clear that a city centre plan was a desirable objective, although in February 1939 the City Policy Advisory Committee had asked the City Architect to collaborate with the City Engineer in the preparation of a limited plan for a civic centre. The outbreak of war in September 1939 interrupted this work, but a joint planning group of architects and engineers continued to function against a background of differing views of the Chief Officers concerned.

The Bombing and Plans for Rebuilding
In 1939 war intervened. Coventry became a target for German air raids

to destroy industrial production. A raid on 14 November, 1940, by 449 bombers became concentrated in the central shopping and Cathedral area; 554 people were killed, many public buildings were damaged; the Cathedral, central library, swimming baths and a cinema were lost, and over 400 shops were put out of action.

Further raids by 237 bombers in April 1941 killed some 475 people and more central area damage was incurred, including St. Mary's Hall, the Police Station and Hospital.

Coventry had been the first British provincial city to be subjected to a highly concentrated air attack. The damage had been grievous, but an opportunity for the previously desired reconstruction had been created overnight. Would the challenge be met with vision and imagination? On 8 December, 1940, immediately following the major air attack, the City Redevelopment Committee requested the City Engineer and the City Architect to collaborate urgently in the preparation of a plan for the city centre. Due to their divergent views this proved impossible; in February 1941 each presented his own proposal.

Ernest Ford, engineer-planner, aimed to avoid disturbing rateable values unnecessarily by retention of the alignment of most of the medieval streets by widening them, rather than by radical restructuring of the road pattern and the basic physical fabric.

Donald Gibson, architect-planner, visualised a comprehensive redevelopment with a more formalised reorganisation of buildings, spaces and circulation. He aimed at a zoning pattern of central area uses, a central square based on Broadgate, and redevelopment near to the Cathedral, similar in principle to the 1939 model. The traditional shopping area was confirmed along Smithford Street, but in the form of a new pedestrian precinct along a formal east-west axis aligned on the hilltop Cathedral Spire. To the north would be an entertainment zone, to the south a market and offices area. South of Earl Street were to be administrative and educational areas.

An important planning evolution was the parallel "working up" of a two dimensional zoning plan indicating different land use areas, together with a three dimensional drawing illustrating integrated building forms, spaces and a reorganised road pattern. This scheme included an Inner Ring Road and parkway, but it was generally limited to approximately half of the eventual central area within the Inner Ring Road. The traditional east–west road link through central Broadgate was to be severed by the proposed pedestrian shopping area to the west, but the southern road link of Hertford Street was to be completely realigned to form a direct approach from the railway station. New Broadgate west and south frontages were to be built including an hotel, offices and shops; and a large new pedestrian area was to be formed between the north–south road in Broadgate and the old Cathedral spire, by clearing the area between Holy Trinity Church and High Street.

The proposals envisaged only medium height buildings and relied

on the vertical features of the spires of the Cathedral and Holy Trinity. ꟿ
Segregation of vehicles and pedestrians was at one level by the adoption
of separate pedestrian areas or precincts with substantial off-street surface
car-parking. The possibility of some limited two- or three-storey car parks
was, however, envisaged in the entertainment and office areas.

The significant feature of this 1941 Gibson plan which was subsequently
implemented in accordance with the principle then proposed was that
part of the pedestrian shopping precinct along the east–west axis, now
the Upper Precinct. The design philosophy included the grand vista
up the slope to the Cathedral spire; safety, amenity and convenience
for the shopper away from danger, fumes and visual intrusion of vehicular
traffic; the intermixture of unit shops and department stores intercon-
nected by covered ways; two levels of shops incorporating an upper
pedestrian gallery overlooking a square; rear servicing to the shops and
ready access to surface car-parking behind the shops. The breadth of
vision of this concept and the scale of it were fundamental to the subsequent rebuilding; it caught the imagination of the Redevelopment
Committee and in February 1941 the City Council adopted the proposals
of Donald Gibson as the Comprehensive Scheme for submission to the
Minister of Works and Buildings. Perhaps one of the best attributes of
the Gibson conception was its capacity to adapt to the evolution and
increasing sophistication of three-dimensional planning and transportation
planning.

The content of the Coventry plan was of a pioneering nature compared
with other British city central area rebuilding proposals of the time; it
influenced subsequent professional planning techniques of redevelopment,
and the speed of preparation between the air raid of November 1940
and approval by the City Council in February 1941 was phenomenal.
However it reflected the urgency of the situation, an evolution of ideas
in Coventry over many years, and in particular of Donald Gibson and
the architect-planners over the previous eighteen months. Whilst the
significance of the proposals were the principles, in particular of the
shopping area, the plans were at this stage little more than sketch proposals. They lacked depth of survey and analysis, and largely ignored the
constraints of existing interests, and legal, financial and conservation
implications. Even accepting these limitations, surely no city could have
been better served by such a positive professional and political response
to tragedy and opportunity. Recognising the need for further detailed
working up of the design, and the benefit of informing the public in a
positive way, Lord Iliffe donated £1000 for a large exhibition model,
and this became available in 1942.

But an imaginative plan would merely cause frustration unless it
proved capable of implementation. Adequate legal powers would be
essential to initiate any comprehensive redevelopment process of compulsory site assembly with compensation. Support would be necessary
to allow exceptional local authority expenditure and to reduce the impact

of the unremunerative land acquisition, clearance, design and rebuilding
period. In 1941 such national powers and aid did not exist.

Fortunately the publication of the Barlow Report (1940), had been
timely in the light of the following war-time destruction. The report
was concerned with the future development of large cities, and the
Cabinet of the Government in October 1940 asked Lord Reith, Minister
of Works and Buildings, to report on laws that would be relevant to the
post-war reconstruction of British cities. He included Coventry as one
of the authorities for detailed study of the problems involved, received
a city delegation in January 1941, discussed the urgent need for more
adequate town planning legislation, and pressed for "bigness and bold-
ness" in immediate production of an inspiring outline plan. Although
this was available within two months, there was much survey work to
undertake. A Ministry of Town and Country Planning was set up in
1943 and it was not until 1944 that a new Town and Country Planning
Act became law. The uncertain intervening years had been frustrating
for government and local government officers alike, but now the city,
as local planning authority, was enabled to define an "area of extensive
war damage" of 183 hectares linked to redevelopment proposals, and
to apply for a declaratory order for an area within which it would subsequently be possible for the Corporation to submit compulsory purchase
orders to acquire land. A public inquiry was held in January 1946.
After considering objections from certain property interests the Ministry
of Town and Country Planning in July 1947 approved a declaratory
order in respect of a reduced area of 111 hectares. Of this some 100 hectares
related to land lying within and including the eventual Inner Ring
Road.

Government confirmation of the Declaratory Order Area allowed the
Corporation to submit a series of compulsory purchase orders for individual sites within it as redevelopment was considered to be ripe.
Objections from interested parties involved in each case a public inquiry,
and time delays could be considerable. For more rapid progress, and to
reduce the betterment effect of new development on adjoining land next
to be acquired, more comprehensive acquisition would have been desirable, but governmental and financial constraints limited the possibility
of this. No total purchase of the proposed rebuilding areas was possible.

The 1944 Act authorised financial grant from Government in respect
of loan charges on capital expended in the first two years, and part of
the loan charges during the next eight years. (Over the years, as war-
time reconstruction became less of a political priority, the basis of grant
became less favourable. In 1970 annual grant stood at 50 per cent of
the net loss incurred in that year on the acquisition, clearing and preliminary development of approved land relating to redevelopment of
areas of extensive war damage.) Grant administration was dealt with in
grant units for conveniently sized areas, having regard to physical
boundaries and the letting of contracts. Similar provisions later applied

G

to land acquired by powers under the Planning Acts of 1947, 1959 and 1962, and the Local Authorities Land Act, 1963. These related to comprehensive redevelopment of areas of bad layout or obsolete development, or development for the benefit of an area.

The legal and financial powers of the Town and Country Planning Act, 1944 were the foundations upon which the implementation of Coventry's comprehensive reconstruction were based. Nevertheless, other constraints affected the progress of rebuilding. In the national situation immediately after the 1939–45 war there were acute labour difficulties for building and licensing controls over critical building materials. Government control of local government capital expenditure could directly affect whether projects proceeded or determine whether they should be municipal development or, if suitable, would need to be sponsored by private enterprise. Such interventions of government control (extended later to include industrial and office development) had a major influence upon Coventry problems, form, development and prosperity.

But any plan requiring many years to implement because of its scale would rapidly become outdated if it were lacking in adequate flexibility to accommodate changing technological and structural influences. The 1941 Plan was to be subject to early evolution. Deeper survey and analysis of central area needs had by 1945 extended the alignment of the proposed Inner Ring Road considerably outwards to the north and west to approximately its ultimate line, and reduced the residential area; had it not done so the central area potential for development to meet growing sub-regional needs would have soon proved inadequate.

Similarly the early plans accepted limited horizontal segregation of pedestrian and vehicle (but a trend in growth of city private car registrations from 15,400 in 1950 up to 73,600 in 1971 was never anticipated). The problem over the years resulted in substantial amendment to the central area highway and pedestrian circulation network, and car parking proposals. There was continuing adaptation and evolution of the earlier plan principles to include civic design and traffic management studies, to reconcile vehicular accessibility and human environment. Regularly from 1945 the traders emphasised the importance of effective public transport convenient to pedestrian areas and of adequate and cheap car-parking accessible to shops. In 1945, in face of these pressures, the Council accepted a new road at right angles and bisecting the planned pedestrian precinct to allow street parking near to the shops. This particular conflict of commercial and environmental views took some ten years to resolve, with significant effect upon the central area layout. The new road alignment (ultimately Smithford Way, Market Way and City Arcade pedestrian ways) fragmented the original larger parking and service areas to the north and south of the precinct, and contributed to a less formal and more integrated redevelopment of this area.

During this period there was recognition that in the light of functional needs, existing interests and financial implications, the 1941 grand design for a substantial central amenity park near Pool Meadow was impracticable. To the north and east of the Cathedral precinct a car park, bus garage and public buildings were therefore proposed. The formal parkway link from Broadgate to the railway station was abandoned. Warwick Road, Hertford Street and Broadgate were to be retained as vehicular streets. The clearance of the whole area between Broadgate, Holy Trinity Church, the Cathedral and High Street was also amended to retain business premises to the north of High Street. The inbuilt constraints were resulting in tighter, less formal development and greater retention of the existing street pattern. Cox Street, Cope Street and Priory Street were all to be retained, and the eastern sector, including the Cathedral, public buildings and clubs, was therefore to enjoy only limited environmental protection.

In all, five main use zones were proposed within the Inner Ring Road and all to some extent reflected the traditional situation. Public buildings were to the east, business premises centre, light industrial in the western and northern peripheral area, a small residential zone to the south near Friars Road, and there would be several dispersed open space areas.

The Minister confirmed this plan in July 1949 as a basis for redevelopment "subject to such improvements as further study and experience showed to be necessary", and this Central Area Plan was incorporated into the Development Plan which Coventry submitted for central government approval in 1951. The Development Plan, with estimates forward to 1971, was approved in principle by the Minister of Housing and Local Government in 1957, subject to amendments to certain aspects.

The Development Plan was based, in part, on the results of a survey in 1949, and a reflection of the Council's appreciation of the evolutionary nature of the situation was its endorsement, in 1965, of a policy plan to review the provisions of the 1951 Scheme. As a result of the detailed proposals which followed, the Council submitted modifications to the Minister in 1967, these were examined at public enquiries in 1968 and 1971, and the Secretary of State for the Environment approved the Development Plan Review in December 1972.

ESTABLISHMENT AND ORGANISATION

The City Council, over many decades and with commendable foresight for growth needs, had purchased areas of land within and without the city for the future benefit of the citizens. In 1945 an Estates Surveyor and Valuation Officer had been appointed for development and management of the Corporation estate. In the central area some 15 hectares were owned prior to the 1947 declaratory order.

A forthright policy of land ownership by the local authority brought the advantages of a more positive promotion of re-development, the enhancement of environment based on sites not limited to haphazard ownership and the opportunity for radical change in road pattern and land use. It also offered the opportunity to consider options of local authority building on acquired land and of leasing the buildings if desired; of disposing of the freehold to developers; or of retaining the freehold and disposing of a 99 year leasehold interest for building de-velopment in accordance with a planning brief and building agreement. The first alternative was adopted when financial resources and govern-ment allowed; when it was desirable for the local authority to prime the pump by initiating a change in environment to attract further investment by developers (as in the initial shopping, restaurant, office block of Broadgate House) when businesses displaced by corporation develop-ment needed urgent relocation (as those affected by the Inner Ring Road were offered accommodation in Spire House); for municipal projects such as the market, swimming baths and multi-storey car parks; or when special form or function was required (as in the Mercia House flats terminal feature of the precinct, the Locarno Dance Hall at the precinct crossing, or the City Arcade). Disposal of assembled freeholds was ex-ceptional and generally restricted to government development, such as offices and the telephone exchange.

Leasehold disposal of sites had the attraction of allowing control of development not only as the planning authority but also as the landlord, a major advantage in achieving a comprehensive three dimensional con-cept of buildings, spaces and materials. It also offered continuing financial return with enhanced value from specified revue dates of rentals. This method was adopted to speed development additional to that for which the local authority had resources, particularly relevant in the commercial field. Examples included the Hotel Leofric, Upper Precinct shops, Owen Owen store, Smithford Way and Market Way terminal blocks of shops, flats and offices, and the professional offices precinct along New Union Street. These methods of land assembly with a continuing muni-

Opposite: Above: 4. The 1942 model looking NE.
This model explained the proposals to the public.
The shopping precinct was to be three linked spaces,
and behind St Michael's Spire, A, appears an early
Cathedral reconstruction idea.

Below: 5. The Lower Precinct.
An axial view to the east, from below Mercia House
flats towards Broadgate and St Michael's spire.
Shops on two levels enclose the Lower Precinct amenity
area and elevated cafe. Service access and car parking
is at the rear of the shops and offices.

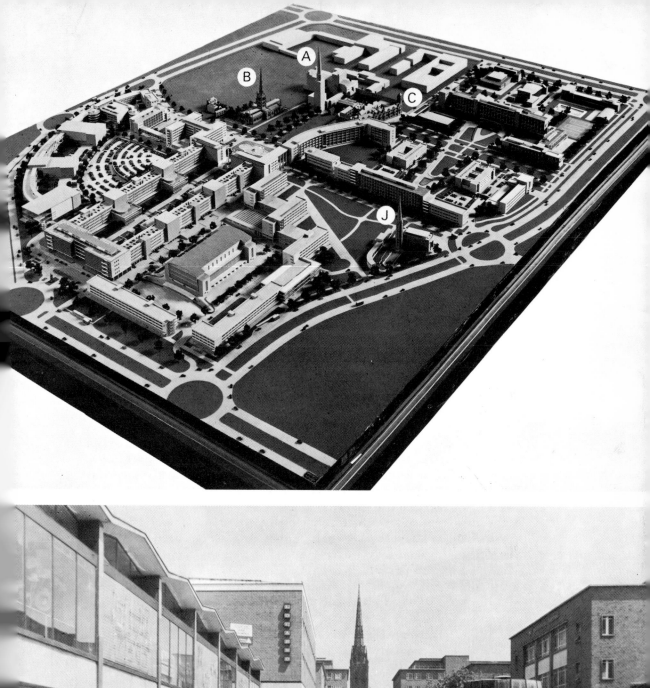

cipal financial interest in the new development fulfilled the political
objective that the city should share in created profitability for the benefit
of its citizens.

Immediately following the air raid of November 1940 the City Council
had resolved that a City Redevelopment Committee should be set up
to consider "the steps which it will be desirable for the municipality to
take to secure a worthy replanning and redevelopment of the city", and
the next month it held its first meeting. The intention was to secure a
unified direction of the process of comprehensive redevelopment. In due
course terms of reference for a Planning and Redevelopment Committee
were adopted to include particular responsibility within the Declaratory
Order Area and Comprehensive Development Areas for matters of civic
design, plans relating to land use, road pattern, making sites available
for development, their programming and relocations, arrangements
with private developers for the erection and leasing of buildings and
schemes for corporation development. Shop and commercial developments were to be undertaken, although transferred to other committees
on completion. The Committee was to act in exercise of powers under
the Town and Country Planning Acts (including development plans,
land acquisition and appropriation), building byelaws (or regulations)
and later certain aspects of legislation relating to public health, land
compensation, factories, offices, shops and railway premises, civic
amenities, highways and licensing. Up to 1967 the chairmanship was
held for significant periods totalling nine years by Alderman George
Hodgkinson.

Procedures required each council committee to submit proposals
annually for a rolling five year capital programme, firstly to the Finance
Committee (to review overall financial implications) and then to the
Policy Advisory Committee to assess priorities. In general the early years
were regarded as the action programme for project design for implementation, and the fourth and fifth years a policy guide related to definition
and acquisition of sites and consideration of any relocation commitments.
Procedural changes were introduced intermittently to relate associated
schemes, or reflect central government control of local authority investment (this was particularly so for example in 1966 and 1970). A most
significant term of Chairmanship of the Policy Advisory Committee was
held by Alderman Sidney Stringer from 1943 to 1967.

Following Conservative control of the City Council in June 1967 a
restructuring of committees was initiated, with the objective of enabling
the Council to study the physical and social environment of the City as
a whole, assess its future needs, lay down major objectives and determine
their priorities. These changes perhaps reflected a growing awareness of
social as well as physical priorities, and a recognition of the progress
already made in central area reconstruction. The Policy Advisory Committee was replaced by a Policy Committee. It was to advise the Council
on all major issues of policy; the development of services, resources and

organisation; the major implications for the community of the Development Plan and other Statutory Schemes; the content of the forward programme of capital works, the level of the annual rate to be levied and allocations to be made to various implementing committees. Alderman Gilbert Richards chaired the Policy Committee from 1967 to 1972 (when another political change promised some reorganisation).

There followed in April 1968 further amendments of committee powers which also reduced the comprehensive redevelopment responsibility hitherto enjoyed by the Planning and Redevelopment Committee. It was renamed the Planning and Development Committee and was no longer responsible for the details of design or actual construction of highways (that is other than formulation of the road pattern) or problems directly relating to transportation, except for the purpose of approving matters of physical development as with the projects of other committees. A new Transportation and Highways Committee now became responsible for all functions relating to detailed highway design, street lighting, traffic control management and regulation, car parking, road safety and transport operation, including their implementation within the Declaratory Order and Comprehensive Development Areas. It was agreed, however, that these two committees should share a strong element of common membership in order to reconcile the relationship between physical development and transportation.

The Council accepted guiding principles as to the division of functions and responsibilities between elected members of the City Council and the professional officers. Ultimately direction in control of the affairs of the authority was to lie with members, who would take key decisions on the objectives and on the plans to attain them. Officers would provide necessary staff work, be responsible for day-to-day administration, decisions on case work and identify problems which had such implications that the members should consider and decide them. The continuing achievements in recreating Coventry City Centre over many years owe much to the complementary teamwork of members' single-mindedness of objectives and of officers' ingenuity in design and implementation.

Following the adoption of Donald Gibson's initial policy for reconstruction, the City Council in May 1941 resolved that the primary responsibility for town planning should be placed upon the City Architect, although he and the City Engineer acted jointly until Ernest Ford's retirement in 1949. Subsequently City Architect and Planning Officers responsible to the Council for development generally have been Donald Gibson until 1955, Arthur Ling until 1964, and from then on the author. Granville Berry was City Engineer until 1967, succeeded by Nathan Rayman, and they made significant contributions relating to civil and highway engineering.

The Department of Architecture and Planning was responsible for all town planning development in the city, civic design matters, together with architectural, landscape architecture, and quantity surveying services related to the implementation of municipal development. A Land Resource and Programme Unit initiated site acquisition and relocation procedures and programmed development projects. Town centre reconstruction only prospers with coordinated interprofessional effort, and from the early years until 1970 integration was achieved by weekly meetings chaired by the Town Clerk (Sir) Charles Barratt. Principal departments involved included Architecture and Planning, Engineer's, Finance and the City Estates Surveyor's. This was the regular "ways and means" meeting.

In March 1970 the Policy Committee endorsed the development of a new management system on a programme budgeting basis, to embrace all local authority activities. Under a Chief Executive and Town Clerk, Derrick Hender, and a Chief Officers' Team interdepartmental groups were formed. Those considering policy formulation were to be known as Programme Area Teams, and there were nine of these, each chaired by a Chief Officer related to a topic. They considered aims, objectives, plan making, five year Capital and Revenue budget implications and output targets, and jointly contributed to the Corporate Local Policy Plan co-ordinated by the Chief Officers team. This was to integrate related special structure, district, and service plans. "Resource Units" advised on finance, land and manpower. The Chief Officers reported to the Policy Committee or Departmental Committees as relevant, and the City Council considered policy issues.

Several interdepartmental officer "Control Groups" were also set up in a parallel organisation to undertake project implementation for different areas of the Capital Programme. A critical path "network" consultancy service operated, and an integrated management information system was under development. This included the City of Coventry Point Data System (1971) which held general information on every property in the city, and detailed information within certain urban topics including manufacturing, retailing, offices and business services. Thus the interprofessional procedures which evolved over many years related to central area redevelopment were now integrated into an expanded system for all development projects involving the local authority.

Such a corporate organisation may be a step towards more ready application of suitable methodology; for example Friend and Jessop (1969) of the Institute of Operational Research had suggested the need in public planning to develop a technology of strategic choice to meet problems of finding solutions, expressing preferences, exposing latent uncertainties, selecting exploratory actions and immediate commitments.

However a local authority must be outward looking as well as inwardly organised in its response to environment. Attention was therefore paid to relationships with the surrounding area, including the need for study of the wider sub-regional and regional context of the city, and positive communication with people comprising the community.

In 1963 the Department of Architecture and Planning published a report, *Coventry City Region*, which appraised the role of Coventry as the focus of a sphere of influence for an area of some ten miles radius with a periphery approximating to Atherstone, Rugby, Leamington, Meriden. It raised the options available for development growth, which would lie outside the city boundary and therefore concern Warwickshire County Council. A further report, *People and Housing*, published in 1966, had made it clear that the anticipated growth of Coventry's population would be only likely to be accommodated within the city until the mid-1970s. Consultations therefore took place with the county from 1965 to set up a joint planning study. The Ministry of Housing and Local Government suggested in 1966 that Coventry, Solihull and Warwickshire set up a study team related to their composite area. In 1968 these authorities agreed to proceed. The independent report in 1971 suggested a short list of four alternative strategies and recommended one as offering the best prospects of meeting the objectives for strategic planning for growth in the sub-region until 1991.

In a wider context still, in 1969, Coventry joined the West Midlands Planning Authorities Conference representing all local planning authorities in the five counties area. Their 1971 report dealt with a broad strategy, including the overspill problems of the West Midland conurbation and was complementary to the sub-regional report. These reports were important in recognising the role of Coventry as the main sub-regional commercial and shopping centre. A related topic was that of ensuring adequate continuing accessibility to the city centre. The proposed Coventry revised road system, approved by the Secretary of State for the Environment in December 1972 as part of the Development Plan Review, evolved over the intervening period from a comprehensive study of traffic and land use by an interprofessional officers team initiated in 1961. The Joint Roads Team comprised Town Planning, Engineer and Transport departments' staffs. The first two groups worked together on a permanent basis in the planning office, with transport staff consultation as necessary. In 1967 a supplementary transportation study group of planners, engineers, economists, and transport officers was formed divorced from day-to-day routines. A phase one report was made in 1969, followed by another in 1973. The study included transportation measures required to implement proposals of the Development Plan Review, including aspects of road construction priorities, parking policy, traffic management measures, bus operations and integration with sub-regional requirements.

Complementary to measures looking at the wider area of influence of Coventry, there was an awareness dating from before 1939, and heightened by the challenge offered by the blitz of 1940, of the need to involve the citizens themselves in planning proposals. The politicians and officers supported positive measures of communication by methods thought to be appropriate to the issues under consideration. Illustrated talks to local organisations were encouraged, and an increasing colour slide

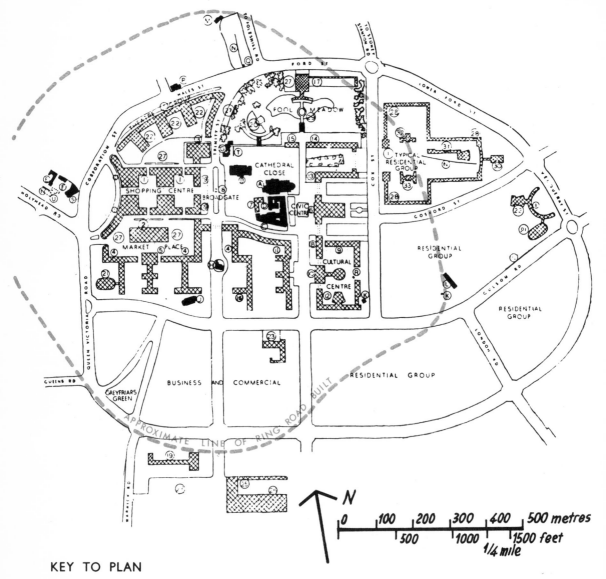

N

| 0 | 100 | 200 | 300 | 400 | 500 metres |

| 500 | 1000 | 1500 feet |

1/4 mile

KEY TO PLAN

OLD BUILDINGS TO BE PRESERVED

A Cathedral
B Holy Trinity Church
C Council House
D St. Mary's Hall
E Bond's Hospital
F Museum
G Bluecoat School
H Ford's Hospital
J Christ Church
K Gate
L Carmelite Monastery
M Cook St. Gate

N Remains of City Wall
P Old Grammar School
Q Swanswell or Priory Gate
R Remains
S St. John's Church
T Old Cathedral
U Suggested Re-siting of Ford's Hospital.

NEW BUILDINGS

1 Arcaded Shops
2 Retail Market

3 Multiple Store
4 Shops and Offices
5 Banks
6 Civic Halls
7 Council House Ext.
8 Art Gallery
9 Art School
10 Library
11 Law and Police Courts
12 University College
13 Council Offices
14 Museum
15 Chapter House
16 Telephone Exchange
17 Covered and Open Baths

18 Godiva Statue
19 Hotel
20 Open Air Theatre
21 Garages
22 Theatre or Cinema
23 Fire Station
25 'Bus Station
26 'Bus Garage
27 Car Parks
28 Flats
29 Band Stand
30 Baths
31 Community Centre
32 Nursery School
33 Health Clinic

collection was assembled in a Building Information Centre in the Department of Architecture and Planning. Voluntary model-making by the architects and planners for the exhibition in 1939, and reliance on a voluntary donation to commission a specific model for public information, as in 1942, were supplanted by the employment of model-making staff from 1950. A sectional model of the whole City Centre area was then prepared to a scale of $\frac{1}{32}''$ to $1'0''$ ($1:384$), and this was normally on display to the public from 1956, within the offices of the department. When new offices were completed in 1959 as part of the Civic Centre development, a permanent exhibition hall was incorporated adjoining the Department of Architecture and Planning with open display to a covered public area adjoining major bus stops. The slowly changing City Centre model (some five metres square) serves as a working tool for project designers, commissioning committees and developers; as a basis for specialist exhibitions and for civics talks to students. It differentiates between buildings to remain or already redeveloped, and future reconstruction. A further development display kiosk in the precinct shopping area controlled by the Planning and Development Committee was completed in 1962 and offered continuous project display.

In 1947 a local authority Public Relations Officer was appointed in the Town Clerk's Department, to act as the point of contact with the press, radio and television. Local press coverage (the Coventry circulation in 1971 was 120,000 copies daily) of development issues has been outstanding, demonstrating a willingness to illustrate and explain proposals (more recently including colour presentation), to promote public comment and to offer considered opinion. When relevant, for example in considering the accommodation requirements for the proposed central area sports hall complex, the press cooperated in publishing questionnaire forms to test public opinion. Similarly, ideas competitions were sponsored, broadsheets distributed, and booklets published. Schoolchildren were involved in ideas projects or competitions and discussion meetings were held with local organisations or in wards of the city when review of development was under consideration.

Opposite: 6. The 1941 Plan.
The essential feature of this study by D. E. E. Gibson, City Architect, following war-time bombing, was the retention of historic buildings; in a formalised redevelopment which provided open spaces to the west and north of the Cathedral. Broadgate would still take north-south traffic, but a pedestrian shopping centre would divert cross-traffic. Later on the residential area was largely excluded and the commercial area extended to the west.

INDUSTRIAL AND COMMERCIAL ACTIVITIES AND INFLUENCES

The 1951 *Coventry Development Plan* summarised "The Main Problems", including the need for "the rebuilding of the city centre with adequate provision for shops, cultural and civic buildings to serve not only a greatly expanded population but also to act as a centre for the surrounding smaller towns and villages. As the reconstruction of the city centre is pressed forward it is becoming increasingly urgent to resite those industries which before the war were mixed up with the shopping and business areas and which must now be resited in order to allow the centre of the city to develop to the size required for the efficient service of Coventry and its environs". Industry then existing within the central area occupied 31 hectares and it was assessed that 21 hectares should be zoned for light industry to cater for firms which needed to remain near the City Centre. These would include goods distribution to the city as a whole, those employing part-time labour, those having some connection with other central area users or processing work from scattered factories. Relocation needs to sites elsewhere were judged to be 32 hectares, an expression of the necessity to promote suburban industrial areas to facilitate central reconstruction.

The existing wholesale market was to be relocated in the suburbs and a new central retail market would be built to replace scattered premises. Compared with the pre-war central shopping floor area of 98,000 sq. m. gross it was proposed to extend this to 191,700 sq. m. by 1971 with a main precinct, free from vehicular traffic, with shopping facilities in two tiers. Central offices were proposed to be provided above shops in the central core and the establishment of offices elsewhere would be discouraged. Main banks and other commercial buildings would be located in a separate area based on the existing grouping. Within the shopping area adequate provision was proposed for car parking.

To meet the needs of an expanding population the three existing cinemas were proposed to be extended to five and the existing Coventry Theatre, with 2,200 seats, for touring shows, was to be supplemented by one about half the size for repertory, possibly with an intimate theatre for amateurs and chamber music. Hotel accommodation was stated to be completely inadequate in 1951; it was proposed to erect a 100 bedroom hotel in Broadgate, and possibly a civic hotel would be established. The pre-war total of 63 licensed premises was to be replaced by fewer and larger premises together with a small number of licensed restaurants.

On the assumption that the central fire station would be relocated elsewhere, a 4 hectare site was proposed near Pool Meadow for a central bus station, including a car park, to cater for local, country, long distance services and coach operators. The possible use of helicopters in the future would be borne in mind. The rebuilding and modernisation of the inadequate main railway station was also envisaged.

It will be appropriate to consider later the degree to which the 20 year proposals of the 1951 development plan quoted above had been achieved by 1971, both as indicative of the planners' judgement and of the buoyancy of the city commercially in recovering from wartime destruction. It was clear at the outset that the local authority would not be given adequate financial sanction by government to erect the majority of buildings of the shopping centre, and therefore complementary phases of development were carried out by public and private agencies over the years in an interlocking manner.

Attempts were made to commence reconstruction in Broadgate privately to the Council's overall design, but these were unsuccessful. The companies to be accommodated were unwilling to promote buildings of a scale and form beyond their own trading interests. The Council therefore set the pattern by building Broadgate House itself during 1949–53, including shops, a restaurant and offices. Subsequently private enterprise cooperated significantly in supporting redevelopment.

It was essential to accommodate trading "magnets" at strategic points, particularly as a new major precinct layout would depend upon induced pedestrian flows for success. Existing department stores and multiples had been trading in temporary or converted premises and their new deployment would be crucial. From 1953 onwards department stores were carefully accommodated at extreme ends of the main precinct, around the precinct crossing of shopping routes, and at the northern end of Smithford Way. To the south the new retail market of 224 stalls was trading from 1958, and the City Arcade of small specialist shops, built in 1962, led to a supermarket in Queen Victoria Road. The cruciform precinct pedestrian flows, accessibility and convenience, were encouraged by bus routes at the extremities (around the peripheral road) and car parks sited within the arms of the cross immediately behind and above the shops.

Certain structural characteristics, apart from the devastation, may have been peculiar to Coventry. After the blitz many shops were housed in temporary units (some still existed in 1973) and redeveloped units carried comparatively high rents. Although every effort was made to relocate existing businesses by offering a variety of shop sizes, complaints were made that early shops offered insufficient small units to encourage variety. This balance was later redressed by the Council itself building smaller unit shops in the Lower Precinct, Smithford Way, Market Way, City Arcade and Bull Yard. Relocated shops earlier included a significant proportion of independent retailers, but these declined at the expense of multiples. Encouraged by planning and estate management controls the shop mix improved so that smaller shops and secondary attractors became dispersed in the links between the magnets.

At times some newly-built shops towards the periphery were slow in letting or trading until adjoining infill proceeded. Measures to help that situation included the demolition of nearby dilapidated properties to improve the local image, the siting of temporary car parks to generate pedestrian flow and, as the centre expanded, the demolition and severance of "fringe" shopping along radial routes that had enjoyed an unforeseen extension of life due to the effect of the blitz on the centre.

Another instance occurred where the Council had to take remedial action. This was to erect temporary buildings for shop and office tenants displaced by a major road scheme approved by one government ministry, because of delay in providing permanent premises due to financial controls of another ministry. (Unfortunately temporary shops tended to be profitable and therefore difficult to remove except for over-riding redevelopment needs.) It was difficult for traders to appreciate the complexities of government in such circumstances.

In the early days the radical change in environment inevitably invoked vociferous comment. The views of the traders in 1945 had led to the adoption of the road bisecting the Precinct. A section of road in Market Way was subsequently constructed, unfortunately with small shops inset into the frontages of Woolworths and British Home Stores with no service from the rear. To maintain the policy of pedestrian and vehicle segregation for the precinct a subway costing some £40,000 would have been required, with ramps to by-pass adjoining shop frontages, but with the completion of the Upper Precinct as a major amenity pedestrian area in 1955, public opposition to the principle diminished. The City Council therefore approved Arthur Ling's proposal that the proposed road, Market Way and Smithford Way should revert to a pedestrian area. This enlarged the amenity precinct area extensively in the form of a giant cross, and encouraged pedestrian flow by opening up circuits for shoppers also using frontages along the peripheral or "inner circulatory road". Unfortunately, the inset shops in Market Way had to continue to be serviced from the otherwise pedestrian area—a memorial to a temporary lack of confidence in the planning principle.

Some years later the Council proposed the pedestrianisation of an existing shopping street, Hertford Street, rather than a total redevelopment as in the precinct area. Here substantial buildings on one side were not yet ripe for redevelopment, but in general rear service accesses were available. The traders accepted that in the light of the constraints of busy narrow footpaths and vehicle no waiting restrictions in force, pedestrianisation would ultimately bring benefits. Their main concerns were that buses should serve each end of the area and that there should be ready access to car parks. Hertford Street was closed to vehicles in 1969. Adjoining redevelopment proceeded, and a further major pedestrian circuit of the precinct was in being.

Another periodic complaint from traders was the level of car parking charges, particularly in comparison with smaller towns nearby. Experience confirmed that the demand for car parking did depend to some extent upon the charges made. However, the use of charges as a regulator had to be seen against the need to define some relationship between the costs of provision (with increasing use of expensive structures rather than surface parking), demand generated by the increasing commercial facilities becoming available and differential charges to allow adequate turnover of spaces for shoppers as distinct from provision for day or half day commuter traffic. Periodic review of pricing and the construction programme was therefore necessary.

Assessment of commercial trends over the period of reconstruction indicated some flexibility in the use of buildings, a fact for consideration in their planning and constructional design and in the form of the review clauses in leases. Rather than demolish Victoria Buildings (an old factory) the Corporation adapted the ground floor as shops, arcade entrance and fish market, and added a clock tower. Another upper section was converted into a bowling alley for some years, but this waned in popularity and a supermarket replaced it. The first floors of Broadgate House and Hillman House reverted in part from shopping to offices; some Belgrade flats were converted into a restaurant; two-storey shops originally designed for different premises became one unit; and there was a general increase in demand for restaurant and entertainment facilities.

There was also change in the relationship between the local authority and developers, particularly where each had significant land interest within the area of a comprehensive development. For example, the Hertford Street West redevelopment of shops, offices and arcade in 1970–72 by Ravenseft Properties was negotiated with the Corporation with an agreed planning brief and ground lease, on the basis of a financial partnership with return related to investment by each party.

National activity exerted varying influence upon the development of the City Centre. In the hierarchical pattern of shopping centres in England and Wales in 1961, Coventry was ranked in relative attractiveness (four rankings) as a second order centre sited geographically between the first order centres of Birmingham and Leicester. The Board of Trade (1961) Report of the Census of Distribution and Other Services quoted shopping turnover in the West Midlands Region as follows: Birmingham, £218,199,750; Coventry, £57,242,860; Nuneaton, Leamington Spa, Rugby and Solihull, each approximately £10–12m. The limitations of facilities imposed by the blitz were being remedied.

In 1967 the Development Plan Review Analysis stated that "even with its rapidly expanding population (or perhaps because of it) Coventry's centre does not give the appearance of serving a sub-regional population of over 600,000. The city centre contains much less evidence of nineteenth-century commercial development than is typical of most English cities. It has been overshadowed by Birmingham but is now emerging as a sub-regional service, shopping and social centre, but despite this the centre still lacks the metropolitan scale in its buildings which might be expected from its tremendous growth and its importance in the sub-region. This is partly due to the imbalance in the provision of local

 Public Buildings

 Business Premises

 Light Industry

 Residential

Open Space

N

0   100   200   300   400   500 met.

500   1000   1500 feet

1/4 mile

service employment and the lack of the central commercial and office development of a typical English city. The realisation of the City's potential as a sub-regional centre would bring advantages economically and socially as well as visually."

In 1970 there were approximately 193,500 jobs within the city, of which one-fifth were occupied by people living outside it. The central area was far less dominant as an employment centre than in most large towns, containing about 21,300 jobs or only about 11 per cent of the total. This has been a major influence on City Centre activities. However, the gradual post-war reconstruction of the central shopping area had by 1970 attracted a higher concentration of activity, with 6,400 jobs (or 45 per cent of the city total) in retailing.

The siting of city industry was widely dispersed and Coventry had a high ratio of manufacturing to service employment—approximately 67:33 compared with an average ratio of 55:45 for cities of a similar size. This reflected the influence of the Birmingham conurbation and the rapid growth of Coventry's manufacturing industry. Most service employment in the city was in retailing, together with professional, scientific and miscellaneous services. In order to improve the imbalance in service employment efforts were being made to exploit potential, diversify and in particular to encourage the increasing demand for office development. However, between 1965 and 1970 national policy (Control of Office and Industrial Development Act, 1965) to restrict the growth of employment in certain areas and government control of office development projects in the city exceeding 280 sq. m. delayed such diversification. The imbalance contributed to the situation whereby Coventry continued to be a "rate deficiency" area, that is, it had a rateable value per head of population appreciably below the national average.

On the other hand, government measures to promote the international tourist industry directly benefited the city. The 1951 Development Plan commented on the local lack of hotel facilities. The Hotel Leofric (100 bedrooms) in Broadgate had been constructed by 1955 but there had been little other progress. After the war Coventry Cathedral itself emerged as a major tourist attraction; within a few miles were the historic towns of Kenilworth, Warwick, Leamington and Stratford; the Cotswolds' countryside was within easy reach and new motorways and the electrified

Opposite: 7. The 1951 Plan.
The proposed ring road had been re-aligned, the formalised road pattern discarded, and open spaces near the Cathedral re-allocated for business premises, car parking and a bus station. A northerly traffic road had been introduced to bisect the pedestrian shopping centre. The key includes zonings for primary uses.

H

railway improved accessibility. The Government offered financial grant
for hotel development physically started before April 1971, and this
resulted in the promotion of eight significant projects in or near the city.
A major hotel (206 bedrooms) was developed immediately north of the
Cathedral and smaller ones developed near the office and railway
station area by adaptation of large residential properties on the original
Cheylesmore Park. Other hotels expanded on radial routes near the city
centre in Warwick Road and Holyhead Road. The prospects seemed
brighter that Coventry might benefit from tourists staying in the city
rather than briefly visiting it, and that conference facilities might be
further encouraged by complementary provision at the University and
Polytechnic.

OTHER ACTIVITIES AND INFLUENCES

In the years immediately following the bombing, the planning philosophy
was generally to redevelop comprehensively around the core of the
Cathedral and Holy Trinity Church and to provide large open spaces,
in contrast to the traditional high density building within the town walls.
In 1946 a public inquiry considered the possibility of removing Georgian
buildings in Priory Row, in order to open up vistas of the Cathedral,
but objection was considerable and restoration followed. The war-
damaged Fords Hospital was eventually restored by 1953, but in 1955
proposals were made to demolish the oldest part of Cheylesmore Manor
House; £12,000 required for restoration was not forthcoming and demolition followed. The late 1960s brought a new awareness of the diminishing
ancient heritage, and positive programmes of remedial works were
undertaken by the Corporation and the private sector. These were later
reinforced by the protective measures of the Town and Country Planning
Act, 1968 for buildings of architectural and historic interest.

In 1966 a survey of medieval timber-framed domestic buildings, once
dominant in the town centre, revealed that only fragments remained.
The local authority proposed to restore the most significant group remaining in Spon Street, which had been made into a cul-de-sac to
eliminate through traffic. Similar isolated buildings elsewhere affected
by redevelopment were also to be reconstructed in Spon Street. This
proved to be a highly contentious proposal, but the City Planning

Opposite: 8. The Development Plan 1957.
This government approved plan incorporated certain
modifications to the 1951 submission. The road
through the shopping centre was to be pedestrianised
to extend the precinct area, through traffic was
still to use Broadgate, and the civic area was
extended to north of the Cathedral, originally the
siting for the bus garage.

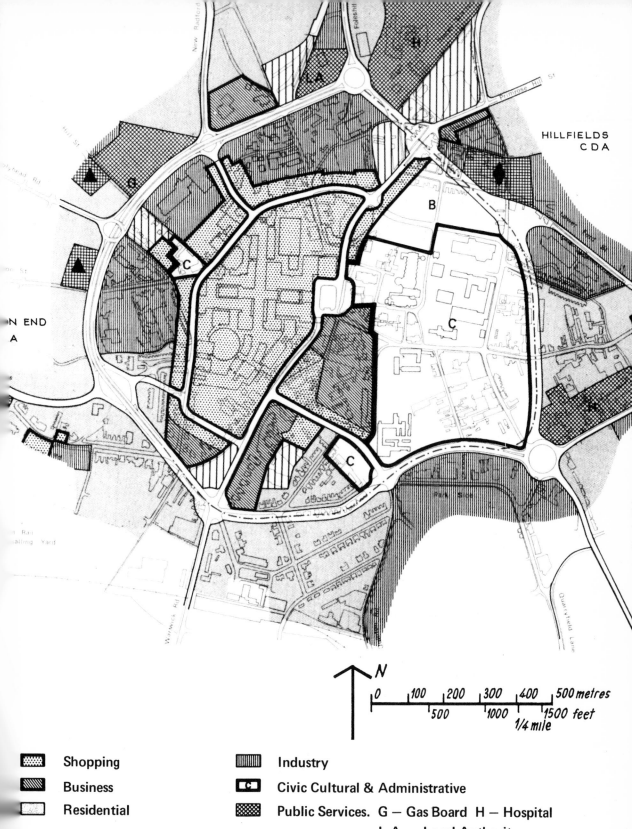

HILLFIELDS
C D A

N

| 0 | 100 | 200 | 300 | 400 | 500 metres |
| 500 | | 1000 | | 1500 feet |
1/4 mile

Shopping		Industry
Business		Civic Cultural & Administrative
Residential		Public Services. G — Gas Board H — Hospital
		L.A. — Local Authority
Primary School		B — Bus Station
Secondary School		Public open space
Further Education		

Department sought support from the Historic Buildings Council of England in 1967, and after inspection they agreed that the Spon Street Townscape Scheme, "involving the large scale dismantling, removal and re-erection of buildings, would be in the nature of an archaeological exercise of considerable potential interest and value". Following the Review Plan Inquiry the Secretary of State in 1972 modified the written statement to include the Council's intention to import into the Spon Street area buildings affected by redevelopment elsewhere in the city.

Number 169 Spon Street was restored in 1970 and to allow Polytechnic development numbers 7, 8, 9, 10 Much Park Street were moved into Spon Street as the first relocations. The Review Plan had also proposed a townscape scheme for the preservation of the group of buildings in Priory Row. Under the Civic Amenities Act, 1967 the Council incorporated these two schemes into conservation areas for enhancement of character and preservation—St. John's Church, Bablake and Bonds Hospital linked to Spon Street; Holy Trinity Church, the Cathedral, the "Golden Cross" and the Guildhall of St. Mary linked to Priory Row. Other conservation areas included Greyfriars Green with the Quadrant, and Lady Herbert's Garden with remains of the City Wall, Cook Street and Swanswell Gates.

These considerations prompted the founding of the Coventry Civic Amenity Society in 1970, a successor to the Civic Guild which, particularly from 1936 until the mid-1950s, had interested itself in development issues.

The early years of working-up the first reconstruction projects had faced frustration and calls for rapid action. In the interim period every possible public relations opportunity was taken to interest the public; a "levelling stone" initiated the pedestrian precinct redevelopment on 8 June, 1946, and construction of the amenity traffic island in Broadgate in 1947 included a landscaping gift from the Dutch Government and an official opening by Princess Elizabeth in May 1948. A "Savings for Reconstruction Exhibition" in 1948 initiated the "Broadgate Standard" as a Coventry symbol to mark the precinct axis. The gift from William

Opposite:
Above: 9. Spon Street and Mercia House Flats. Spon Street, once a busy radial route, is now a cul-de-sac along which medieval timber framed domestic buildings are to be preserved. The view is towards the east and Holy Trinity spire.

Below: 10. Holy Trinity, The Cathedral and the Polytechnic The spires of Holy Trinity and St. Michael, with the ruins and the new Cathedral. In the left foreground is the City Reference Library, and on the right are the Lanchester Polytechnic residential tower and administration block.

harmony!

Bassett-Green of the Lady Godiva statue in Broadgate by sculptor Sir William Reid Dick was unveiled with ceremony in 1949.

Some proposals during this period became highly controversial. The animated Godiva clock overlooking Broadgate (later to prove a considerable tourist attraction) drew protests, meetings and a petition. Some projects were completely reappraised. The new art gallery and museum, sponsored with gifts from Sir Alfred Herbert, had commenced construction in Earl Street in 1939, with some opposition to its pseudo-classical style. Later the donor agreed to a new site in Jordan Well, and a revised design, and this building was completed in 1959.

The problem of the war-damaged Cathedral was of more than local concern. Rebuilding plans by Sir Giles Gilbert Scott did not prove satisfactory to the Royal Fine Art Commission in 1946. Should the original building be restored, or cleared and redeveloped, or should the ruins be retained? It was decided to hold a major architectural competition and the design of (Sir) Basil Spence was selected in 1951. His conception retained the ruins as an open paved place, a link with the past, a monument to war but with a message of reconciliation, and dominated by the magnificent late medieval steeple. The new structure was sited to the north and at right angles to the old, both now forming the Cathedral, retaining a major public footpath, St. Michael's Way, between them. A landscaped close was formed adjoining Priory Row; a frontage was created along Priory Street and a new north front overlooked Pool Meadow.

The planning authority were not convinced of the high priority for cathedral reconstruction related to other pressing needs, but the Minister of Works, Sir David Eccles, sanctioned an immediate start as a special priority of more than local significance. The new Cathedral was completed in 1962 and as Sir Nikolaus Pevsner (1966) wrote "even internationally speaking, the Cathedral acts with a high emotive power . . . it has moreover plenty of subtleties which can be appreciated coolly . . . such as the interlocking of old and new building".

The land characteristics of the centre include a low hill on which is sited the Cathedral, Holy Trinity Church and Broadgate. This allowed exploitation of certain levels and views. The two spires are quite dominant and development was planned to retain certain views of them from Greyfriars Green, Warwick Road and Spencer Park. The main precinct axis was aligned in 1941 onto the Cathedral spire in a grand vista and the drop in level allowed the design of two-level gallery shopping in both the Upper and Lower Precincts. There is a valley below the north end of the Cathedral, and part of it has been developed as a pedestrian square, enclosed by halls of residence and a hotel. The latter included a first floor pedestrian gallery linking it to the Cathedral north terrace in 1973. The levels at Hertford Street allowed a tunnel to be driven under the upper end to give vehicular service access under the pedestrian shopping. The shallow valley of Pool Meadow allowed almost one-third of the

Inner Ring Road to be elevated by 1970 so that local roads and pedestrian routes ran underneath where landscaping and certain other uses such as car parking could be accommodated.

The area immediately to the east of the Cathedral had been proposed in the 1951 Plan for civic, cultural and administrative public buildings. A first block of a new College of Art had been opened in Cope Street in 1955 but this became inadequate within 10 years and a new College of Art and Design was completed to the east of Cox Street by 1967. This education buildings expansion changed zoning policy for social clubs within the ring road and a new clubs area was developed outside (off Queens Road) in the late 1960s. The 1951 Plan for a new central College of Technology was implemented in a phased programme of blocks adjoining the Cathedral (the first being completed in 1961) in the form of a landscaped precinct. Government policy to expand higher education in the public sector grouped the colleges of art and technology (and the Rugby College of Engineering Technology) into the Lanchester Polytechnic in 1970. The growth of the city colleges were such that by 1971 they occupied 8 hectares with 54,800 sq. m. of accommodation. They had sought additional areas to the south of Jordan Well (which caused a Crown Office site to be moved to Pool Meadow) and more outside the Ring Road to the east. The rapid evolution of the Polytechnic in the central area was very significant as a functional and environmental contribution to redevelopment.

In this area a change from the 1951 Plan was the decision to build central swimming baths and displace the zoning for a bus garage to outside the City Centre. A war damage claim on the Government, loan sanction availability and general accessibility determined central facilities. The Coventry Baths, opened in 1966, included three pools (one of international size), seating for 1174, restaurant and games area and meeting rooms in an outward-looking, exciting design and overlooking a parkway near to the Polytechnic and Cathedral. Also completed in 1958, was the civic Belgrade Theatre in Corporation Street, seating 910, managed by a Theatre Trust supported by the City Council and the Arts Council for Great Britain.

Within the Inner Ring Road the 1951 Plan retained only one significant residential area, that existing near Friars Road, together with existing almshouses and a tiny group near Lady Herbert's Garden. However, considerable residential redevelopment by the local authority, private developers and housing associations has taken place in adjoining comprehensive development areas at Hillfields and Spon End. An area to the east of the railway station also remained zoned residential. The relatively small centre offered diminishing residential accommodation, other than in the special categories of hotels, hostels, halls of residence, small business flats, old people's accommodation and the like. Financial constraints and readily accessible suburbia generally discouraged developers and housing associations from providing central family housing.

Townscape improvement is a positive concern of the City Council, and there has been an annual programme of tree planting since 1966. Action was also taken in 1951 to declare 12 hectares in the centre a smokeless zone (under Local Act powers), and this was extended by stages under the Clean Air Act, 1956.

A major factor upon the post-war activities and layout was the influence of the vehicle. The trend towards larger container vehicles delivering goods to shops led to public support for pedestrian areas but required adequate and increasing consideration for segregated service areas for shops. The layout discipline imposed by the Coventry plan over many years provided rear service roads to the shops, with some communal use for access to adjoining car parks. However, it is intended in due course to provide additional direct overhead links from car parks to the Inner Ring Road or circulatory road system. Certain major buildings employed basement storage (e.g. Owen Owen, Hillman House, the retail market) and the upper precinct included service ramps to several levels.

In order to limit congestion the commercial requirements of the central area were seen to be: rapid access from the national, regional and local road network for all vehicles; deflection of through traffic; convenient bus stops, efficient commercial vehicle access; car park accessibility for different users; and safe pedestrian circulation. Development and traffic management measures were designed to meet these requirements. Special design needs in precincts, arcade areas, multi-storey buildings and car parks emerged for emergency services and for the disabled.

Car ownership in Coventry proved to be higher than in any other major city in Great Britain. Nearly half the people using the shopping area car parks came from outside the city. A city centre pedestrian survey in 1967 indicated that 70 per cent of midweek and 60 per cent of Saturday shoppers came by bus. For all these reasons accessibility had to be maintained. Unfortunately the Pool Meadow main bus station, with few facilities and peripheral to the shopping centre, proved to be too far away for some shoppers. Improvements and supplementary routes or interchange points were called for. The railway station, outside the central area, was rebuilt in 1962 with excellent facilities, an impressive concourse, and a linked multi-storey car park. With the introduction of electrification in 1967 it became an important sub-regional railhead but suffered somewhat from its peripheral siting, although it was linked by railbus

Opposite:
11. The Review Plan 1966
This review was submitted in 1967, and approved by government in 1972. It introduced multi-level junctions for the Ring Road and an Inner Circulatory Road which extended environmental areas by eliminating through traffic. Townscape conservation areas and a Lanchester Polytechnic zone were defined.

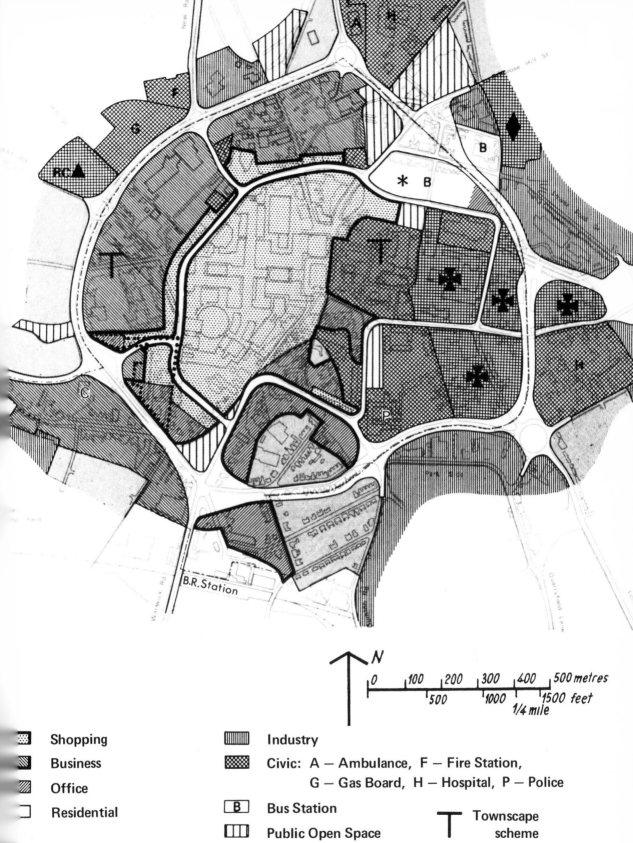

N

0	100	200	300	400	500 metres
	500	1000		1500 feet	

1/4 mile

Shopping

Business

Office

Residential

R.C. Primary School

Secondary School

Further Education
Polytechnic

Industry

Civic: A – Ambulance, F – Fire Station,
G – Gas Board, H – Hospital, P – Police

B Bus Station

Public Open Space

* Recreation centre

Townscape
scheme

C Clubs Area

Boundary of area for land use
calculation purposes

Boundary of Queen Victoria Road Extension,
Comprehensive Development Area

to the centre and the bus station.

The Coventry Canal Basin, immediately to the north of the Ring Road, was no longer in use industrially but was designated as a leisure cruiseway under the Transport Act, 1968. This offered opportunity for development as a recreational centre to the benefit of the central area.

EFFECT OF NEW BUILDING TECHNOLOGY

The 1941 conception was of a central area which, for the size of city, would not need very high buildings, and which could rely on the Holy Trinity and Cathedral spires for visual focus. Twenty years later there was increasing concern to build up the scale to reflect the sub-regional role of the City, to change a lingering image of small town character, to add interest to newly created spaces with vertical elements, to give the central area visual identity and variety of skyline, and to introduce residential accommodation.

High buildings technology generally offered alternatives of vertical towers with central lifts and services, or slab blocks with corridor circulation. The basic philosophy that evolved between 1960 and 1972 was to accept blocks over 7 storeys as of more than local significance to adjoining spaces, to control their disposition and orientation related to the central area as a whole, to adopt tower blocks as offering vertical elements of a compatible scale, complementing rather than detracting from the central spires, and to prefer light colours offering visual contrast to the darker materials of the spires and of the lower development.

From the 1960s a series of definitive 17-storey tower blocks were sited peripherally outside the Ring Road, and of related scale to it; one group being located to emphasise the topography of the northern city slopes and to offer a sense of identity. Within the City Centre, terminal flats blocks were provided to the axes of the shopping precinct in Smithford Way and the Lower Precinct and twin office towers were proposed in Market Way in 1971. Towers were also sited as focal elements for the railway station in 1965, the Polytechnic in 1966 and the civic offices in 1973.

The planning authority encouraged the introduction of high buildings within the disciplines of a visual design philosophy. However developers increasingly exerted pressures for maximum commercial exploitation of high value central sites, with less regard for a neighbourly relationship of form and scale than for financial return. High building techniques increasingly made possible uncoordinated approaches for business expansion which were often at variance with civic design preferences.

A visual skyline problem in high building was related to lift rooms and services situated on flat roofs. A variety of solutions emerged: a major design feature giving a predominant character to the whole building (Hillman House); a simple addition (Mercia House); integration by application of superimposed fins (Polytechnic); and silhouette interest by form of parapets (Spire House). Slab construction of buildings also allowed flat roofs to be used for other purposes, in the case of precinct shops and the market for roof car parks connected to the upper floors of multi-storey car parks. The heating of access ramps proved advantageous for all-weather use; and the ability to tunnel and ventilate roads (as under Hertford Street, 1971) or elevate them on structure for considerable distances (Inner Ring Road, 1970), allowed the complete segregation of pedestrian and traffic circulations.

Constructional techniques of bridging openings allowed a more integrated relationship of buildings and spaces. Pedestrian routes through buildings were increasingly utilised as in Shelton Square (1960) and Market Way, and also from Fairfax Street under the halls of residence into Cathedral Square (1972). Substantial buildings crossing streets were also adopted in order to create townscape, for example Broadgate House and Hertford Street (1953), Station Square offices (1965 and 1970), and the hotel in Fairfax Street (1972).

The flexibility of new building techniques facilitated the close integration of differing accommodation. The rigid separation of different use zones, if not required in functional terms, was now far less constrained by structural factors. Interlocking shops, offices, flats, car parks, footways and roads were in some circumstances advantageous.

Variety in the urban scene in many cases reflected the ability to match functional needs with a structural solution. The wide span market was built in circular form, to prevent the establishment of prime stall sites. The swimming baths roofed large spaces with elegance and interest using steel structure. The ability to glaze extensive areas gave particular character to certain buildings; the entrance screen to the new Cathedral, the south side of the swimming baths and the Owen Owen store, the entrance to the Locarno ballroom, the concourse of the railway station and Belgrade Theatre, all inviting the world in and contributing atmosphere by illumination after dark. Visual interest was also offered by an increasing variety of materials used for artistic features of buildings and spaces.

Increasingly, illuminating engineering provided more flexible opportunities for lighting public areas. It became possible to light whole spaces with one high mounted source (as in Station Square, 1966, and similarly in multi-level junctions of the Ring Road), although where practicable, parapet-mounted strip lighting proved less visually obtrusive in the daytime. Arcaded shops offered potential for illuminated signs, and the floodlighting of selected buildings enhanced the urban scene after dark. Planning policy in 1968 recognised defined areas of "concentrated brightness and advertising" in the commercial area in order to promote interest and variety.

The principle of weather protection for shoppers included a variety of technical solutions over the years, simple cantilever canopies, arcaded shop frontages with or without accommodation over, and covered shopping arcades; the continuity achieved in new shopping areas was substantial.

DEVELOPMENT PLANS, ACTION AREAS, ACHIEVEMENTS

The Central Area Plan accepted by the Ministries of Local Government and Planning, and Transport, in July 1949, was incorporated into the Coventry submission of their Development Plan in 1951. This, with proposals looking towards 1971, was approved by the Minister of Housing and Local Government in 1957. He confirmed certain amendments, including elimination of the road through the heart of the pedestrian precinct shopping area. The plan allocated primary use zones, proposed a ground level Inner Ring Road, severed east–west but retained north–south traffic through Broadgate, and adopted a shopping circulatory road and surface car parks. Within the City Centre, streets were intended to carry public service traffic as well as private car traffic, and a radial city road pattern utilised intermediate and outer ring roads.

The city's Development Plan was subsequently reviewed in the light of changing circumstances since the original survey of 1949, in an attempt to assess city requirements for 1981, particularly in the light of continued population and traffic pressures. The Council approved a policy plan in November 1965. Local detailed proposals followed, and after exhibition and the receipt of 2,000 comments the Council introduced modifications and the Review Plan was deposited with the Minister in May 1967. Formal deposit was followed by further advertisement, public exhibition, comment, and objections to the Minister. The Council then made further modifications (to which some counter objections were received!). In all 80 meetings had been held, with three exhibitions attended by 11,700 people. 732 formal objections were made, but 322 of these were withdrawn by the time of the public inquiry, held from October to December 1968. The *Development Plan Review* was approved by the Secretary of State for the Environment in December 1972, with certain modifications proposed by him which were not significant to the central area.

The Review summary of problems to be solved had stated:

Opposite:
Above: 12. The North South Shopping Precinct 1966.
A view along Market Way after pedestrianisation
towards the Hillman House flats. Seen here are
the precinct shops with their continuous canopies
and the roof top car parks.

Below: 13. Hertford Street.
The street was closed to vehicular traffic in 1969
and redeveloped on the western side with shops,
offices, cinema and an arcade. Traffic is now
diverted along the Inner Circulatory Road.

"The number of vehicles has increased much more rapidly than was originally forecast. Government plans for a national motorway network have become clarified. It has therefore been necessary to completely revise the City road pattern proposed in the 1957 development plan and to provide a radical solution to future traffic problems. The road pattern included in the review plan will form an adequate structure to deal with anticipated off-peak period flows but further studies are being made of the problem of providing sufficient facilities for commuter movement and the role of public transport in the comprehensive transportation plan.

"Progress on central area reconstruction was delayed after the war because of the priority given to housing and schools. Considerable central redevelopment was envisaged in the 1951 Plan and much of this has now been achieved. The most significant problem remaining in the city centre is the further development of the traffic circulation system and provision of further car parking space, together with extensions to the shopping area.

"In order to minimise the burden on the City's finances the emphasis has been on revenue-producing development. Many of the central shops and offices are built and leased by the City Council. These will provide a satisfactory return on capital, and the earlier schemes are already showing a surplus which will eventually be available to return to the general rate fund."

The adoption of pioneering computer-based land use–transportation techniques from 1961 produced an advanced city highway network designed to give easy access to employment areas and the City Centre from the national and regional road system. These new links were a change from the former concentric pattern around the City Centre, and formed tangential routes which would reduce congestion and improve accessibility from the sub-region.

The Review Plan adoption of inner ring road multi-level junctions, and cuttings or elevated sections, achieved greater flexibility for pedestrian and local traffic movement. The road will be completed by 1974 and will allow approach to any central sector; to the railway and bus stations; and will promote ease of movement by police, fire, ambulance and hospital services. Even partial completion of the ring up to 1966 reduced through traffic and cars within the central area by 3·8 per cent per year, and an analysis of accidents on the Inner Ring Road showed a potential reduction in accidents per million vehicle-miles per year of one-fifth.

A major circulation proposal of the Review Plan included provision of an extended Inner Circulatory Road, primarily for buses and service vehicles, not only round the shopping area but also servicing the other central sectors. Three completely new roads were constructed—Fairfax Street (1965), New Union Street (1966) and Greyfriars Road (1968). A pattern of environmental areas protected from circulating traffic was thereby formed both within the inner circulatory route and as outer cells bounded also by radial connections and the Inner Ring Road. This allowed the restructuring of circulation and extension of pedestrian segregation within the environmental areas, including implementation of the Review Plan proposal to sever the north–south traffic route through Broadgate via Hertford Street. These radical changes from the 1957 Plan made for considerable relief from central traffic congestion, particularly noticeable from 1969. The only roads within the Inner Circulatory Road still carrying more than service traffic were then the linked streets of High Street, Broadgate, Trinity Street, Cross Cheaping and Burges.

In the central area, according to the 1966 review plan written statement relating to transportation, "provision will be made for the continued development of the comprehensive public parking system. The number of parking places will be limited to 10,000 spaces within the Inner Ring Road. Wherever possible direct links will be provided to and from the car parking areas to the Inner Ring Road independent of the Inner Circulatory Road system. It is not proposed to introduce parking meters; provision for short-stay parkers will be made within the parking complex, and will be controlled by pricing policy. Freehold developers will not be encouraged to provide independent car parks but will be expected to contribute towards the provision of comprehensive car parking in the central area."

The *Traffic and Transport Plan 1970*, a City Council report to the Ministry of Transport, included the following policy appraisal:

"The provision of car parking space has been an integral part of the planned comprehensive reconstruction of the Central Area of the City based on the following principles:

That it was desirable to have a Civic Centre as a focus of the City's civic, cultural, business, shopping, social and education activities;

That public car parks should be provided as close as possible to these activities and any charges so arranged as not to deter car drivers from using them;

That the provision of car parks should be the responsibility of the Local Authority so that there would be control over parking duration and charges and to a lesser extent traffic generation;

That there should be a comprehensive parking system, because piece-meal and haphazard development of small private car parks is wasteful, particularly where land values are high, and would increase traffic congestion due to a multiplicity of accesses;

The acceptance of a positive and continuing role for public transport. The subsequent policy implemented has had to have regard to changing circumstances but the main features have been:

A positive programme for public car park provision to meet increasing demand;

Discouragement of the provision of non-operational private parking spaces;

The maintenance of charges at a level which would not seriously

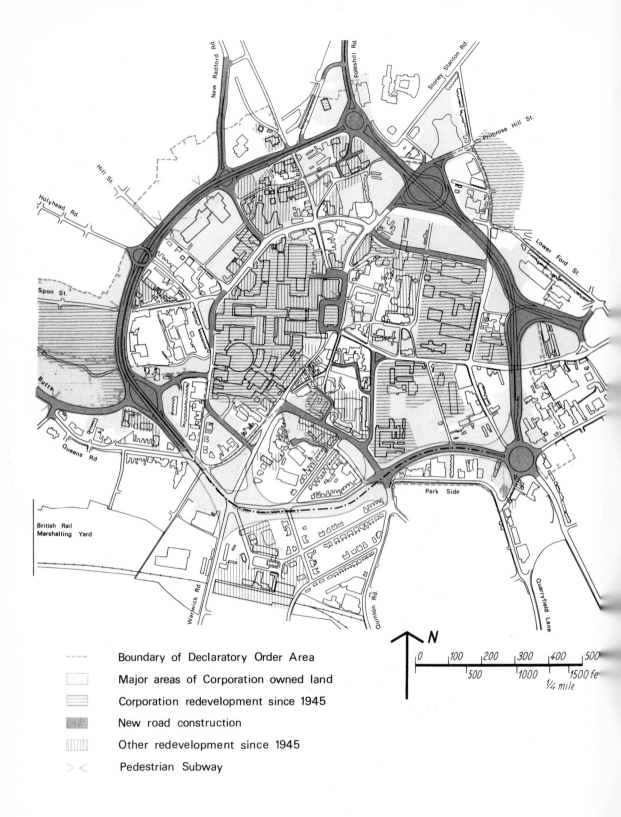

New Radford Rd.
Foleshill Rd.
Stoney Stanton Rd.
Primrose Hill St.
Hill St.
Holyhead Rd.
Lower Ford St.
Spon St.
Butts
Queens Rd
British Rail
Marshalling Yard
Park Side
Warwick Rd
Quinton Rd.
Quarryfield Lane

N

| 0 | 100 | 200 | 300 | 400 | 500 |
| 500 | | 1000 | | 1500 fe |
¼ mile

- - - - - Boundary of Declaratory Order Area

☐ Major areas of Corporation owned land

☰ Corporation redevelopment since 1945

▨ New road construction

▥ Other redevelopment since 1945

> < Pedestrian Subway

discourage the attractiveness of the Central Area to private car users;
The acceptance of contributions from private freehold developers in
lieu of the provision of private car parking; and
The safeguarding of direct connecting links from the Inner Ring
Road.
More recently the differentiation between long-stay and short-stay
parking provision by different scales of charges.
The successful implementation of this comprehensive parking system
has produced the following benefits to the community at large, which
would not otherwise have occurred:
Increased income to the Central Area business and shopping establishments;
An increased floor space can be permitted in new private leasehold
and freehold development as a result of waiving any requirements for
private off-street parking provision;
The most economical provision of car parking space by multi-use
giving maximum turn-over of spaces and comprehensive management
of traffic generation;
The acceptance by the Corporation of capital sums from private
freehold developers in lieu of the physical provision of parking space.
These benefits have already cumulatively assisted the successful and
continuing reconstruction of the city centre in a form which provides
for a wide range of functions and maximum accessibility to them."
By 1971, complemented by waiting restrictions on roads, the parking
in the central area and station area was for 8,804 vehicles. Of this total,
2,707 spaces were provided in multi-storey, basement or roof-top structures
conveniently related to redevelopment. These achievements should be
compared with the 1951 Plan target requirements for some 3,000 spaces
by 1971.
    In order to meet emerging tourist and entertainment needs in the
area, including the Cathedral, baths and theatres a coach park was
provided in 1970 at the White Street interchange of the Ring Road.
    The 1966 Review Plan did not increase the total shopping area for
1981 above that previously planned, but substantially extended the

Opposite:
14. Redevelopment Progress 1971.
The Corporation (£32m) and others (£12m) had spent
£44m on redevelopment from 1948 to 1971. 99
compulsory purchase orders had been confirmed, the
Corporation owned 76 ha. of land, and a new road
pattern had been structured. Buildings catered
for a wide variety of civic, commercial, educational
and residential development, and included the new
Cathedral.

precinct area within it. By 1971 the comprehensive pedestrian area offered a weather protected shopping frontage without crossing any vehicular road of 4366m., and accommodated 314 shop units and 224 market stalls. These impressive figures did not include shopping frontages along the Inner Circulatory Road, and within it there were some 2000 car park spaces.

The office floor space achieved by 1971 was more than double the 1957 Plan estimate. This appears to have been largely due to the existing low density prior to redevelopment, and the realisation of greater site floorspace than anticipated at the time of the 1951 survey. It also reflected pressures to redevelop offices due to the effect of other major reconstruction schemes, particularly new roads. New professional and commercial offices outside the shopping area tended to concentrate on the south side in New Union Street and Warwick Road near to the railway station and car parks. The achievements were of visual significance in promoting a commercial image. The 1966 Review Plan set a higher floorspace target for 1981, reflecting continuing service employment needs.

The civic, cultural and administrative area of the 1957 Plan was divided in the Review Plan to allocate a separate further education area to recognise establishment of the Lanchester Polytechnic, which by 1971 had 5000 students. Very substantial progress was made towards creating a new environmental area north of Jordan Well towards Fairfax Street by buildings for the new Cathedral, art gallery, museum, reference library, Polytechnic, halls of residence, swimming baths and hotel.

The civic area to the south, developed up to 1960, had two groups of municipal offices, a police headquarters and telephone exchange, but for ten years progress was delayed by other financial priorities and the findings of the Royal Commission on Assizes and Quarter Sessions, set up to determine the accommodation of the proposed Law Courts. In 1971 the Polytechnic library and in 1973 a civic offices tower in Much

Opposite:
Above: Left, top: 15. Model of the North East Central Area 1971. Key numbers are as for the City Centre Structure Plan and also: 31 Holy Trinity; 32 Polytechnic Halls of Residence; 33 Hotel (under construction 1972); 34 multi-storey carpark, with shops under; 35 coach park beneath elevated Inner Ring Road; 36 future Crown Offices; 37 future Commercial Offices; 38 Entertainment area above future car park and bus station.

Below: 16. Model of the South East Central Area. Additional key numbers are: 41 Civic Offices; 42 Professional Offices; 43 Civic Square. In these views of sections of the City Centre Model, dark roofs are buildings existing in 1972; light roofs are future proposals.

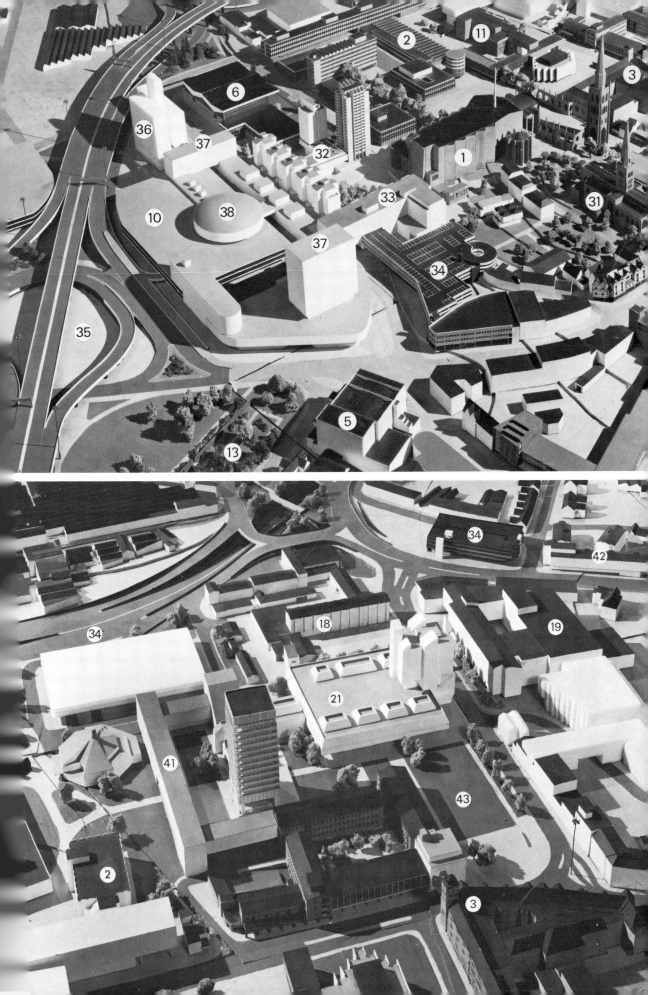

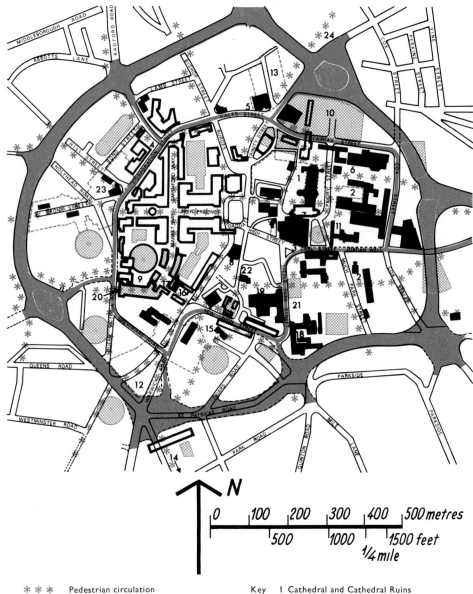

N

| 0 | 100 | 200 | 300 | 400 | 500 metres |

| 500 | 1000 | 1500 feet |

¼ mile

* * *	Pedestrian circulation
	Car Parking
	Inner Circulatory Routes
	Inner Ring Road
-------	Boundary of Conservation Areas
	Commercial Buildings
	Public or Historic buildings

Key
1 Cathedral and Cathedral Ruins
2 Lanchester Polytechnic
3 Council House
4 Belgrade Theatre
5 Coventry Theatre
6 Swimming Baths
7 St. Mary's Hall
8 Head Post Office
9 Retail Market
10 Bus Station – Pool Meadow
11 Art Gallery, Museum and Library
12 Greyfriars Green
13 Lady Herbert's Garden
14 Railway Station
15 Cheylesmore Manor
16 Bull Yard
17 Shelton Square
18 Police Headquarters
19 Telephone Exchange
20 City Arcade
21 Proposed Law Courts
22 Ford's Hospital
23 Bond's Hospital
24 Swanswell Park

Park Street were completed, to recommence redevelopment in a sector which, although then dominated by temporary car parking, will be almost entirely reconstructed as a civic offices complex.

The area designated for industrial use in the 1957 Plan was, in the Review Plan, redesignated as more appropriate to business uses. Steady progress was maintained in the expansion of this area on the north-western periphery, but due to fragmented commercial needs this was not in a comprehensive form. By 1971 the target of the 1957 Plan for that date had been exceeded by some 50 per cent, and the Review Plan had further increased the 1981 planned area after survey and assessment, related mainly to the distributive trades, display and storage.

A wide variety of urban spaces of differing size, floorscape and character were created. In 1972 a significant link between Lady Herbert's Garden and Swanswell Park was landscaped under the elevated Ring Road. Positive rehabilitation was also under way in the Spon Street conservation area, which should offer prospects for the development of small specialist shops.

The philosophy of reconstruction reflected concern not with single plot developments but with the relationship of building forms linked with spaces and circulation, consideration for overall civic design, for the amenity, safety and convenience of people, and for a rationalisation of functional activities having regard to the human scale. In 1972 the Council codified twenty visual policies to guide development of the Central Area (*City of Coventry-Corporate Planning Survey Reports, 1972*). They formed the basis for the evaluation of specific proposals together with other design standards such as the provision of adequate servicing, access, parking and daylighting.

The City of Coventry has been unique in the extent of its own involvement in central area redevelopment. This has included positive action in land assembly, provision of infrastructure, and the use of buildings to promote the fulfilment of objectives. The coordinated partnership between town planning, estates, engineering, architectural, together with legal and financial functions has been a remarkable achievement. By 1971, in implementation of the post-war redevelopment programme 99 compulsory purchase orders had been confirmed, the City Council owned 76 hectares of land in the central area and had spent some £32 million with major expenditure on land, roads, sewers and buildings. In the process many old thoroughfares completely disappeared including

Opposite:
17. Proposed City Centre Structure 1971.
Through vehicular traffic has been diverted from Broadgate, while accessibility is retained. The four conservation areas, and the pedestrian dominated environmental areas are conspicuous, as are the Inner Ring Road and Inner Circulatory Route. Car parking is to be directly related to the road network capacity and Area Traffic Control.

Bablake Street, Cow Lane, Freeth Street, Market Street, New Street, Vicar Lane, West Orchard, City Arcade, Drinkwater Arcade.

In retrospect over 25 years it may not be difficult to be critical, but regard must be had to the factors relevant in a rapidly expanding city, government controls of finance and development and post-war problems of materials licensing; changing architectural concepts, traffic pressures and retailing methods; the inherent risks of pioneering new ideas and the need for politicians to heed public opinion. City development is a process of evolution but the scale of change in this generation was phenomenal in Coventry City Centre, and is continuing.

Perhaps the greatest factor was the ability to adapt ideas in a flexible way to changing circumstances, rather than slavishly to implement an outdated plan. Opportunities were taken to reduce the physical constraints of the inner ring road, to restructure central circulation, to increase pedestrian amenity areas, to improve townscape quality, to retain the old Cathedral ruins and integrate historic buildings, to increase car parking and commercial floorspace and to develop a Polytechnic. Mistakes were made, such as the difficulty of access to the upper precinct gallery shops, but the lesson was learned in the lower precinct. The Broadgate traffic island introduced a major bus interchange with a severed amenity area in the central place and remains an environmental challenge. But, overall, the Coventry achievement has been a major one. International experts Pevsner (1966) and Mumford (1964) commented, "The scale of the city centre plan is still among the most impressive in Britain, is very complete and functions well" and, "that it has brought back both social activity and aesthetically rewarding open areas to its once cluttered and sordid commercial centre and in doing so has intensified civic pride".

THE FUTURE

Severe national financial constraints upon general development in the years from 1965 caused local authority capital investment to be orientated towards basic city infrastructure related to growth: school places; sewage disposal; trunk sewer and road network facilities. These projects will themselves provide a springboard for a further leap forward in city development.

The 1971 reports of the West Midlands Regional Study and the Coventry–Solihull–Warwickshire Sub-regional Study confirmed the substantial growth opportunities in the area over the next 20 years. The latter study found that the greatest potential for growth was in and around Coventry, where half the labour force was employed in growth industries, and recommended a strategy that sub-regional growth should include locations both north and south-east of Coventry, and that the city should be fostered as the main sub-regional commercial and shopping centre. Such possibilities reflect a logical evolution of past trends.

Implementation could, however, be influenced by the form of political and administrative changes contained in the Local Government Act, 1972, to be effective from 1974. The city has lost the town planning policy function it once enjoyed, as a county borough, to a metropolitan county based on the West Midlands conurbation. Coventry has become a second tier metropolitan district council, and the determination of relative powers and functions will be critical to the continuance of the comprehensive redevelopment policies the city has used so positively and successfully. The city hinterland has also been subdivided, for the purposes of policy planning control, between Warwickshire and the metropolitan county council. Consolidation of the communication system in the sub-region is already materially committed in a form that is focused around Coventry and will benefit the city centre. On one axis, the M6 motorway (linking to M1 and M5) was completed in 1972, supported in this direction by the A45 and the electrified railway from London to Birmingham and the north-west. From the south-west, direct links from the A46 by-passes to Warwick, Kenilworth, Stivichall and Cheylesmore were partially complete by 1973. Approval in 1972 of the revised city road pattern in the Review Plan should assure fast, convenient access to the central area for private and public transport from all directions, separated from local traffic.

Such improvements in mobility could, of course, also be used to support the establishment of shopping centres in locations away from traditional centres. There are pressures to set up out-of-town supermarkets with relatively cheap sites and buildings, generally in areas controlled by county councils; they could affect a centre such as Coventry, and the situation emphasises the regard necessary to a sub-regional strategy related to the hierarchical pattern of shopping centres. The degree of interaction would relate to the level and variety of the services offered, and the post-war consolidation in Coventry should carry major advantages, but must be continued. Similarly, the relative attractiveness of out-of-town shopping should not be as extreme near a redeveloped non-congested centre, where there has been high regard paid to accessibility and convenience for private and public transport, to the pedestrian, amenity and supporting leisure services.

The location of the city in regional, national and international terms related to the network of communications and to the national corridors of economic growth, is extremely favourable for office and commercial development, and sites can be made available. The rapidly expanding services offered in Coventry by the University of Warwick, the Lanchester Polytechnic and other further education institutions will give increasing support.

The growing importance of the city as a tourist centre of international significance based on the Cathedral (world-renowned for its architecture and the theme of reconciliation), and on the rebuilt City Centre (world-renowned for its innovation in physical planning implementation), is

Pedestrian + vehicular accessibility in
the Ring Road multi-level junction
with a pedestrian park way under
adjoining the preserved city wall.

reflected in the growing provision of and demand for hotel and restaurant facilities, and a wider range of shopping and services. Coventry has a considerable future for conference activities, and as a tourist, advanced industrial, educational and technological centre, and the Council's development programme recognises this.

These opportunities will create a changing demand for related special retail outlets, and phased redevelopment is creating suitable sites in the City Centre. Even further opportunities might be created by enlarging the shopping precinct, by considering traffic restraint in the Burges and by revitalisation of the adjoining area.

Coventry's policy is to expand quality and specialist shopping and department stores to achieve a well-balanced centre, related also to the function of district centres to which some "daily" shops might be displaced. The Review Plan reappraised the potential total retail floor space up to 1981, calculated on the basis of spending power converted into a floorspace/turnover ratio. Whilst this assessment included a range of uncertainty, and depended considerably upon policy considerations, the process confirmed the target of the 1951 Plan as reasonable for a monitored series of intermediate decisions for expansion with avoidance of overshopping. Certainly the Coventry Point Data System, established in 1970 and tailored to current computer and planning authority requirements, gave a firm information basis for future decisions related to all relevant topics.

These growth activities require support in related educational, leisure and administrative services, and the municipal capital programme includes such projects. The Polytechnic will continue by stages; an indoor sports and recreational centre will be developed, possibly by extension of the central swimming baths; the central fire station will be relocated and this will facilitate a multi-purpose development with commercial and Crown offices and an entertainments centre integrated with the Pool Meadow bus station and car park; the Belgrade Theatre will be extended to provide experimental theatre, and the central lending library will be relocated. Consideration will continue to be given to opportunities to provide ice skating and concert hall facilities.

New Law Courts will be provided and the library and court relocations will free other sites which will then offer possibilities comprehensively to redevelop Broadgate and the area adjoining Holy Trinity Church and the Cathedral. This will offer a challenge to link that area with the shopping precinct, to create a unified amenity area which will need

Opposite:
18. Pedestrian and vehicular accessibility
The Ring Road multi-level junction with a pedestrian
parkway under, adjoining the preserved city wall.
To the west are car park spaces under the road decks,
and beyond them the Polytechnic.

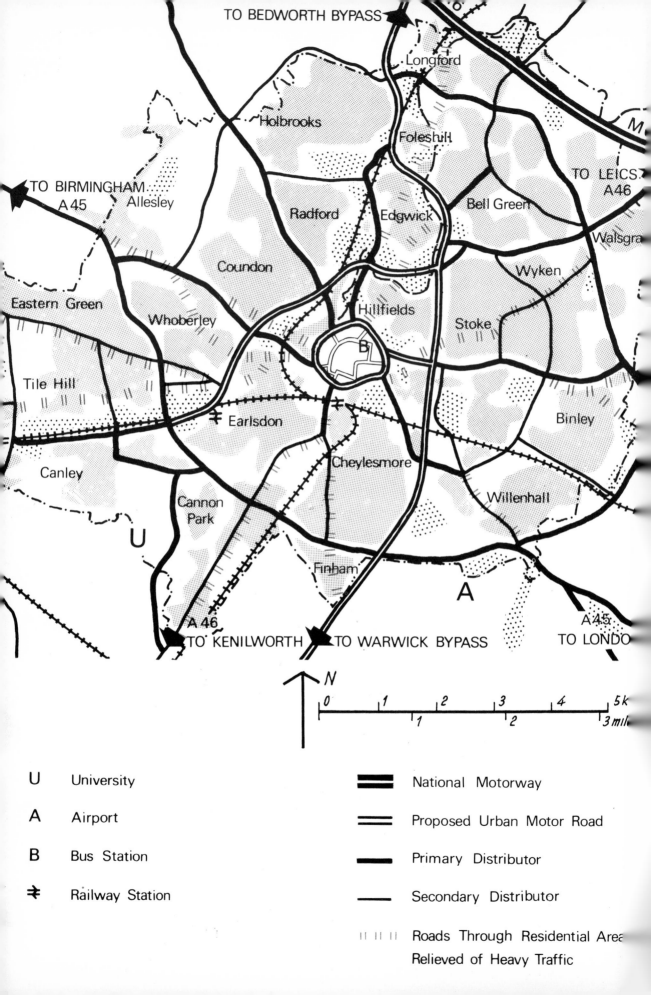

TO BEDWORTH BYPASS

Longford

Holbrooks

Foleshill

TO BIRMINGHAM
A45

Allesley

Radford

Edgwick

Bell Green

TO LEICS.
A46

Walsgra

Coundon

Wyken

Hillfields

Stoke

Eastern Green

Whoberley

B

Tile Hill

Earlsdon

Binley

Canley

Cheylesmore

Cannon
Park

Willenhall

U

Finham

A

A45
TO LONDO

A46
TO KENILWORTH

TO WARWICK BYPASS

N

| 0 | 1 | 2 | 3 | 4 | 5 k |
| 1 | | 2 | | | 3 mil |

U	University		National Motorway
A	Airport		Proposed Urban Motor Road
B	Bus Station		Primary Distributor
⇌	Railway Station		Secondary Distributor
		II II II	Roads Through Residential Area Relieved of Heavy Traffic

consideration of restricting traffic to buses and service vehicles.

The major pedestrian square to be created immediately to the north of the Cathedral will provide it with a more worthy setting, and the closure of Priory Street will offer the opportunity for a landscaped space joining the Cathedral, Polytechnic and baths precincts.

Advantage will be taken, by coordinated highway and landscape design of the multi-level Inner Ring Road junction adjoining Greyfriars Green, to double the "green" area, with separated pedestrian movement. Thus is the 1941 principle of a shopping amenity area free from traffic being extended widely within other sectors of the central area. The Canal Basin will offer leisure opportunities. These projects will offer positive improvement of a townscape endowed with limited natural advantages.

An Area Traffic Control system will be installed, in order to reduce congestion, aid public transport, increase pedestrian safety and protect environmental areas. Computer control will service linked traffic signals, car park marshalling and diversionary routing. Delays will be reduced, and accessibility in the central area will be further improved by purpose-built links to multi-storey car parks from the Inner Ring Road. Design constraints imposed on highway and car park capacities will demand complementary support from public transport. Steps will therefore be taken towards the provision of an improved public transport system, even though it is more difficult to operate effectively in a city of dispersed patterns of activity and movement than in more densely developed towns. As a car manufacturing city, Coventry will continue to come to terms with the implications in a realistic way.

These projects include further physical and management measures to continue the process of rejuvenation of the town centre fabric and activities, in the words of the resolution of 1940, "to secure a worthy replanning and redevelopment of the city".

The evolving Central Area Plan has been subject to regular review over the years, submitted to or approved by central government in 1941, 1943, 1947, 1949, 1951, 1957, 1967, 1972. Opportunities afforded by the Town and Country Planning Act, 1968, should eventually simplify future procedures.

In spite of the uncertainties beyond its control the City Council believes that the future holds great promise, and is confident that Coventry, because of its traditions of skill and innovation, its pioneering spirit and enterprise, its outstanding potential for further expansion, its

Opposite:
19. Coventry city-wide Review Plan 1972.
This city movement system was approved by the
Government in 1972. New Urban Motor Roads
will remedy the existing concentric pattern, reduce
central congestion and improve accessibility from
the sub-region and national highway network.

excellent communications and its care for people will continue to rise
to opportunity and challenge.

4
Leicester

*"A city should be built for the convenience and satisfaction
of the people who live in it and for the great surprise of
strangers."*

—Sansovino (1460–1529)

A walk in the central area of Leicester today would give an impression
that the city has undergone a recent bombardment by enemy action.
A great deal of demolition work which is taking place on the sites in the
city centre, broken up carriageways and pavements, bulldozers everywhere and the noise of pneumatic drills—give an appearance of a "blitzed"
city. To this should be added the chaos brought into the city by the
invasion of motor cars—the traffic congestion and the visual clutter of
traffic signs and notices.

Rapid changes are taking place in the structure of the central area,
affecting its scale and its sky-line—vacant shops, well-established firms
closing down but also new firms moving in, the appearance of multi-
storey parking garages and tower buildings. These changes are certainly
not the signs of decline but of the vitality of Leicester. The scale of a
"market town" is being transformed into that of a true "city".

The public is bewildered and critical about these changes. Elderly
ladies write rude letters to me: "Why do you hate Leicester? Why are
you destroying this once gracious city?"

There are many reasons for these changes and they can be traced to
the influence of the commercial forces, the economic situation, the
political climate and the city council's initiative in planning. Some of
these changes are inevitable and they would have taken place whether
there was any city planning or not. But the town planners maintain that
the purpose of planning is that these changes should follow a definite
pattern, a logical and consistent *Plan*.

Leicester was one of the first cities in the country to establish a separate
City Planning Department, which was set up in 1962. Its activity falls

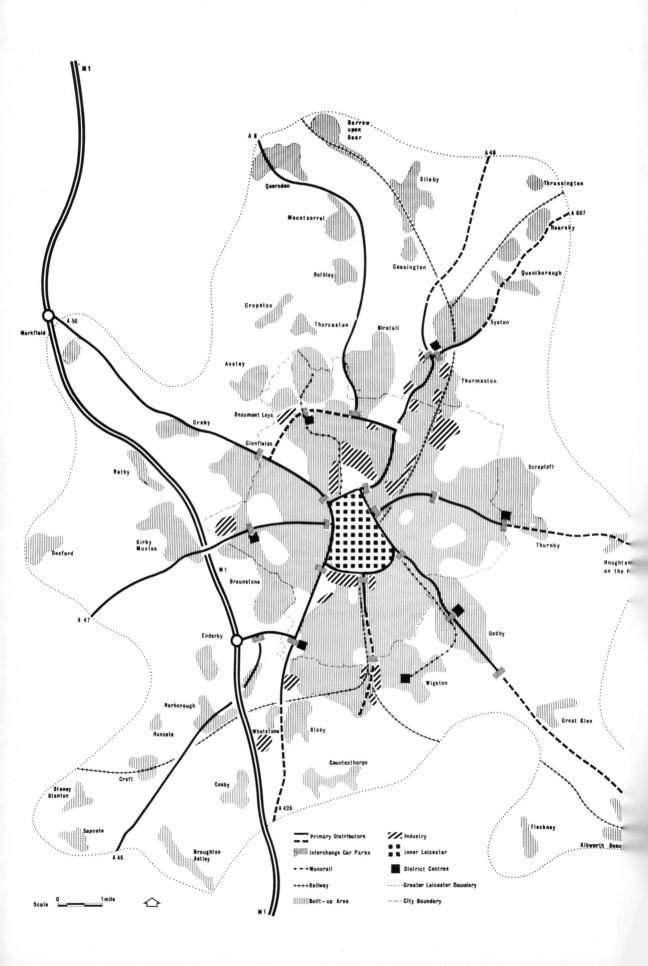

M1

A 6

Barrow
upon
Soar

Quorndon

Sileby

Thrussington

A 46

Mountsorrel

A 607

Rearsby

Queniborough

Rothley

Cossington

Cropston

Thurcaston

Birstall

Syston

Markfield

A 50

Anstey

Thurmaston

Beaumont Leys

Groby

Glenfields

Scraptoft

Ratby

Thurnby

Desford

Kirby
Muxloe

M1

Houghton
on the

Braunstone

A 47

Enderby

Oadby

Narborough

Wigston

Great Glen

Huncote

Whetstone

Blaby

Countesthorpe

Croft

Fleckney

Stoney
Stanton

Cosby

Sapcote

A 426

Kibworth Beau

Broughton
Astley

A 46

▬▬▬ Primary Distributors	▨ Industry	
▬ ▬ ▬	▦ inner Leicester	
▨ Interchange Car Parks		
◆◆◆ Monorail	■ District Centres	
+++ Railway	⋯ Greater Leicester Boundary	
▥ Built-up Area	— · — City Boundary	

Scale 0 ___ 1mile

M1

into two fields: development control and preparation and implementation of town planning schemes, short-term and long-term.

Development control is concerned with the many separate enterprises undertaken by individuals, which play a vital role in the development of the city. No building or civil engineering works can be carried out, nor can the use of any existing building or land be changed, without planning permission having first been obtained from the local planning authority. In Leicester this is the City Council, under which the Town Planning Committee has delegated powers. Over 200 planning applications every month are dealt with by the City Planning Department. It is difficult to measure the effect and success of development control as it is only a matter of conjecture as to what would have happened if the control had not been exercised. It is not, however, an overstatement to say that without it there would be chaos.

Development control is an important tool in the implementation of the planning policy but it must be supplemented by creative, positive planning. This second field of activity of the City Planning Department plays the most important role in influencing the pattern of future Leicester. This activity embraces the preparation and continuous revision of the Development Plan for the whole city, production of comprehensive development schemes for action areas and conservation schemes for historic districts.

City planning is concerned with the shaping of the extremely complex, living and ever changing organism of the city. Its total result may not be evident to the general public of today because the fruits of city planning are always in the future. The city planners are confident that out of the upheaval which the city of Leicester is now undergoing a new order and consequently a better city will emerge.

This is the story of the city centre of Leicester, one of the important provincial cities of Great Britain. As the city centre cannot be treated in isolation, the first part gives a brief survey of the whole city in its national and regional setting and a summary of the long-term traffic plan. In the second part the anatomy of the central area in its present state, the political, social and commercial forces, the administrative machinery, the Plan with its short-term and long-term proposals, what has already been achieved and finally what are the prospects for the future, is considered.

The world is becoming more and more urban. The quality of our cities reflects the quality of our civilisation. Therefore, it is hoped, that this story of town planning in an extremely interesting and critical period of the motor revolution, should be of interest not only to a professional but also to a general reader. For this reason an attempt is made to avoid professional jargon.

Opposite:
1. Master Plan for Greater Leicester, A.D. 2000.

NATIONAL AND REGIONAL SETTING

Geographically, Leicester is in "the centre" of England. The city is situated approximately 100 miles from both the east and west coasts, and roughly halfway between London in the south, and the Lancashire and West Riding industrial towns in the north. Its excellent national communication links include the adjacent M1 motorway from London to Yorkshire and a fast rail connection with London. Adequate air links are available through Birmingham airport and the East Midlands airport at Castle Donington.

In terms of population, Leicester is the fourth largest city in the Midlands region, being exceeded in size by only Birmingham, Nottingham and Coventry. Its population is approximately 285,000 and its area is nearly 26 square miles. Situated about 200 feet above sea level Leicester is a natural centre and provides the link between industrial west and rural east.

CHARACTER OF THE CITY

Leicester is a county town and a centre of industry, agriculture, distribution, commerce, justice and administration. For the most part, its inhabitants earn their living in factories or in other occupations related to manufacturing. The chief industries are hosiery, footwear and various types of engineering which together provide almost half of the 200,000 employment opportunities that exist in the Leicester Employment Exchange Area. The city is a centre of higher education with a Regional Polytechnic and a University.

As a shopping centre, too, the city has considerable attraction. The catchment area is about 600 square miles with a population now in the region of 700,000 people. According to the Board of Trade Census of Distribution, trade turnover in 1961 in the central area of Leicester exceeded £27 million. The claim frequently heard that "Leicester is the richest city in the United Kingdom, and the second richest city in Europe after Lille in France" (Annals of the League of Nations, 1920), would be difficult to substantiate; but certainly it is one of the most prosperous cities in England.

In a sense, Leicester during the last hundred years has been a static city. Perhaps its motto "Semper eadem" comes very near to the truth. For the most part its pattern of land use is well established, having emerged gradually rather than dramatically. Similarly for the future, although the city can cater for its own natural increase in population, it is reasonable to assume that no fundamental change will come about in its basic land use and social structure.

Owing to its favourable geographic position, mild climate, good educational facilities, compactness and an attractive surrounding country-side, Leicester is a good city in which to live.

DEVELOPMENT PLAN

The City Planning Department, established in 1962, inherited the statutory Development Plan for the City of Leicester of 1952, and one of the main duties of the new Department was to undertake the revision of this Plan. It soon became evident that in the light of the motor revolution and the profound changes in the many fields of life which have taken place in this country since the war, the available Development Plan could no longer form a basis for planning in Leicester. Instead of undertaking its revision, the City Planning Department produced in 1964 the "Leicester Traffic Plan", the first attempt in formulating a long-term urban policy reaching beyond the administrative boundaries of the city and embracing the whole built-up area plus the agricultural hinterland, which could be described as Greater Leicester.

The next stage was the initiation jointly by the City and the County of a sub-regional study, which resulted in the publication of the "Leicester and Leicestershire Sub-Regional Planning Study" in March 1969. The recommended strategy was to concentrate the future growth of the sub-region into the Greater Leicester Area.

The Town and Country Planning Act, 1968, introduced a new form of development plan, described broadly as a Structure Plan. This new type of development plan will have to be more scientific, with built-in provision for change and requiring consideration of alternative strategies. The Act is a very unusual piece of legislation as it does not prescribe any date for its operation. In fact, the Department of the Environment has invited a few chosen planning authorities to prepare their development plans under the new procedure. Leicester and Leicestershire were included amongst those authorities.

In December 1969, a joint team staffed from the City and County Planning Departments was set up to undertake the preparation of the new Structure Plan for Greater Leicester and the County. Thus the City of Leicester has entered into a new and exciting phase of planning for the future.

LEICESTER TRAFFIC PLAN

Immediately after my appointment as the City Planning Officer in 1962 pressure was put on me by the City Council to prepare a city traffic plan as the most urgent requirement. The Leicester Traffic Plan (1964), was one of the first city plans to say *NO* to the motor car scientifically. The plan was based on a new type of comprehensive land use–traffic survey which utilised the latest computer techniques. Instead of motor cars being counted, people were interviewed in their homes about their travel habits, and for this purpose 100 women interviewers were employed and trained. This was more than a traffic survey as not only traffic but the land use, the social and economic structure of the city were analysed and fed into a computer programme. This technique, first developed in U.S.A., is now widely accepted but at the time Leicester pioneered the application of the new technique to a traffic plan and a long-term urban policy.

The following assumptions, resulting from the traffic survey and the analysis of physical and economic factors governing the life of the city, were made:

The plan should embrace the period of 30 years (1995) when the saturation level of car ownership in Leicester will almost be achieved, with 0·4 cars per head of population, or 1·2 cars per family. The present number of cars would increase more than fourfold.

The present population of Leicester is 285,000 and that of the whole urbanised area (Greater Leicester) about 475,000. In the thirty-year period the estimated population of the city would be about 340,000 and of Greater Leicester 640,000.

The chief source of conflict in an existing city is the lack of balance between the land uses, as traffic generators, and the available traffic accommodation (roads and parking). In thirty years time this lack of balance will bring a state of complete breakdown unless some measures on a formidable scale are undertaken. The task is complicated and the analysis did not point to one clear-cut solution. There would seem to be various ways of achieving the aim, but each with different economic and social consequences and a different effect on the environment.

First solution—unlimited use of motor cars
As the first exercise a solution allowing for uninhibited use of the private car throughout the whole city, including the central area, was produced.

This would involve the construction around the central area of an elevated inner motorway of gigantic size (16 lanes) with enormous multi-level intersections. The city centre would consist of a small shopping core surrounded by huge "car stacks"—monuments to the private car— and these in turn would be surrounded by an intricate pattern of elevated access roads. Parking garages for the private car—a thing of personal convenience, which for most of the day would be lying idle on a fantastically expensive "shelf"—would be the dominant buildings, the motor age cathedrals, in this Leicester of the private car. The historic environment would be almost destroyed. The cost of the scheme would be over £400 million, not counting the cost of additional local distributor roads.

This solution was found unacceptable on economic, social and environmental grounds.

Opposite:
2. Master Plan for Inner Leicester, A.D. 2000;
major road network and system of pedestrian ways.

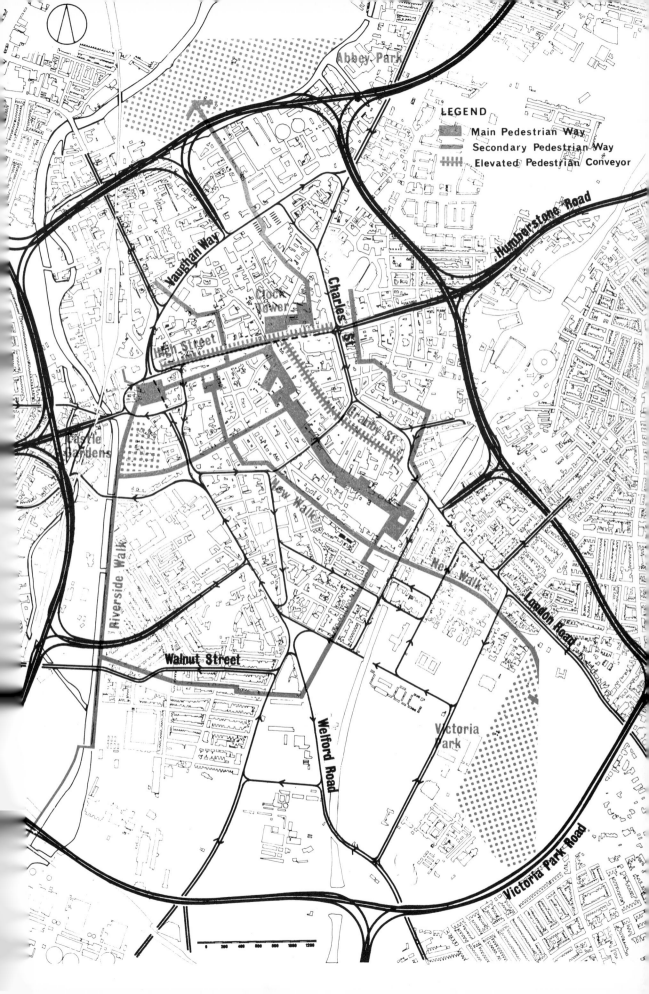

LEGEND

Main Pedestrian Way
Secondary Pedestrian Way
Elevated Pedestrian Conveyor

Abbey Park

Humberstone Road

Vaughan Way

Charles St.

Clock Tower

High Street

Granby St.

Castle Gardens

New Walk

New Walk

London Road

Riverside Walk

Walnut Street

Welford Road

Victoria Park

Victoria Park Road

0   200   400   600   800   1000 1200

Second and recommended solution—Integrated Transport System
The recommended solution proposed a balanced interplay of the following
elements: interchange car parks; high capacity road network; and
public transport.

Interchange car parks ("Park and ride"). In order to relieve the pressure
upon the city centre and to reduce the enormous traffic flows on radial
roads predicted for the thirty year period, a system of "interchange car
parks" was proposed. These would be attached to radial roads with the
function of intercepting car drivers and transferring them into the central
area by means of a modernised and efficient public transport system.
These car parks would be linked with suburban shopping, entertainment
and sports centres.

Road network. The interchange car parks would reduce the traffic
density both on the radials and on the inner motorway so considerably
that instead of 16 lanes only four to six lanes would be required. A high
capacity elevated inner motorway, embracing the area of Inner Leicester
and only five miles long, would replace the three ring roads of considerable
mileage in the present Development Plan. The inner motorway would
be linked with the seven radial roads.

Public transport. A unified city transport comprising under one control
bus services, a monorail and a taxi service was proposed.

Three types of buses including a special city centre bus—a small
"crush" type of vehicle where standing only is allowed—was envisaged.

The proposed monorail would be in the form of a double track line,
tangential to the city centre, linking the concentrations of residential
population in the north-west and in the south-east. In the central area
it would be erected in Charles Street. It would be possible to add feeder
routes extending radially from the city centre to the proposed fringe car
parks situated at key points on the outskirts of Inner Leicester.

A new kind of taxicab—a small vehicle electrically driven, for circulation
in the central area—was recommended.

Central area
Pedestrian conveyors, along the routes of the greatest concentration of
pedestrian movement, either in the form of pedestrian bridges or of
elevated, continuous walkways down the centre of the main shopping
streets, would provide additional means of public transport.

The central area would be preserved with historic buildings intact and
without the necessity of widening existing streets. The outworn parts
would be redeveloped in a comprehensive way.

The traffic which would be allowed to enter Inner Leicester is *the
essential minimum* (all commercial vehicles and external traffic having an
interest in the area) and cars on firms' business together with some cars
on personal business and shopping. This traffic would be carried by a
network of secondary distributors assisted by computer controlled traffic
lights designed to utilise the existing streets. The secondary distributor

network is supplemented by a pattern of service roads forming one-way loops.

The upper ceiling of parking accommodation was established at 22,500 car spaces (as against 67,000 car spaces for unlimited use of private cars) destined mainly for short-term parkers. This would be easy to provide without straining the existing urban structure and without overloading the street network.

General

The cost of the recommended solution was estimated at £135 million and this represented the total capital investment from all sources including private enterprise.

The proposed "Integrated Transport System" would fulfill the following conditions:

It would allow for a healthy growth of this prosperous city without destroying its historic heritage and local identity. The process of development would take the form of gradual evolution and replacement of outworn areas rather than of the revolutionary transformation of the urban structure.

It would allow for the unlimited use of the private car throughout the whole area of the city with the exception of Inner Leicester. The maximum level of circulation would be achieved at the minimum cost.

The conditions of life created by the new system should make living easier, more comfortable and more attractive. The basic needs of the motorised society with its continuously growing standard of living would be fulfilled.

Implementation of the Traffic Plan

The City Council accepted the philosophy of the Leicester Traffic Plan and agreed that it would be impossible to achieve full penetration of private cars into the central area.

A new programme of major road construction in accordance with the Leicester Traffic Plan for the next 20 years was approved. This included the construction of the first phase (eastern part) of the Inner Motorway, for which working drawings and a detailed study of its impact on the immediate environment were prepared.

After a long campaign on my recommendation, the City Council approved the abandonment of the Central Ring Road, proposed in the Development Plan of 1952.

A double roundabout on the western approach to High Street, which was proposed by the City Engineer, was abandoned and replaced by an underpass with a gyratory system of roads. This big road construction venture (Southgate intersection), which included an extensive underground pedestrian ways system (Newark), is now virtually completed.

The City Council approved the change of the first shopping street

(Loseby Lane) into a pedestrian street and also the first steps are taken towards the transformation of the main shopping street (Gallowtree Gate) for pedestrian circulation. Gradually in the city centre the priority will be given to the pedestrians over any other form of traffic.

According to the new parking policy, approved by the City Council, parking accommodation is divided into two categories: short-period (off-peak hours) parking for shoppers and long-period (peak hours) parking for commuters.

Short-period parking is being encouraged and gradually all public parking garages in the central area will be only of this type. Six multi-storey parking garages with a total capacity of 3,800 car places are now in operation and the seventh is under construction.

A first interchange car park ("Park and ride") was established at Welford Road as an experiment and eventually more will be built at other radial roads around the central area. This is now accepted as the only effective method of dealing with the commuter traffic and parking.

Public transport is being continually improved by the City Transport, which under a vigorous and progressive management is still a debt-free and commercially viable undertaking in spite of the fact that Leicester has the cheapest bus fares in the country.

With regard to implementation of the monorail no progress has been made up to now. There are many reasons for this. The monorail is still technically undeveloped. There is no encouragement combined with financial help from the central government, and the transport managers look with suspicion at the new and untried forms of public transport. The matter is not politically ripe. However, in all long-term plans for Leicester the possibility of the introduction of a monorail at some future date is not excluded.

HISTORIC EVOLUTION

Leicester, as its name suggests, is a city with a long historic tradition, which is reflected in the beautiful names of streets and places—De Montfort Square, Grey Friars, Black Friars, Holy Bones, Haymarket, Silver Arcade—full of evocative associations. But on the evidence of the scant remains of historic environment it can hardly be called an "historic" city in the same sense as Oxford, Cambridge and York.

Judged on the basis of old prints and the few historic buildings which have survived—St. Mary de Castro, the medieval Guildhall, some Georgian buildings—Leicester must have been a very pleasant although quite small town maintaining continuity of historic tradition up to the end of the eighteenth century. But during the Industrial Revolution Leicester experienced a quite extraordinary growth of population, which from 1800 to 1900 multiplied nearly thirteen times, from 17,000 to 212,000 people. A quiet market town was rapidly transformed into a prosperous industrial town. In the process many of the historic buildings were swept away and replaced by the contemporary buildings of the time (Victorian) which in turn have become "historic" buildings of today.

Periods of expansion and vitality are always characterised by disrespect for the old and the obsolete and Leicester, not being an exception from the general rule, has a grim record of destruction of historic buildings. One must remember that even the more distant great historic periods have had little regard for historic heritage. The ancient Basilica of St. Peter in Rome was ruthlessly demolished by the Pope Julius II to make room for the contemporary conception of Bramante—Michelangelo. What a pity that we could not have both.

The idea of conservation of historic buildings is modern and the view that not only individual historic buildings but also the whole areas forming an historic environment, should be preserved has crystallised only recently. We are now more "conservation conscious" than in any past period of our civilisation.

The plan of the Leicester central area as it is today is not the result of conscious planning but the result of organic growth during a long period of historic evolution.

A small settlement occupying the crossing at the river Soar attracted the attention of the Romans because of its strategic position. The Roman city built in A.D. 43 left no substantial imprint on the street pattern of Leicester as in Lucca or Florence. A quiet period during the Anglo-Saxon and Danish occupations followed and it was only after the Norman conquest—500 years after the Roman period—that Leicester re-awakened to progress and change. Gradually a Medieval street pattern was established which has survived until the modern times in the area of the Cathedral precinct, the Market Place and Castle Gardens.

During the eighteenth century the development of the manufacture of hosiery brought new prosperity to Leicester and the town's population trebled. Most of the Medieval gates were demolished in 1774 as they had become an obstruction to traffic! Another expansion of Leicester was the laying out of "New Walk", a magnificent pedestrian promenade almost three-quarters of a mile long, a great contribution to town planning in Leicester. In the nineteenth century the Town Hall Square was formed and the city centre was expanding, following more or less a chessboard street pattern. At the beginning of this century Charles Street, a parallel road to the main shopping streets—was built and for almost half a century performed a successful role as a relief road. Today this relief road has reached the saturation level and the third parallel route, Eastern Motorway, will provide a new "relief road".

The Development Plan of 1952 has made a mark on the structure of the central area by the proposal of the Central Ring Road, the northern part of which has been built. The Central Ring Road, both its concept and route, was not acceptable to the new City Planning Department, established in September 1962. Our criticism could be summed up as follows:

The Central Ring Road was advanced for its period and was known in the Ministry of Transport as the "Leicester solution". However, in the light of the motor revolution this basically intuitive proposal became equally obsolete as a horse-drawn carriage. This road proposal if completed, would have fatal town planning repercussions. The Ring Road was too tight and did not embrace all the central area uses, leaving out to the south the proposed civic centre, the cultural centre (Museum and Art Gallery) and the main railway station.

The most drastic was the western route, a surgical operation, cutting the central area into inorganic parts and severing it from the river. The river development should be an integral part of the city centre.

The southern route would plough through the conservation areas destroying some important historic buildings (the Georgian Crescent) and cutting through New Walk.

The proposed double roundabout on the western approach would introduce additional through traffic to the already congested High Street.

As the result of the above criticism and after a prolonged and bitter campaign the City Council decided to abandon the continuation of the Central Ring Road. This was the first contribution of the new City Planning Department—preventing the wrong things being done.

COMMERCIAL AND POLITICAL FORCES FOR CHANGE

A city centre, the heart of an urban community, is the area of concentrated activities, the most intensive land use and the highest land values. Its development or decline is conditioned not only by the interaction of the various commercial and political forces but also by the general economic climate of the local community and the nation at large.

In post war years the city centre of Leicester was for a long time almost static. The central area shopping was compact and well established, the many one-family businesses were flourishing without a pressing need for modernisation. There was no urban renewal or comprehensive development taking place. But gradually the pressures for modernisation and initiative in town planning started to build up. This was expressed in the establishment of the new City Planning Department in 1962.

In that period the general economic and commercial climate combined with free economy and no restrictions on development was favourable. But there were no plans for the central area. The new City Planning Department was compelled to apply a policy of restraint on development pending the preparation of the plans.

When the plans were produced the economic and political climate changed radically. The national economic crisis resulted in a curb on

Opposite:
3. Inner Leicester, A.D. 2000; photograph of model.

148 CITY CENTRE REDEVELOPMENT

public expenditure. The Labour Government strengthened the policy of directing development to the declining North and restricting it in the congested and overpopulated Midlands and South-east of England. The city of Leicester found itself in the area where restriction on industrial and office development applied.

The total effect of this changed situation was stagnation in the city centre and the speeding up of the forces of disintegration which were already at work. The vacant shops in the city centre and particularly in the High Street started to alarm the public and the local Chamber of Trade. The favourite object of attack were "the planners". In October, 1969, the number of vacant shops in the city centre reached 10 per cent.

It was less evident to the general public that simultaneously the obsolete central area shopping was undergoing a painful process of adaptation to the new conditions. Death and birth go together in the biological process. Some retail shops were unable to compete with the well-organised departmental stores and supermarkets, offering the same goods at lower prices and with better service. The doom of these retail shops was inevitable. The other, more old-fashioned shops, frequently one-family businesses, were unable or unwilling to adjust themselves to the changes in shopping habits.

But gradually, as the result of implementation of the schemes in "action areas" and a more free economy caused by a change of Government, the situation started to improve. Already in May 1970 the number of vacant shops in the city centre had decreased to 7 per cent. When in 1971 the Conservative Government abolished restrictions on office development in the Midlands, this had a stimulating effect on development in Leicester. The empty sites started to fill up with office development, some in the form of towers. This in turn had a beneficial effect on shopping. The city centre suddenly experienced a commercial revival and this trend continues.

ESTABLISHMENT AND ORGANISATION

It is fashionable now to criticise the local government of this country, particularly as its reorganisation is under consideration. There is little doubt that in spite of its shortcomings British local government is the strongest and the most efficient in the world. It is the result of a long evolution of local democracy and it is one of the greatest institutions of Great Britain. British local authorities build roads, sewers, schools and houses. On the continent, most of these enterprises are the responsibility of the central government. The success of town planning depends on a strong local government. Local authorities of this country are invested with considerable powers and have adequate resources at their disposal.

The City Council of Leicester, composed of unpaid elected citizens under the chairmanship of the Lord Mayor, meets normally for a one evening session each month.

But the real work is done by the nineteen City Council Committees and twenty Sub-committees, each with a chairman and vice-chairman.

The character of the City Council is strongly political—in a way, it is a microcosmic parliament with basically a two-party system. In Leicester, whether there is a socialist or a conservative City Council makes little difference to town planning. More marked differences appear in housing and educational policies.

Town planning is under the control of the Town Planning Committee, but indirectly, other Committees, such as the Traffic, Transport, Public Works and Finance Committees, are also involved in planning.

The Corporation Departments are under Chief Officers with the Town Clerk as the chief executive and co-ordinator. The main technical Departments are: the City Engineer's Department, the City Architect's Department and the City Planning Department. The Chief Officers in charge are on an equal footing.

Co-ordination of the work is achieved by frequent officers' meetings under the chairmanship of the Town Clerk or one of his deputies. There is a "Project Co-ordination" Section in the Town Clerk's Department.

Outside the Corporation there are numerous social and cultural associations concerned with local problems. There is a Chamber of Commerce (for industry) and a Chamber of Trade (for shopping).

There is a very influential local newspaper, the *Leicester Mercury* with its famous "Page Four", on which the readers' letters voicing their grievances against the City Council are published. "The planners" are often accused of crimes which they have committed and also of those which they have not committed. There is also a very active local radio station.

EXISTING TOWNSCAPE

The physical and emotional heart of the city is the Clock Tower area, a triangular space formed by the intersection of the main historic routes. This is the most congested spot in Leicester, where formidable local traffic is mixed with through traffic and very intensive pedestrian circulation. The use of the surrounding buildings is shopping. The scale of the area is that of a market town and rather incongruous if related to the present role, size and prosperity of a city of almost 300,000 people.

The main shopping street (Gallowtree Gate) extends south, and High Street, which is of secondary importance, west from the Clock Tower. The Market Square, containing one of the largest open markets in the country under a permanent roof, is situated south of High Street. The Town Hall Square with the handsome Victorian Town Hall is the present civic centre, inadequate in size. The Cathedral is set in a quiet office precinct.

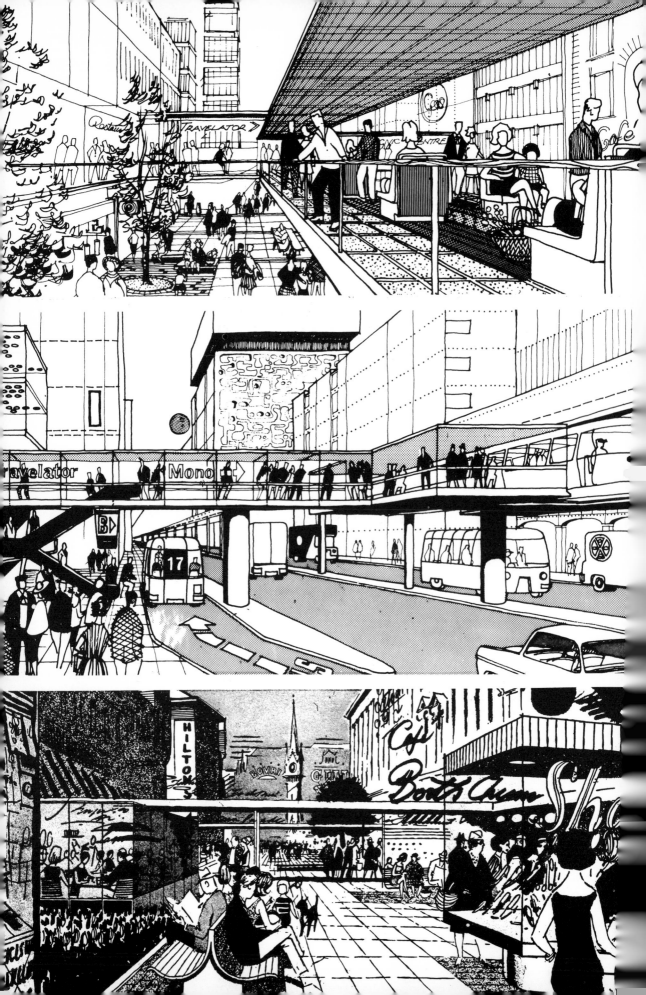

At the river there are two isolated areas of architectural quality, the modern Vaughan College, built over the ruins of the Roman Forum, and the Castle Gardens with an historic group of buildings around St. Mary de Castro Church.

New Walk, a pedestrian promenade, built during the Georgian period, linking the city centre with Victoria Park, is a unique feature of the city.

Although the commercial core is concentrated in a compact rectangle formed by High Street, Market Street, Belvoir Street and Charles Street, the cultural and civic uses such as the Art Gallery and Museum, De Montfort Hall and the University are extending the Inner Leicester area south towards Victoria Park.

The central area, although containing some parts of historic and architectural quality, is rather disjointed and an attempt will be made to link the unrelated parts into a logical civic composition.

This is what Kenneth Browne, the townscape consultant, said about Leicester:

"Semper eadem: always the same. Leicester's motto sums up the city to an outsider; the first view inevitably feels flat. There are no high spots, no dramatic sites and gestures and no obviously endearing local traits. Only later does he realize the deep and lasting virtues that are the other side of 'semper eadem': an unhysterical balance, a willingness to accept new ideas, and a fair hearing for all points of view. These qualities have produced remarkable things—the first modern public library, a first-rate museum, first-rate schools, a city almost without slums and with perhaps the highest average standard of living in the country."

MASTER PLAN FOR INNER LEICESTER, A.D. 2000

The evolution of the Leicester central area plan, described in the previous chapters, was the result of natural growth and isolated, piecemeal planning. There was never any preconceived plan on paper for the whole city centre.

The first comprehensive conception of the central area was produced by the new City Planning Department in connection with the preparation of the Leicester Traffic Plan. It was in the form of a long-term Master Plan in which the various short-term schemes (some in the process of realisation) and the long-term schemes (not yet designed in detail) were

Opposite:
Proposed types of pedestrian walkways for Leicester
city centre; Top: 4. elevated covered walkway with
moving floor in Granby Street; Middle: 5. elevated walkway
in Humberstone Gate linked with a monorail stop in
Charles Street; Bottom: 6. Transformation of Gallowtree
Gate into a pedestrian street (drawing by K. Browne).

fused into a coherent whole. It was also the first attempt to create a three-dimensional composition of the city centre and this was expressed in the form of a model. Some parts of this plan were later modified in the light of the changed conditions by detailed design and some may never materialise.

This first Master Plan, as the subsequent events proved, served as an invaluable guide for redevelopment and provided the basis for the identification of the "action areas". Town planning is meaningless and negative unless there is a *vision* embodying the main objectives. It is interesting to note how many of the "dreams" of this Master Plan, conceived in 1964, have become a reality during a seven year period.

The Master Plan covers the whole area surrounded by the proposed Inner Motorway which is greater than what is generally considered as the "central area". Therefore, it was necessary to introduce three terms related to three distinct and well defined areas—"Inner Leicester", "central area" and "city centre".

"Inner Leicester", surrounded by the Inner Motorway, is an area of intensive and diversified land-use and high land values. It includes in the north, an industrial zone; in the south, Victoria Park; in the east, commercial and high density residential areas, and in the west, a linear, mostly industrial development along the river.

The "central area" refers to the inner shopping and commercial core containing the Clock Tower, the Market Square, the Cathedral precinct, Town Hall Square, the Southgate with Castle Gardens and the area of the proposed Civic Centre.

The "city centre" indicates the innermost heart of Leicester and is limited to the area of three squares: Clock Tower, Market Place and Town Hall Square.

The Clock Tower area—Leicester's Piccadilly Circus—was proposed to be redesigned as a formal pedestrian square. The triangular block to the east would be redeveloped as a multi-level shopping and entertainment centre (Haymarket). This would become the real commercial heart and the chief meeting place of the city.

From the Clock Tower a pedestrian link (Cheapside) would lead to the revitalised Market Place with new roofs and a small forecourt in front of the Corn Exchange. From here the pedestrian route would pass through a new shopping arcade to the Town Hall Square, redesigned in the long-term with an underground parking place. Town Hall Square, would be linked to the south by a series of shopping arcades and small squares terminating in the new civic centre. The described urban route starting at the Clock Tower and ending at the new civic centre would be the backbone of the central area and its new compositional axis.

Opposite:
7. Central area, major land use (1964); proposed central
ring road (1952) superimposed in colour.

LEGEND

▦ Shopping

▤ Public Buildings

▥ Commercial

⬩ Industry

░ Residential

⣿ Open Space

River Soar

Vaughan Way

High Street

Charles Street

Parallel to this main route another pedestrian way from the Clock Tower along the main shopping streets, Gallowtree Gate and Granby Street, to the railway station was proposed. The transformation of these streets into pedestrian shopping streets would gradually take place by providing service roads at the rear of properties. Gallowtree Gate would be filled with kiosks, flowerbeds, seats and all the excitement of colour and lights. In the long-term, an elevated covered walkway with a moving floor and frequent pedestrian bridges to the department stores on both sides of the street could be built. This would provide an "express" pedestrian route from the railway station to the Clock Tower, the commercial heart.

The traditional New Walk would be the third parallel pedestrian route, providing a quiet, green promenade, linking Victoria Park via the Civic Centre to the Cathedral precinct.

Two east-west pedestrian routes were proposed: first an elevated walkway with a pedestrian conveyor in Humberstone Gate and High Street, linking the monorail in Charles Street via Clock Tower to the Southgate redevelopment area (St. Nicholas Circle); secondly a pedestrian way from the Clock Tower along Guildhall Lane via Southgate redevelopment area to the riverside walk.

This generous provision for pedestrian movement was consistent with the philosophy of the "Leicester Traffic Plan", according to which in the city centre the priority should be given to pedestrians and full use be made of modern technology capable of providing more efficient means than motor cars of moving people in the concentrated areas.

ACTION AREAS

Since 1962 within the central area the following five action areas were defined: Market Place, Loseby Lane, St. Nicholas Circle and Newarke, Haymarket and Civic Centre. These enterprises are now in various stages of implementation and their total impact on the central area will be felt in the next 2–3 years. Each action area has its own interesting story to tell.

Market Place
The main idea of the redevelopment scheme for this area is the modernisation of an open market in the heart of a prosperous industrial city. The open market, although the oldest form of shopping and considered by many as a medieval anachronism, can play a vital role in the life of a modern city along with the retail shop, department store and supermarket.

The open market occupies the whole of what used to be in the historic past the main square of Leicester. It is commercially successful and is reputed to be one of the finest open markets in the country. It sells amongst a variety of local produce that great cheese Stilton, "le fromage du pays". The shops surrounding the market square are well-established businesses relying to a great extent on the continued success of the open market. Several shopping arcades leading into the market provide a clear and useful system of pedestrian ways.

Up to the beginning of this century, the market square was a civic space for the enjoyment of the people as shown in old prints and photographs. In front of the handsome and dignified Corn Exchange, in the style of the Italian Renaissance, with its monumental flight of steps— there used to be a piazza and even a monument.

The scheme proposed the redevelopment of the area by leaving the present pattern of streets intact. The open market was proposed to remain in its present position but new roofs over the stalls were designed to be built and a small paved forecourt in front of the Corn Exchange to be formed. Goods would be distributed from the peripheral service road by means of motor trolleys throughout the whole market, which would be virtually a pedestrian area.

The historic Corn Exchange, reconditioned and redecorated, would be put to new uses—cafes, bars, restaurants—which would keep this centrally located building alive day and night. The block behind the Corn Exchange would be redeveloped mainly for market uses.

The scheme is now being implemented and the first phase (rehabilitation of the Corn Exchange, the piazza and the new market roofs) has been completed.

This is just a dry summary of the redevelopment scheme, but its history is a long and turbulent one.

To outline only the highlights: until the beginning of this century, the Market Place was a magnificent civic square for public meetings and trade, a symbolic heart of the city. Today Leicester is a city without a focal point, without a heart. When in 1930 for purely utilitarian reasons the ugly permanent roof was constructed over the whole area, the civic square was disposed of overnight, an act of cultural barbarism, probably unique in Europe.

In the late 1950s a development company purchased a considerable number of private properties behind the Corn Exchange and in the immediate vicinity of the Market Place, and hoped that they and the city would benefit from their comprehensive development scheme, which included the transfer of the market to a less dominant position and re-development of the area for supermarkets and other profitable uses.

Overleaf:
Left: 8. Central area as existing (1964); black – historic buildings; colour – civic spaces and pedestrian ways

Right: 9. Central area as proposed (A.D. 2000); pedestrian ways and spaces in colour; civic centre according to the modified scheme of 1969.

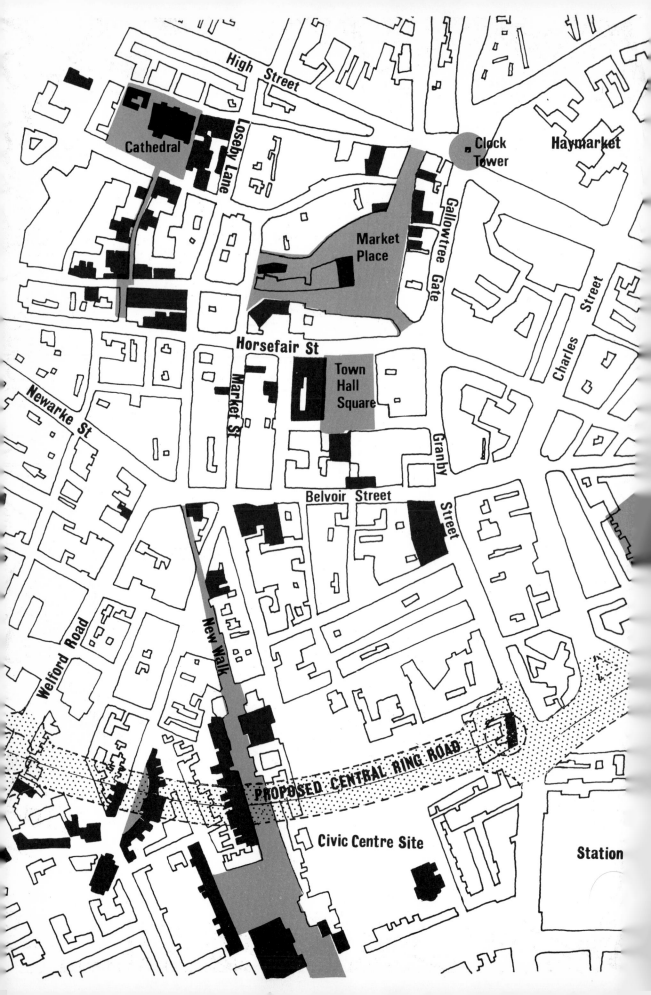

High Street

Cathedral

Loseby Lane

Clock Tower

Haymarket

Market Place

Gallowtree Gate

Charles Street

Horsefair St

Market St

Town Hall Square

Newarke St

Granby Street

Belvoir Street

Welford Road

New Walk

PROPOSED CENTRAL RING ROAD

Civic Centre Site

Station

The scheme provoked violent opposition from stallholders and shop-keepers, which was vented in the *Leicester Mercury* over a long period. One of the stallholders chained himself to the gallery of the Council Chamber to voice a dramatic protest.

The City Council did not approve the developers' scheme but in 1962 appointed Mr. J. D. Trustram Eve, a consultant surveyor, to prepare a report on the economic aspect of redevelopment of the Market Place area and to co-operate with me in producing a new redevelopment scheme. After six months of work the conclusion reached jointly by us was that the open market should remain where it is without any substantial reduction as a powerful shopping magnet and that the whole area was not suitable for radical redevelopment.

The scheme produced by me in March, 1963, proposed modernisation of the market with new roofs and a small piazza in front of the Corn Exchange. This scheme was received with great surprise but also with relief by the City Council and the stallholders.

But the "honeymoon" with the stallholders did not last long. Opposition started to build up against the scheme and particularly against the "piazza", which was planned to be carved out of the profit producing area. The opposition of the stallholders became so powerful that it delayed the implementation of the Market Scheme for four years. Pressure was put on the City Planning Officer to abandon the piazza and even to consider the demolition of the historic Corn Exchange. However the scheme survived and the "piazza" was smuggled in, reduced in size and under the term of the "service forecourt". But the proposed fountain in front of the Corn Exchange was rejected by the City Council; one of the reasons was that it would attract pigeons.

Loseby Lane area

Loseby Lane, located north-west of the Market Place, is a secondary shopping street. Although the individual buildings are of no outstanding architectural or historic value, the environment of Loseby Lane as a whole is picturesque and a part of old Leicester. To the east is an area of decayed and substandard properties on which, according to the Leicester Traffic Plan, a shoppers' parking garage was proposed.

In 1970 a private developer produced a scheme, proposing the widening of Loseby Lane on the eastern side and redeveloping the land for super-markets and a parking garage. The City Council declared their intention to proceed with comprehensive redevelopment and the compulsory purchase of land. The private developers' scheme and the City Council's

Opposite:
Three phases in the history of Leicester Market Place;
Top: 10. View in 1855 when the Market Place was a civic square.
Middle: 11. View of the ugly roof built in 1930.
Bottom: 12. Rehabilitation scheme of 1963.

decision caused strong public opposition and vigorous criticism, even the long extinct civic society was re-formed with the aim of defending "the historic Loseby Lane".

The City Planning Department produced an alternative scheme, proposing the retention of the existing properties on both sides of Loseby Lane with a new service road running parallel on the east side. This would allow for transformation of Loseby Lane into a pedestrian street. On the land to the east a supermarket with a small office block and a shoppers' parking garage for 450 cars was proposed. This scheme however would cost £60,000 more than the private developers' scheme. The City Council approved this scheme in spite of its financial disadvantage, taking into consideration the social and environmental factors in favour of retaining Loseby Lane. *Leicester Mercury* triumphantly announced the victory of public opinion in saving Loseby Lane.

In fact, the City Planning Officer, had this scheme for a long time in his file but did not submit it for approval because of the financial aspects. But when the political climate, fostered by public pressure, changed radically it was the right time to bring this scheme forward and get it approved. This is a classic example of the fact that even the best scheme on paper will have no chances of realisation unless it is produced at the right time and under favourable political and economic conditions. A similar lesson was provided by another action area, St. Nicholas circle redevelopment.

St. Nicholas Circle and Newarke
On the western fringe of the central area a major intersection in the form of a gyratory system of roads combined with an underpass was designed in 1964. This ambitious road construction scheme, costing £1,115,000, has now been completed.

An area of about five acres of land above the underpass was released for development. The City Planning Department produced several alternative schemes, some for commercial and some for residential development, in order to test the potential of this valuable site. The residential development fell through because the Ministry would not grant an "expensive site subsidy". A scheme with a cluster of office towers could not be realised because the Ministry would not give "an office development permit" (O.D.P.). It was a period of frustration.

Finally, the Americans came to the rescue with the proposal for a large hotel and a practical although possibly not the most attractive scheme emerged, which is now in an advanced stage of realisation. The scheme consists of an American hotel, "Holiday Inn", with 204 bed-rooms, a multi-storey garage for 700 cars, some commercial development and a tower block of offices. A system of elevated walkways at first floor level will link this development with High Street and the surrounding areas.

To the south around the historic Newarke Gate an extensive system of pedestrian underpasses has recently been constructed. It is composed of pedestrian passages and landscaped piazzas, providing for an intensive pedestrian movement from the Polytechnic to the city centre.

Clock Tower and Haymarket

The commercial heart of the city is the Clock Tower area, which in its present state is an area of intensive use, containing the most inflamed traffic intersection in the city centre. The buildings are of poor architectural quality, but the land is of considerable value.

In the long-term period it will be possible to transform this traffic intersection into a pedestrian square with stepped walkways around it. Shops at ground and first floors with an entertainment centre above are the main uses proposed. The tower on the square would contain offices. North-west, a group of smaller tower buildings containing luxury flats joined together by roof gardens is proposed. On the square itself, conceived as a formal urban space, the Victorian Clock Tower will be preserved for the continuity of tradition rather than its artistic merit, but other accents—a reflecting pool and modern sculpture—will be added. The windowless elevation of the dance hall on the top floor will be covered with advertisements and lights in order to give the appropriate character to this commercial heart of the city which should be alive by day and night.

To the south the square is linked by means of pedestrian ways with the Market Square and Gallowtree Gate, the main shopping street, which will be transformed into a pedestrian street.

As the first stage in the redevelopment of the Clock Tower area the triangular area to the east (Haymarket) is being redeveloped in a comprehensive way with shops grouped along a system of shopping arcades and a large covered pedestrian concourse. The upper floors will be occupied by an entertainment centre composed of a theatre, a dance hall, restaurants, cafes and roof gardens. The basement will form an underground service area. A multi-storey garage for 600 cars will be approached by ramps from the rear. Three pedestrian bridges will link this triangular block with the surrounding central area.

While the redevelopment of the Clock Tower intersection itself is a long-term proposal to which the City Council at this stage is not committed, the development of the triangular block east of the piazza, known as the Haymarket scheme, was approved by the City Council in 1966. The corner of this block fronting the square (Littlewoods store) has recently been built and the remaining area is now being developed as a joint enterprise of the City Council and the private developers, Taylor Woodrow Property Company Limited. The whole scheme was due to be completed in the Spring of 1973.

The history of the Haymarket scheme is a story of success. Pressures for development started to build up about 1960 when Littlewoods Stores purchased the strategically placed corner site fronting the Clock Tower.

The Town Planning Committee was reluctant to grant planning permission for development of this site because there was no comprehensive plan for the area.

As a matter of urgency the new City Planning Department produced a comprehensive scheme for the whole Clock Tower and Haymarket area and on its basis planning consent was given to Littlewoods for redevelopment of their site as a freehold property. Theoretically it was wrong to give permission to this somewhat "piecemeal" development when it was already decided to go for comprehensive redevelopment of the whole Haymarket area. But life had to go on, and to freeze all development in the city centre pending preparation of plans could have had negative and serious repercussions.

It is true that this commitment complicated the comprehensive scheme and was a source of some difficulties. But judging now from the distance of eight years the decision was correct as it speeded up the development. The usual procedure for comprehensive development and compulsory acquisition of land followed and then some leading development companies were invited to submit their ideas and tenders on the basis of the City Planning Officer's scheme. Taylor Woodrow Limited was the winner in the competition.

Afterwards followed several years of co-operation between the developer and the city officials in the preparation of the final scheme. Nineteen alternative solutions were produced jointly by the City Planning Department and the developers' architects (Building Design Partnership) and were tested on the commercial and financial sides. The final scheme which was agreed, closely resembled the City Planning Department's original scheme, which served as a brief to the competing developers.

Civic Centre

As early as 1942 the City Council realised that the Victorian Town Hall was inadequate for civic functions and that it was inconvenient for the various Corporation Departments to be housed in separate buildings all over the city. The idea of a new civic centre, comprising all municipal offices and a civic theatre, was born.

The first site was considered in the immediate vicinity of the Victorian Town Hall along Market Street. But this proposal was quickly abandoned because of the necessity to acquire the extremely expensive central area properties.

Opposite:
Clock Tower and Haymarket.
Bottom: 13. Model of proposed redevelopment.
Top: 14. View of the interior of the Haymarket centre.
Middle: 15. Haymarket entertainment centre.
Left: 16. Clock Tower against the background of Littlewoods development.

The next proposal (1953) was a free-standing building in Victoria Park designed by a consultant-architect.

The third scheme (1958) was produced by the City Architect on the site located at the southern fringe of the central area between the Museum and Art Gallery and the railway station and fronting the proposed Central Ring Road. On the advice of the Fine Art Commission this scheme was not approved by the City Council and Mr. Peter Chamberlin, consultant-architect, was appointed in 1960.

About four years elapsed until Mr. Chamberlin produced his scheme in the form of a large building, 680 feet long, and extending from the Museum and Art Gallery to the railway station. It was a highly monumental conception, containing in one single building all Corporation Departments grouped along a central covered courtyard. The intention was to build the shell of the whole building in one operation and to provide for future extension by adding mezzanine floors. The estimated cost was £5·6 million and phasing of construction was not possible.

The Chamberlin conception was out of scale with Leicester (one single building one and a half times the length of the National Gallery). However, the City Council approved the project and paid architects' fees. As it was, the project could not be realised, mainly because of the prevailing economic climate, for the country had just entered a period of economic crisis with strict restrictions on public expenditure. The Government would not grant loan sanction for a civic centre. The city of Leicester had missed the boat.

In order not to sterilise the whole of the land allocated for the civic centre, the City Planning Department produced a revised scheme in 1969. The grouping of the civic buildings around two squares, following the north-south axis, was proposed. This would allow for better integration of the civic centre with the city centre and it was in more appropriate scale with Leicester. The eastern part of the site was released for private commercial development, which saved the City Council £855,000 on the acquisition of land. The scheme aimed at maximum flexibility as it was possible to break down the development into separate though interrelated buildings, which could be erected either singly or in groups as and when required.

The City Council approved the reduced civic centre site and also the construction of one office block to provide the urgently required accommodation for Corporation Departments. This block was scheduled for completion in January 1973. This was the happy but rather inglorious

Opposite:
St. Nicholas Circle and Newarke Redevelopment.
Below: 17. Model of St. Nicholas Circle viewed from the north, in the foreground "Holiday Inn".
Top left: 18. View of the main piazza.
Top right: 19. Steps leading to underground pedestrian areas.

ending of the long story of the Leicester civic centre marked by a series of failures and frustrations.

Pending the reorganisation of local government, which is taking place, the implementation of the civic centre will remain in abeyance. But the civic theatre will be built within the Haymarket scheme, planned to be opened in the Spring of 1973.

CONSERVATION OF HISTORIC ENVIRONMENT

Introduction

Britain has a reputation for being a conservative and tradition-loving nation. This is one of those generalisations which is only partly true. How do we explain the record of destruction of historic buildings and buildings of local character in every city, town and village since the war?

European countries and even communist countries (where one could expect contempt for historic tradition) could put Britain to shame with regard to the preservation of historic buildings. Dubrovnik, Prague, Cracow could serve as models of how a medieval city as a whole should be preserved. Poland has almost completed a gigantic reconstruction of historic buildings to the neglect of their housing programme. During the last war Warsaw was completely wiped out and Goebbels reported in the Reichstag that it was only a geographic point. Immediately after the war, half-naked human skeletons, creeping out from the ruins, rebuilt old Warsaw, the largest reconstruction work of an historic area in Europe. The Poles went so far in their love for historic tradition that where historic buildings did not before exist they built them!

Historic buildings are a liability as most of them are obsolete in their function and often structurally substandard. But they must be maintained for all time—if we are a civilised society—for the sake of their historic, architectural or even sentimental value and for the sake of the continuity of tradition.

It is extremely important in our cities to secure the past, to plan for the future and to maintain the continuity of this process for, in the words of Lewis Mumford, "the past never leaves us and the future is already here". The city's function is not only to provide for the physical needs of the community, but it is a highly complex organism, reflecting our failures and our achievements, our dreams which became frustrated and our dreams which are becoming reality. A city without old buildings is like a man without a memory.

The legal machinery for protection of historic buildings—the "listed" buildings procedure of the Town and Country Planning Act, 1947, the

Above: 20. Civic centre, revised scheme of 1969.
Below left: 21. Plan of Town Hall Square improvement.
Below right: 22. Treatment of areas under the trees.

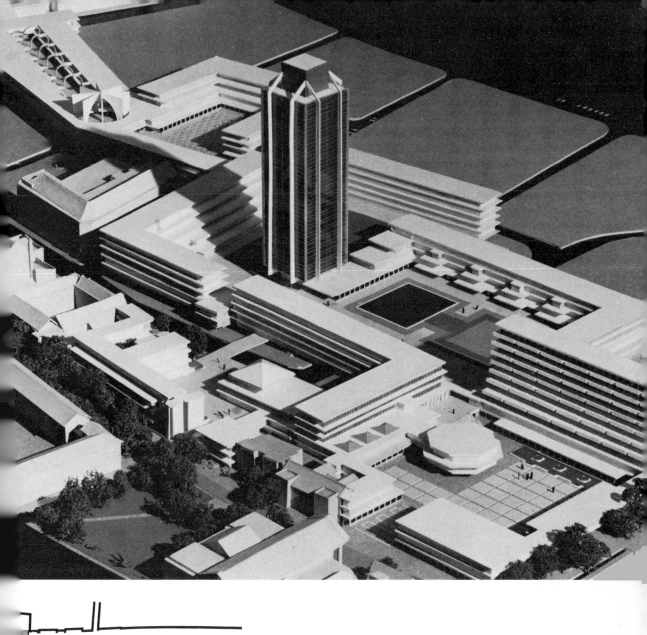

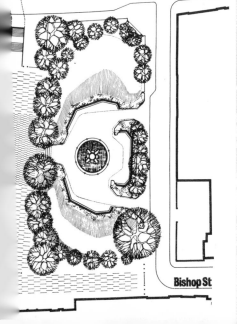

Horsefair St

Bishop St

Civic Amenities Act, 1967, and the Town and Country Planning Act, 1968—has been greatly improved. Consent for the demolition of a "listed" building is now required and the Department of the Environment has to be informed. Lord Kennet has said that the number of "listed" buildings destroyed (400 in 1966 and 266 in 1969) has been considerably reduced owing to the improved machinery. This may be so but a cynic could comment that this commodity is becoming rapidly scarce and probably in the year A.D. 2000 not one historic building will be destroyed because none will be left!

Conservation policy in Leicester

On the basis of the analysis of the urban environment it was necessary to define certain areas where the historic character has survived and where the local identity is intensified. Following the provisions of the Civic Amenities Act, 1967, four areas in the city have been designated as "conservation areas": The Town Hall Square, New Walk, Cathedral precinct and Castle Gardens.

The Civic Amenities Act defines the "conservation areas" as "areas of special architectural or historic interest, the character or appearance of which it is desirable to preserve or enhance." The importance of these new provisions is that for the first time statutory powers are given to planning authorities to protect not only individual historic buildings but the environment as a whole. Also a new concept of "conservation" as distinct from "preservation" has been introduced whereby the historic areas are treated as living organisms where changes have to be accepted provided they are sympathetic to the historic environment. Applications for development in these areas must be advertised and must be open to inspection by the public during the period of twenty-one days. This element of direct public participation is a new and important one.

In practice, the total effect of the designation of "conservation areas" is largely psychological as no extra powers for protection of historic buildings are given. But of considerable importance is the enforced delay for the new development and the opportunity for the general public to express their views, resulting frequently in vigorous controversy in the local press, to which both the planning authority and the private developers are sensitive. On the intensity and quality of this controversy

Opposite:
Improvement of New Walk.
Left: 23. Plan of long-term proposals; 1, pedestrian subway; 2, tower of offices; 3, commercial; 4, R.C. church; 5, offices; 6, civic centre; 7, Museum Square; 8, Art Gallery; 9, railway in cutting; 10, De Montfort Square; 12, The Oval.
Top: 24. Before improvement.
Middle: 25. The same area after reconstruction.
Bottom: 26. After improvement, pedestrian forecourt to Art Gallery (previously car park).

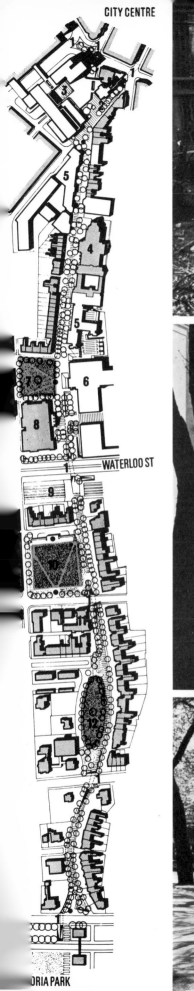

WATERLOO ST

ORIA PARK

may sometimes depend the fate of the buildings of historic interest or architectural value, which are not "listed" yet vital in those areas.

The designation of "conservation areas", in a city such as Leicester, where very few historic buildings of outstanding quality have survived, is of particular value. This is the only procedure which may prevent the destruction of areas with strong local character but with individual buildings of secondary importance. But will it prevent?

In spite of new developments and considerable changes the city of Leicester has done more conservation work in the last five years than in the previous hundred years—The Crescent saved by the abandonment of the construction of the central ring road, the historic Corn Exchange revitalised, the recent improvement of Town Hall Square and of New Walk and the rehabilitation of the Market Place.

Although the Market Place is an historic environment, it was not considered appropriate to designate it as an "conservation area" because of substantial changes taking place there now and planned in a not-too-distant future.

The four "conservation areas" and the Market Place are the most important areas where the historic and local character of the city has survived and continuous vigilance will be required to prevent them from being swept away by new development in an expanding and prosperous city.

Town Hall Square

Town Hall Square is a very pleasant urban square located right in the heart of the city, which has preserved a unity of traditional styles, mainly Victorian, and quiet dignity in its domestic scale. None of the buildings has outstanding architectural value but they all have "good manners" and fit in admirably with the whole environment. The fountain with seats around and the small landscaped areas attract crowds of people and this certainly is the most popular meeting and resting place, particularly in summer.

The City Planning Department produced an improvement scheme—consisting of new permanent seats, removal of fences and hedges, new pavings and overall tidying up—which has now been implemented.

The square is a classical example of a "conservation area" where the environment as a whole needs protection, particularly as the commercial pressures for redevelopment are building up.

Quite recently an application for the demolition of the Sun Alliance, an attractive Victorian building, and its replacement by a modern building was refused by the Town Planning Committee and the matter was the subject of a vigorous public controversy. As an example, here are two opposing views (published in *Leicester Mercury*):

Prof. J. Simmons:

"I wish to support Mr. Smigielski very strongly in his effort to retain the Sun Alliance building in Town Hall Square.

It is a work of real distinction. Anybody who doubts that has only to look at the brickwork, which is extremely refined, in the very best tradition of English craftsmanship. The stone carving too is good; and the whole building has a dignity, in proportion and scale, that is fully worthy of the Town Hall, which adjoins it. To take it down would gravely injure the pleasant domestic character of Town Hall Square."

Mr. P. Leonard:

"The old Sun Alliance building is a Victorian monstrosity and the Clock Tower a nondescript heap of stone, both catering for the superfluous bad taste of the Victorian era. Both are architecturally worthless as they owe their design and concept to a mixture of styles. The architect was a man catering for the stifling trends of his time."

New Walk

New Walk is a fine example of a Georgian pedestrian promenade, almost three-quarters of a mile in length, linking the city centre with a public park. To this promenade, three squares, each of different size and character, are attached. There is a consistent continuity of scale and although the buildings themselves have no outstanding architectural merit the environment as a whole is attractive and quite unique. This area has been allowed to fall into a state of dilapidation and neglect, which for several years was a source of embarrassment to the City Council and a favourite subject of criticism in the local press.

In 1967 I produced a scheme for conservation and redevelopment of this area which falls into two parts: short-term improvements comprise co-ordinated colour schemes of elevations of Council and private properties, removal of the clutter of superfluous traffic signs and notices, repairs to the road surface, additional tree planting, proper landscaping, replacement of unsightly street lamps, seats, etc. In the long-term proposals pedestrian underpasses under all roads cutting across New Walk and an underground car park with landscaped roof in De Montfort Square are planned.

The scheme was exhibited in the Art Gallery and at the opening of the exhibition I made scathing remarks about the people of Leicester for neglect of this environment in order to make them angry and to provoke them to action.

The City Council agreed to the expenditure of £20,000 for improvement of New Walk and also to the establishment of a special "Amenity Fund", £6,000 annually, for small improvements of the environment.

Rehabilitation of New Walk is now in a very advanced stage of implementation and it would be interesting to quote the impressions of a recent visitor:

"May I congratulate the City Council and those concerned in the restoration of New Walk? This haven of peace is now being restored to its rightful dignity, and surely it must be unique.

I have travelled to many towns and cities and have not seen a walk

M

quite like it.

My daughter and I recently walked its length and enjoyed every minute of our stroll, from Upper New Walk with its railed, now neat garden, its railings now painted white and gold and—in the autumn— abounding squirrels.

Then the tall elms, stout sycamores and lovely beech trees on either side fronting the gracious houses, many of which are now offices but very well kept, as are the lamps which stand at intervals down the Walk.

The pathway newly laid makes for easier walking, and even the new office façades breathe an air of the gracious living in Georgian times.

The Museum looks magnificent with its entrance pillars and neat gardens at the side. Indeed it looks as important as it should.

Another surprise is the new office block farther along where stood the most awful delapidated buildings.

Soon New Walk could be the pride of the city, not an embarrassment as of late years. Given back its old dignity, it will be a delight to walk through even if the maxis, midis and minis have replaced the crinolines." (H. E. Padfield, *Leicester Mercury*, 4th February, 1971.)

EPILOGUE

City planning is a creative activity influenced by the many forces operating in an urban community. Its success depends on the quality of the political, social and administrative system. But even the best system will give no results if there is no *idea*, no general conception of the city embodied in a *Plan*.

The Plan should not be too rigid and too technical. The town planner operates on a living and highly complicated organism undergoing a process of continual change, to which apply the laws of biology. An ecological approach to city centre planning would reveal some analogy with nature. In agriculture a "one-crop system" is fatal. Equally a successful development plan for a city centre must secure the diversity of shopping, industry and entertainment, which would provide the diversity for employment.

Our urban design techniques will have to be more subtle and more flexible, allowing for the rapid and unpredictable changes of the technological age. We know how to destroy and we know how to build on new lines. We still have not learned how to develop a method whereby a continuous process of revitalisation of our urban environment would be secured without destroying heritage.

The urban crisis caused by the motor revolution has left us bewildered and uncertain. But gradually a new approach to the urban traffic problem

27. Aerial view of Leicester City Centre, 1970. In the south end of the Market Place can be seen the beginning of change, the new roof under construction.

and a new philosophy of planning with exciting possibilities is emerging.

Town planning in the city centre of Leicester has entered a new phase. The general political and economic climate appears to be very favourable to meet the challenge. Private developers have faith in the future of Leicester and are willing to invest money in this city. There is a boom in office development. The city centre shopping is modernising rapidly. The prospects for the future are bright.

In the not too distant future Leicester will have a new multi-storey shopping and entertainment centre (Haymarket), a revitalised Market Place and a new civic theatre in addition to the two existing theatres. There will be at least seven parking garages in strategic positions. The freeing of Loseby Lane from vehicular traffic, to which the City Council is already committed, will inevitably be followed by changing Gallowtree Gate, the main shopping street, for the sole use of the pedestrian. Gradually in the whole city centre the priority will be given to pedestrians.

Following the successful revitalisation of New Walk, improvement work in "conservation areas" will secure the preservation of old Leicester for all time.

If these trends continue, the city centre of Leicester will become highly concentrated, with a great diversity of uses, virtually free of motor cars, with a strong civic composition, full of vitality and colour, and very close to the idea of the best continental cities. There is even some hope that it may become the object of "the great surprise of strangers"!

5
Liverpool

The fortunes of Liverpool and its City Centre have always been closely associated with the life of the port. Histories of North West England make no reference to Liverpool until the twelfth century and, for a considerable time after this, Chester and the Dee estuary continued to play the dominant role. This was partly because of Chester's military importance, near the Welsh Marches, and partly because that city stood at a centre of the land communication system which had been largely developed during the Roman occupation.

The eighteenth and nineteenth centuries, however, saw the emergence of Liverpool as Britain's principal exporting port. This change resulted from a series of national and international developments whose effects combined to enhance Liverpool's economic importance. The Industrial Revolution and, in particular, the growth of the industrial areas of the Midlands, Yorkshire and Lancashire, greatly increased the volume of foreign trade. The development of the American continent and, later, the growth of British interests in Africa south of the Sahara Desert, increased the importance of ports on the western seaboard of Britain. The development of the railway system made Liverpool very accessible and the fact that the Mersey could accommodate ships in great numbers and of large tonnage also contributed to Liverpool's strategic economic position. A position which was reinforced at the time of maximum growth by the plentiful supply of cheap labour from Ireland.

Thus a great deal of Liverpool's current economic and physical structure was laid down in the middle and latter parts of the nineteenth century on the basis of the city's life as a port. Import and export business of all kinds were established, commodity exchanges were opened, banking and insurance flourished, ship building and repairing expanded and there developed a variety of industries which processed imported materials.

At first the port, the industries and the commercial buildings were intermixed in the City Centre, but as the port activities grew the docks and associated industries extended, first along the Lancashire bank of the River Mersey and subsequently on the Chester side at Birkenhead, thus leaving the site of the original city to develop as a major commercial and regional centre.

The city population grew rapidly as a result of Irish immigration during the nineteenth century and since then the economic structure of the area has largely influenced the development of the population structure. The manning of ships, the handling of merchandise in the port and the warehouses and the port associated industries of raw material processing and ship building all required large numbers of low paid workers. Similarly, banking and insurance required large numbers of poorly paid clerks, with the result that, compared with other cities, Liverpool in the nineteenth century had very many low wage earners, a few very prosperous people and a disproportionately small number of the middle classes. Although the economic base of the city has now substantially changed, the aftermath of this situation can still be seen. The city contains large areas of cheap housing, situated near to the centres of employment, each provided with its complement of shops, pubs and schools. In many areas the strong attachments to the Protestant and Roman Catholic Churches has led to the growth of very strong local community ties.

The legacy of that era is that approximately one third of the city's housing stock was assessed as slums or potential slums in 1966. But in contrast to the areas of cheap housing, the City Centre contains a fine collection of large and distinguished commercial office buildings, the remnants of a very extensive club life, a rich collection of civic and cultural buildings, such as art galleries and concert halls, and the vestiges of a high quality shopping centre.

The fortunes of Liverpool and many ports of North West of England took a sharp downward turn during the economic depression of the 1920s. Since that time there has been a continuous process of adjustment. Some industries have been in a state of absolute decline and many others have been mechanising and shedding labour, to such an extent that there has been a chronic unemployment problem for the past forty years (excepting 1939–1945). The effects of labour shedding have been combatted by energetic programmes to introduce alternative job opportunities, the most notable of which have been the establishment of industrial estates on the periphery of the city and the attraction to Merseyside of the major motor manufacturing plants. It must nevertheless be acknowledged that despite these efforts the area has failed to keep abreast of national growth rates and the gap has increased between the standards on Merseyside and those in the country's most prosperous areas.

Although these new industries have done much to alleviate the problems of unemployment, they have not completely met the need for jobs and they have only contributed to the development of the City Centre by increasing regional purchasing power. New industries have usually come to Merseyside as a result of a general national growth or as an expansion of an industry centred on some other part of the country. The result is that Liverpool's importance as a commercial and administrative centre has diminished, and, while many old and large businesses retain their offices in the city, there is a tendency as mergers take place for the head office elements to move away either to Manchester, which enjoys a geographically more central location, or to London.

National trends in the distribution of wealth have reduced the influence and number of very prosperous families in the city and this, coupled with the relatively modest growth of senior managerial and administrative activity, has tended to reduce the demand for club life and high quality shopping which, in turn, has affected the character of the centre. Similarly, the outward movement of owner occupiers to the Wirral peninsula and South West Lancashire, and public housing tenants to the new towns and peripheral estates, has reduced the frequency with which people visit the City Centre for shopping and other purposes. However, this effect is somewhat offset by an increase in the population within the centre's catchment area and rising purchasing power.

One other historical event which has had an important, but not easily measurable, effect upon the city and its centre is the transfer of the control of the port installations. Until 1857 the port was administered by the City Council and port revenues were available for the Council to use as they saw fit for the improvement of the city or the port. As a result of allegations that the city was not devoting sufficient funds to port development and that charges levied on ships passing through the port to Manchester were excessive, the port was placed under the control of a separate board. Whether or not these allegations were justified is a matter for debate, but it is certain that from the time of the establishment of the Mersey Docks and Harbour Board the prosperity of the port and city was no longer seen as one administrative and governmental problem.

Overleaf:
Left: 1. Liverpool Central Area from the North West showing the floating landing stage in the foreground; Pier Head on the right; Royal Insurance/Liverpool Post project on the left; St. John's Precinct and Beacon in the middle distance; and the Metropolitan Cathedral of Christ the King distant centre.
Right: 2. River Mersey and Pier Head with St. John's Beacon to the left and St. James' Cathedral to the right.

THE FORCES OF CHANGE

In the early part of the period since 1947 the forces of change in the central area were oblique and negative. Both the port and the city suffered very extensive war damage, and the problems of an impoverished and inadequate urban fabric were aggravated by the large proportion of housing which was old and in need of replacement. It is estimated that in 1950 there were approximately 100,000 houses over 80 years old and that this amounted to 40% of the total housing stock accommodating 50% of the population.

Faced with an urgent need for a massive housing programme, and probably influenced by the cultural tradition of large scale initiative by private enterprise, the Council, very understandably, decided to concentrate its own efforts on the housing programme and to leave commercial reconstruction to the resources of private enterprise and grants for war damage repair and reconstruction.

This decision of the Council was in line with the city tradition. In 1869 Liverpool built the first local authority housing in Britain and its continued efforts resulted in a public housing stock of 3,000 dwellings by 1918 and 54,000 by 1951.

The single minded pursuit of a massive public housing programme had several consequences for the central area. The creation of large new housing estates with minimal shopping and other facilities generated an artificially high demand for secondary shopping in the central area. The concentration of local authority effort outside the City Centre meant that little thought was given either to the need or opportunity for restructuring the central area. Furthermore, because of the obsolescent character of parts of the Merseyside economy, initiative on the grand scale did not materialise from the private sector and was not fostered by the local authority. Consequently, much city centre development was piecemeal, circumscribing obsolete buildings which should have been demolished, and reinforcing the historical pattern of roads and street blocks.

During the period up to 1960 much of the main shopping street was reconstructed on its original lines and a number of office blocks were constructed on cleared sites in the heart of the office area, but there was insufficient economic momentum for all the war damaged areas to be redeveloped.

The effects of increasing car ownership were modest, partly because the city had inherited a rather generous road system, partly because there had not been a rapid increase in central area use, and partly because car ownership rates were below the national average. Additionally, the undeveloped central area sites could be used for car parking further to reduce congestion of the street system.

Another de-pressurising factor was the overall size of the conurbation. Distances from the centre to pleasant semi-rural areas were, and are still, sufficiently short for there to be very little demand for central area accommodation by the home owning section of the community. In the public sector also, high land and building costs coupled with central government controls and the Council's own rented structure all militated against central area residential development if other sites were available.

The total effect of these trends was that central area growth and redevelopment was very slow until about 1960 but, around that time, a number of indirectly related events combined to increase the pressure for, and tempo of, change.

In 1961 the City Council decided to revise its committee structure in May 1962. The main purpose of the reorganisation was to streamline the decision-making process in relation to building projects. Prior to that date, non-controversial proposals had to be approved by several committees before submission to the City Council. It was, therefore, decided to form a new committee which would deal with all aspects of development proposals. Considerable importance was attached to this new Development and Planning Committee and membership comprised some of the most prominent and distinguished members of the political parties which made up the City Council.

It is difficult, if not impossible, to prove direct cause and effect, but it seems significant that shortly after prominent Council members had come together in a committee whose central responsibility was the subject of development, the Council began to express concern about the City Centre. By that date many other cities had embarked upon seemingly grandiose redevelopment schemes, many of which were a blend of private investment developments and public sector improvements. The Council was concerned that the private sector had not shown much interest in Liverpool's central area. The Council was also conscious of the fact that it had not prepared any schemes in anticipation of such an interest and it suspected that this state of unreadiness might have contributed to the lack of private enterprise activity.

The involvement of private capital was of importance to the Council for three reasons. First, although the country was, at that time, in a state of economic buoyancy it was not realistic to expect the public sector to find the whole of the required capital. Secondly, some of the commercial activities which the Council sought to encourage had their own preference for private investment. Thirdly, and of considerable significance, was the fact that the majority party in the City Council was the Conservative Party and the encouragement of private enterprise was a matter of doctrinal importance.

In addition to these political developments, some pressures for physical change had begun to emerge. Traffic problems around the entrance to the road tunnel under the Mersey and in the shopping centre had generated a proposal from the then City Engineer and Planning Officer for an Inner Ring Road. Littlewoods mail order and multiple shop organisation was seeking to build a large block of offices, and Ravenseft Developments were showing interest in developing an area around St. John's Market.

None of these proposals related positively to each other and there was considerable opposition to the Inner Ring Road from property owners and bodies with environmental interests.

The effect of these pressures has been to set in motion a whole chain of organisational rearrangements, which have not yet ended, and which have extended far beyond the City Centre. These operational developments will be discussed in the next chapter, but, before moving on to this topic, some reference must be made to the political developments which have occurred since 1960.

In 1963 political control of the Council passed into the hands of the Labour Party, for only the second time, and there was then concern amongst the planners that the work, then well in hand, might be set aside. To some degree this concern sprang from the fear that a planning organisation which had been created by one party might be politically unacceptable to another. But the major cause of concern was that Alderman J. Braddock, the then leader of the Labour Party, was a pragmatist, with a considerable suspicion of intellectuals and professionals, and who was not prepared to devote any time to sophisticated planning. For some months a state of uncertainty prevailed, but the sudden death of Alderman Braddock led to the emergence of a new leader, Alderman W. H. Sefton, who saw the planning process as a positive tool for improving the social and physical well being of the city.

There were, however, ideological differences: the Conservative dominated Council had sought to achieve redevelopment by encouraging private initiative, whereas the Labour dominated Council sought to achieve similar ends by direct action. There have been no substantial political differences over the proposed physical structure of the city or the central area, but changes in priorities and methods of achievement have affected a number of projects in ways which will be discussed later.

ORGANISATIONAL ARRANGEMENTS

At the time when the City Council became concerned about the slow rate of development of the City Centre, the planning services of the local authority were provided by a small division of the City Engineer's Department with an establishment of 39 professional, 7 technical and 4 administrative staff, but only half of these posts were occupied.

Such a staff resource was clearly insufficient to undertake a searching reappraisal of the central area and to prepare a detailed plan for redevelopment. The City Council, therefore, in February 1962, appointed Graeme Shankland as planning consultant for the City Centre and instructed him first to advise the Corporation on the planning of the inner area of Liverpool and on matters relating to it, and to prepare proposals for the City's inner road system, together with three-dimensional proposals for the redevelopment of the areas within and adjoining it;

and secondly to assist in the initiation of studies leading to the revision of the Liverpool Development plan.

Mr. Shankland worked in collaboration with the planning section of the City Engineer's Department but, upon the retirement of the City Engineer, the Council decided to create a separate City Planning Department with an establishment of 140, and in December 1962 Walter Bor took up his appointment as the City Planning Officer. The proposal to create a new department had been supported by Mr. Shankland, because it was abundantly clear that a more intensive application of the planning process to the whole city was necessary if the central area was to be soundly planned and effectively developed.

There were, however, difficulties in phasing and synthesising the work on the central area and that on the rest of the city. One difficulty was that work was further advanced on the central area than on the rest of the city and the consultant had to be retained for a fourth year to allow the time lag to be overcome. Another difficulty was that, since both the Planning Consultant and the City Planning Officer had direct and independent access to the same Development and Planning Committee, there was no machinery to ensure that the planning advice of the two planners was always consistent and compatible.

There was, however, a great deal of goodwill between the two principal planners involved in this situation and, as a result, they agreed to set up a joint office of their two staffs for the last year of the work on preparing the City Centre Plan.

The catalytic effect of appointing two distinguished planners to work on city problems was very marked. In the first place, they attracted well qualified and enthusiastic staff. Secondly, they attracted and exploited considerable public interest, so that an air of confidence and optimism was instilled in some key sections of the city's economic and social structure and, no less importantly, among potential developers.

As a consequence, the city found itself having to make decisions on major city centre development projects submitted to the Council before the completion and approval of the City Centre Plan. It was the view of both elected representatives and planners that wherever possible these proposals should be encouraged, and a substantial number of schemes which required some local authority participation were approved at an early date. The implementation of these projects in practice placed an additional burden on the Town Clerk's Department in relation to legal agreements, property transactions and the co-ordination of the work of various corporation departments. It therefore became necessary to set up a Development Unit, within the Town Clerk's Department, to deal with the managerial aspects of these projects.

The establishment of the joint City Centre Planning Group was of great value in ensuring the full integration of the City Centre Plan into the overall Interim Planning Policy prepared for the whole city, and in ensuring a smooth transition of responsibility when Graeme Shankland's

Opposite:
Above: 3. Chapel Street, Liverpool, showing from left to right Newcastle Breweries' hotel under construction, Richmond House offices, old property about to be redeveloped and No: 1 Old Hall Street offices. An elevated pedestrian route passes through these properties and is incorporated in the new development. A ramp can be seen in the distance leading up to the pedestrian level. A bridge will cross Chapel Street at the top of the ramp and another bridge will cross Old Hall Street from the set back in the frontage of the new building.

Below: 4. Cook Street/North John Street, Liverpool. A recently built outfitters store designed to receive two pedestrian bridges at the points where the window detail varies on the first floor. The different widths of these provisions reflect different volumes of predicted pedestrian movement.

Above: 5. St. John's Precinct, Liverpool, showing the two shopping levels connected by escalators in the foreground and a third shop level exploiting the rise in the level of the site at the far end. Above the shops can be seen the carcass of a new hotel which surmounts the project.

major involvement came to an end in 1966. Since then, the planning arrangements specially relating to the City Centre have remained unchanged although some external events have had their impact on the City Centre Plan.

These external factors include the Merseyside Area Land Use and Transportation Study between 1965 and 1969, which subjected the City Centre Plan's implications for the sub region to rigorous examination and which caused some changes in the Plan's priorities. Another factor was the resignation of Walter Bor in September 1966, and his succession by the author, who has tended to place greater emphasis on strategic issues and economic and social development, with the result that the Plan has been supplemented by a number of "non-physical" policies.

The external factor with the most far reaching consequences is, however, the introduction of a new committee and departmental structure designed to improve the Corporation's decision making and managerial efficiency. This reorganisation has abolished the Development and Planning Committee and placed all major planning decisions in the hands of the Policy and Finance Committee (the policy and strategy committee of the whole Council). This arrangement ensures that financial and physical planning decisions are made together and that resources are allocated so that development in one sector is not outstripped by development in another. Because of its involvement in these resource allocation and programming operations, the City Planning Department has now had to add an implementation team to its establishment.

From time to time major planning problems have arisen in the City Centre, either in relation to a particular site or project, or in relation to a topic, such as car parking or residential accommodation. These frequently require inter-departmental collaboration, and ad hoc project teams are set up for the purpose and disbanded as soon as their work is completed. These have proved to be very effective in securing a synoptic approach and solution to a problem, but have had no lasting effect upon the organisation of the authority.

The essential principles of the City Centre Plan which have withstood the test of time are based on the intention to exclude unnecessary vehicular traffic. To effect this, around and at some distance from the core of central area activities, an inner motorway is to be constructed which will provide direct and easy movement between all the radial routes, the tunnel entrances and a series of major car parks which extend up to the central core. Within the motorway there are separate circulation systems for vehicles and pedestrians, and substantial areas are allocated for office, shopping, residential, cultural and recreational purposes. Land is allocated for the expansion of these uses, mainly in areas of obsolete warehousing, industrial and residential property.

The Plan anticipates that all movements cannot be by private car in the future and therefore incorporates an underground railway system, an improved bus circulation system and a car parking policy designed to ensure that business and shopping visitors will not be excluded by commuters.

Particular attention is paid to the question of environmental quality, both in terms of exploiting the advantages of a riverside location, and in relation to the internal character of the area. Special proposals are made to integrate the major new road works into the urban fabric and policies for future design work are prescribed. In addition, the Plan contains detailed proposals for several comprehensive redevelopment sites where action is imminent.

INDUSTRIAL AND COMMERCIAL ACTIVITIES

As was said earlier, much of the economic and physical structure of the City Centre was laid down in the nineteenth century; nevertheless, since then there have been significant changes.

The most important of these changes has been the decline in the number of head offices within the city. Since this is largely the result of company mergers and the creation of larger commercial organisations both nationally and internationally, it is not a trend which the city could hope to reverse. The effect of this trend is not merely a matter of prestige. In terms of employment, growth in numbers and quality of jobs is more certain at head offices than elsewhere. The reduction of the number of firms, and increased vertical integration have reduced the need for provincial commodity markets and much of the associated brokerage business. Thirdly, but most importantly, with the exodus of business the heads of large commercial organisations have ceased to show the same interest in, and concern for, the city and its future.

The situation in respect of head offices is not entirely black. Some firms have remained and have played a major part in the growth and re-development of the central area and particular mention will be made of the Royal Insurance Company at a later stage. In other instances, new businesses have been established and developed in the city, of which Littlewoods mail order and shop organisation, is the most notable both for its size and for the involvement of its founding family in city affairs.

Another activity which has gone from the City Centre is the wholesale markets, but in this instance the loss has benefited both the central area and the city. Until 1966 there were two wholesale fruit and vegetable markets and a fish market in the City Centre. These markets had the combined effect of causing early morning congestion and creating dead areas in the centre for the greater part of the city's day. In addition, the market buildings and the associated traders' accommodation were obsolete and unsightly. The question of resiting the markets had been the source of much controversy since the late 1950s, largely because attempts had been made to reach agreement with each market unilaterally. In 1964 the planning department made an appraisal of all the market operations and was able to propose one new suburban site for the three

N

markets which received the approval of the City Council and of all the trading organisations.

The importance of the removal of the markets was not merely that it got rid of a central area problem. The vacated sites presented some of the first opportunities for the city to consider comprehensive redevelopment of substantial areas. It also set the scene for the relocation of the fruit and vegetable exchange which originally claimed that a central area location was essential, but which is now considering a move to the site of the wholesale markets.

Retail trade in the central area has been subject to changes arising from national trends and from local pressures. The increasing influence of the multiple stores and the decline of the individual trader, together with a shortage of car parking facilities, have accelerated the disappearance of quality shops, which were already at risk because of limited growth of population in the upper socio-economic groups. In addition, the higher trading efficiency of the multiples results in floor space increasing at a slower rate than turnover. These changes have been given additional impetus by the increased rate of redevelopment and because individual traders can seldom afford the high rents which are charged by investment developers.

The loss of individual traders reduced the variety of shops and of goods available in the central area and may eventually reduce the attractiveness of the shopping centre. Unfortunately, these traders constitute an interest group which cannot look to either of the major political parties for adequate protection or assistance. On the one hand, they are the victims of market mechanisms whose operation is a major element of right wing doctrine: on the other hand, they represent a sector of the capitalist system which is abhorrent to the left wing philosophy.

Much more critical to the Liverpool scene has been the shift in convenience shopping habits. Until the early 1960s, most new housing was constructed either on inner area clearance sites near to existing shops or on the periphery of the city without adequate shopping facilities. As a result, many residents of these new areas would frequently travel back to the old inner areas to visit friends and relatives and to do their shopping. One end of the City Centre shopping area extended into the older residential areas along both sides of London Road, the busiest radial bus route, and, consequently, this section of the shopping area became a thriving centre for convenience goods and low price consumer durables.

During the early 1960s the remaining friends and relatives moved away from the inner areas, public transport fares increased, and shops began to operate in quantity in the new residential areas. At the same time, shops in the remainder of the central shopping area had increased their

Opposite: 6. Routes of pedestrian and vehicle circulation which are projected for 1981.

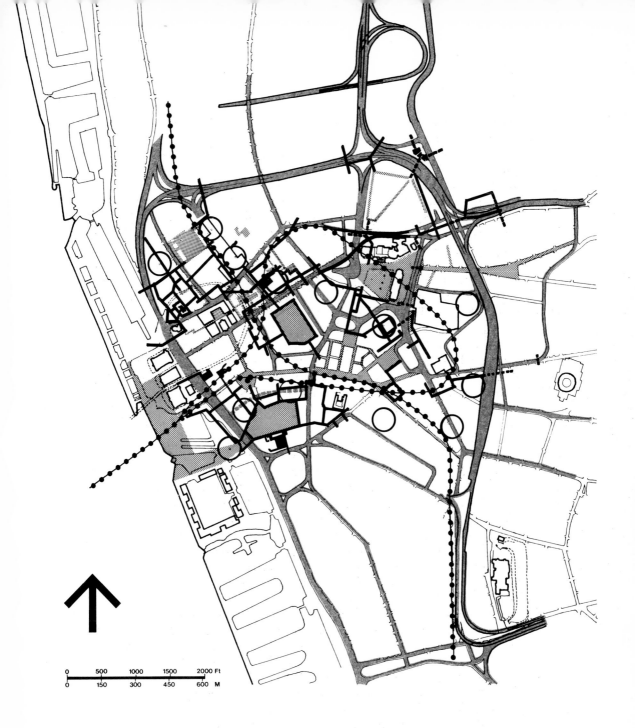

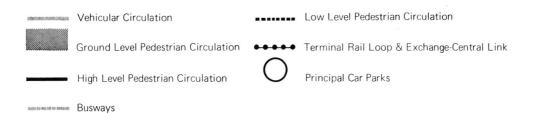

0   500   1000   1500   2000 Ft
0   150   300   450   600 M

Vehicular Circulation   Low Level Pedestrian Circulation

Ground Level Pedestrian Circulation   Terminal Rail Loop & Exchange-Central Link

High Level Pedestrian Circulation   Principal Car Parks

Busways

Circulation 1981

efficiency and attractiveness so that the London Road area began to decline. Once the London Road area compared unfavourably with the remainder of the centre the deterioration accelerated, and it has now reached a point where the majority of the area is ripe for redevelopment. The local authority now faces the problem that site assembly will be expensive because of the established shopping use values, yet, in a period of economic retrenchment, the prospect of new investment and development is limited. There is, therefore, the risk of this area remaining in a depressed state for some time.

Two other central activities have also declined in importance. One of these is warehousing, which has declined both because it is no longer commercial practice to stock pile large quantities of goods at the port, and because retail traders now rely more upon rapid delivery from manufacturers and less upon the holding of large stocks of goods.

The other declining activity is industry, which falls into three distinct categories. First, the industries which are closely allied to other central area activities which need to remain in the area. These include printing, tailoring and office equipment repairers. Secondly, there are industries which have no particular tie to the central area and which are flourishing businesses. Thirdly, there are those which may or may not be tied to the central area and which are only marginally profitable; these may vary from rag sorters to violin makers.

Most of these industries are in old buildings on the outer edge of the central area and, as a consequence, lie in the path of the proposed Inner Motorway and are therefore bound to be disturbed. The Council has surveyed all the affected firms and has made available to them a variety of options. In and around the centre, sites have been made available for firms to erect new premises of their own; new flatted factories have been erected for rental to displaced firms, and an old multi-storey warehouse building has also been converted to low rental flatted factories. Sites and, in some cases, buildings are also available in other parts of the city for firms who wish to move out from the centre.

Experience has revealed that about 55% of firms close down when they have to leave their old premises, but that the others become more efficient. One of the factors contributing to this high proportion of firms going out of business is that, if compensation for disturbance is to be obtained, the move must be made just before the Council requires the site. Thus, if a firm moves early it gets less money from the Council but, if it waits until it can get the greater compensation, there may be other obstacles to moving which force or induce the owner to close down. Other causes of closure are, of course, scarce financial resources and owners approaching the age of retirement. In some instances, the industries which close are businesses which are obsolescent, and disturbance only accelerates the inevitable; but the loss of some craft and specialist service may diminish the attracting power of the City Centre, in the same way as the loss of speciality shops.

OTHER ACTIVITIES AND INFLUENCES

Transport

The essential character of the transport system is described in an earlier section, but some more detailed comment is necessary to describe how modifications have occurred.

The Inner Motorway, as originally conceived, was an elevated structure divided into a number of lineal phases, each of which contained ground and elevated works which would be implemented simultaneously. The different phases were to be built sequentially over a period of fifteen years, partly because this was expected to reflect the increased rate of car use, and partly so that too large an area would not be disrupted by development at one time.

Whilst powers were being obtained in Parliament and land was being assembled, the Merseyside Area Land Use and Transportation Study (1969) was carried through and, although it generally confirmed the desirability of constructing the motorway, it did have certain implications for its design and phasing. The MALT Study put forward two alternative conurbation strategies. One, the "restrained" system, assumed that funds for transport development would be limited to such an extent that the use of the private car for central area commuting would be restrained to a point below the level of free choice. The other, the "choice" system, assumed that the road capacity would be available for all who chose to travel, in the peak period, to the central area by private car. The number of car parking spaces which could be provided in the central area was physically limited to about 30,000 for either system, but their use and disposition varied according to their use as commuter or business/shopping/leisure short stay parks.

The decision whether to design for the "choice" or "restrained" system was to be based on the rate of economic expansion. Consequently, one of the benefits of the unfortunate state of the national economy has been to make it abundantly clear that the restrained system must be adopted. Additionally, the national economic situation is such that the original fifteen year programme is not practical, and other matters have emerged which influence the phasing.

One of these factors is the grant arrangements in relation to land assembly. Under the local act authorising the construction of the motorway, any affected owner could require the local authority to acquire his property within three years. As a result, the city has bought large quantities of land along the whole length of the route as well as the whole of the land for the first phase. The cost of this land amounts to over £5 million on part of which a grant of 75 per cent is payable by the Department of the Environment. But the grant is not payable until the commencement

Overleaf, Left: 7. Land use in Liverpool's central area, March 1972.
Right: 8. Proposed pattern of the allocation of land for primary uses in the central area.

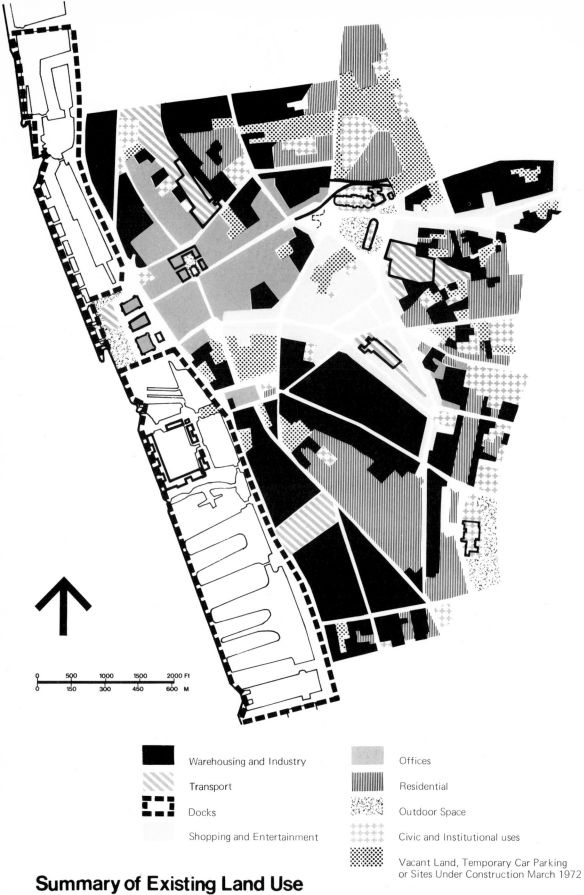

■	Warehousing and Industry	▦	Offices
▨	Transport	▥	Residential
▪▪	Docks	⠿	Outdoor Space
	Shopping and Entertainment	✛	Civic and Institutional uses
		▦	Vacant Land, Temporary Car Parking or Sites Under Construction March 1972

0   500   1000   1500   2000 Ft
0   150   300   450   600 M

Summary of Existing Land Use

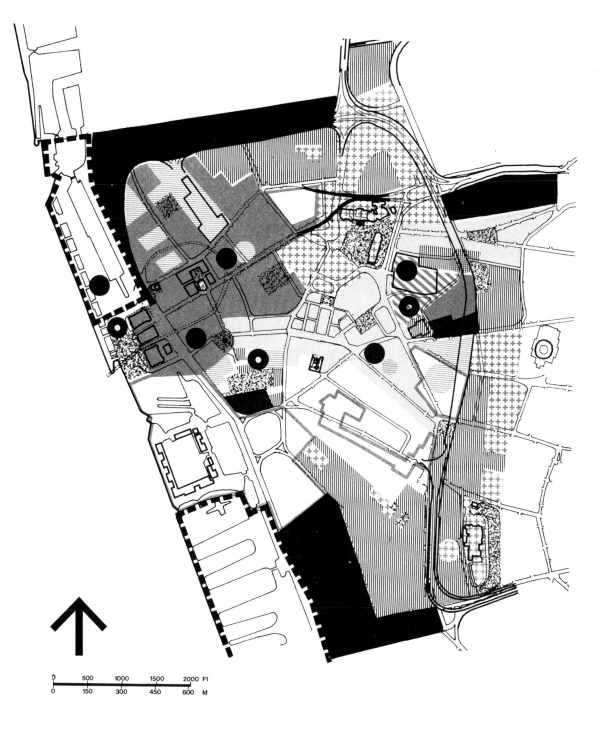

■	Warehousing and Industry	▦	Outdoor Space
▨	Transport	✛✛✛	Civic and Institutional Uses
⬚	Docks	▭	Study Area
	Shopping and Entertainment	●	Railway Station
▨	Offices	◉	Bus Station
▥	Residential		Public Car Park

Proposed Primary Land Use Pattern

of construction.

The City Council is, therefore, anxious to start construction, throughout the whole length of the route, at the earliest possible date for two
reasons. On the one hand, large areas are beginning to look semi derelict
because of advance acquisitions, on the other hand, the local authority
must carry the burden of debt charges on the whole of the land costs
until the grant is received. As a result, the motorway has been modified
so that ground works can be completed throughout the whole length
in advance of the elevated works. Not only does this remove dereliction
and secure the grant; it also provides a central area periphery route at
an early date. There is a further advantage which is certainly not part
of Council policy, but which one cannot ignore in the light of changing
public opinion. If public attitudes favouring the restriction of the use of
cars in central areas become sufficiently strong, it might not be necessary
to build the elevated sections at all.

The associated car park development has not progressed as fast as had
been hoped, largely because the City Council decided that, wherever
possible, these facilities should be provided by private enterprise. Although
these car parks would have shown a positive return on investment, the
rate of interest compared unfavourably with other investment opportunities, so that the car park provision lagged behind other development.
In 1969 the lag had become so serious that it appeared to be depressing
the volume and quality of shopping potential in the central area and the
Council decided to build car parks from its own resources. Sites for
5,890 cars are now being designed or constructed. This will bring the
total number of spaces in the City Centre up to 17,860 by 1976.

As in many other cities during the twentieth century there has been a
disproportionate emphasis on the development of bus public transport
to the detriment of suburban rail services. The consequent duplication
has resulted in losses on bus services and in rail access to the central area
becoming so uneconomic that numerous proposals have been made for
the termination of train services. Fortunately, the Minister of Transport
required a stay of execution until the findings of the MALT Study
were available. Subsequently these findings revealed that there was
great potential in the rail system and that if all modes of public transport
were properly integrated an optimum communication system would
carry far greater numbers of passengers by rail. It is too early to experience
the full benefits of the MALT Study proposals but the greater co-
ordination achieved through the formation of the Merseyside Passenger
Transport Authority has already brought about economies which have
checked the escalation of operational deficits.

The major railway element of the central area system is a loop line
connecting the four radial line termini and giving an improved passenger
distribution system. This project was first postulated in the early part of
this century, but it had to await justification in the overall communication
context of the MALT Study, and a more flexible government attitude

towards government investment before construction could commence.

A further element of the communication system is the separate system of pedestrian routes linking the stations and car parks to the main office and shopping areas. Substantial parts of this system have now been completed within new development projects but few of these lengths are of much value until they are linked together. In areas where the pedestrian routes are above or below ground, the Corporation is building the necessary bridges and subways. But, in other areas the continuity is broken by substantial buildings, constructed before these routes were planned. To overcome this problem the City Council has also obtained power from Parliament compulsorily to purchase spaces for routes through existing buildings where these can be proved to be necessary.

Housing
The amount of residential accommodation in the central area is limited but certain aspects of the city-wide housing activities have important implications for the central area.

The most significant factor has been the Council's changing attitude towards housing densities. Up to the beginning of the 1960s it was contended that the occupants of slum clearance properties should be re-accommodated as far as possible in the inner areas because their jobs were in the port or inner area industries and because of intense local loyalties. As a consequence the Council built to the highest densities they could achieve in the inner areas and thereby kept overspill to the minimum. This had implications for shopping facilities which have already been described but it also meant that the central area was the best location for many other services and particularly those administered by the local authority.

During the 1960s many obsolescent inner area industries closed down, others have moved away and yet others have become more capital intensive and have shed labour so that the job opportunities in the inner areas has diminished. During the same period the Council has found that local loyalties were not as strong as had been believed and that high density housing (up to 500 persons per hectare) is not suitable for many households needing local authority accommodation. It has also found that the high costs of high density accommodation, even after central government subsidies, have seriously strained the Council's rental structure, which itself depends upon a system of internal cross subsidisation. The resulting rent increase has consequently reduced the demand for public housing, notwithstanding the availability of a rent rebate scheme.

The sum effect of these events has been for the Council to reduce housing densities to around 200 persons per hectare and to turn its attention to improving the internal and environmental amenities of its older housing stock. The resulting dispersal of population has also meant that many services previously provided in the City Centre have now had to be dispersed to the districts which have received the overspill population.

Within the inner motorway there are three residential areas, two of which were built in the 1930s and one partly in that period and partly in the early 1950s. All are adjacent to industrial and commercial uses and in recent years traffic congestion and car parking difficulties have resulted in the areas being used for short cuts and for uncontrolled commuter parking. There is, therefore, an urgent need to improve the environmental quality of these areas but the need conflicts with other priorities. The Council is anxious to maintain the attractiveness of the central area and does not wish to aggravate problems of accessibility and car parking by excluding all but essential traffic from these areas. Additionally some adjacent activities are unsuitable neighbours to residential areas but their disturbance could be damaging to the local economy.

The Housing Act of 1968 has, of course, encouraged the Council and residents to take more interest in improving existing dwellings and their surroundings. Community councils and residents groups in many parts of the city have been active in promoting self help schemes and in putting pressure on the Council to achieve such improvements. Most notable amongst these has been the Shelter Neighbourhood Action Project where the operation has achieved considerable momentum through the concentrated input of professional advice by Shelter, the national organisation concerned with homes for the poor. Similar trends can be detected amongst the central area residents groups and it is likely that some environmental improvements will accompany the internal improvements which are now proposed for the dwellings.

The general problems of economically developing expensive sites for public housing have discouraged the Council from building central area dwellings and at the same time more attractive and cheaper sites in outlying areas have diverted the interests of private enterprise from either central or inner area projects. However, the Council has been anxious to expand central area residential activities so that the City Centre facilities are used to the fullest practical extent and so that the central area remains populated and attractive during the evening hours.

Several attempts were therefore made to provide luxury high rise, high density dwellings in the Strand Paradise Scheme adjacent to the central core on a site with excellent views across the river. Unfortunately, two obstacles were encountered. The most serious of these was the fact that the dwellings cost more than £5,000 each and the Ministry of Housing and Local Government would not give the approval which any housing association then had to have before embarking on a project of that order of cost. A less serious problem was the fact that the project needed to be sufficiently large to make an effective residential precinct and although market research revealed that there was a demand for such accommodation it also indicated that the demand might not be present in sufficient quantity.

The events of the past decade seem to suggest that it is unlikely that there will be any significant increase in central area residential use, although existing local authority estates are likely to remain and be improved. Additionally, the reductions in population of the inner areas is likely permanently to reduce the need for local services to be provided in the central areas.

The Polytechnic

Mention has already been made of the Council's intention to secure appropriate redevelopment adjacent to the Inner Motorway. This policy proved to be of special significance in the case of the Polytechnic which the Department of Education and Science decided should be formed out of the existing colleges of Art, Building, Commerce and Technology. Of these four colleges, the latter was housed in a substantial new complex adjacent to some obsolescent local authority walk-up flats, and a large tract of land acquired under the special motorway legislation for redevelopment. There were numerous reasons for choosing a central area location and the land adjacent to the College of Technology re-presented the only available uncommitted fifty acre site in the City Centre. The City Council, therefore, decided to allocate this land for the Polytechnic, but it has generated considerable opposition.

Many of the staff of the existing colleges suffer from traffic noise in unsuitably designed buildings and some of these staff do not believe that adequate sound insulation and vibration protection will be in-corporated into the newly designed buildings. Others do not believe that the Polytechnic should be in the central area, and hanker after a "green fields" location. Both are opposed to the current site and are interested in a riverside site which has subsequently become available and which will be referred to later.

Another source of opposition to the Polytechnic stems from the local residents, who wish to remain despite the fact that the walk-up flats have many internal inadequacies and are likely to be cut off from other residential areas and services by major roads. This is largely because they fear that rehousing would result in their being moved away to a different area, distant from their places of work, and their places of worship.

The Council have given assurances to the academics about the level of protection from the effects of traffic, and to the residents that they would be rehoused locally, but both parties remain sceptical and it is not likely that opposition will disappear until it becomes clear that the Council has honoured its undertakings.

Civic and Social Centre

Another project which has aroused controversy is the proposed Civic and Social Centre. This sprang from a need to accommodate most Corporation office staff under one roof and for a site near to St. George's

Hall and from a sketch brief prepared by Graeme Shankland. Colin St. John Wilson was appointed as the architect, and originally produced a cruciform building of ingenious design which bore little relationship to the Shankland brief. This design had to be abandoned because the cost of £30 million was excessive, but not before it came in for criticism for its lack of neighbourliness. A new £10 million scheme has now been produced which, at the time of writing, is also being criticised for un-neighbourliness and for its extravagance. The Council is anxious to proceed, in view of their urgent need for accommodation, but in the light of these criticisms and the impending reorganisation of local government, there must be some uncertainty about the future of this project.

Albert Dock Area
Except for a small frontage at the Pier Head, the City Centre is cut off from the River Mersey by the dock system. The docks, administered by a separate statutory undertaker, are free of any local planning authority control over their operational uses. This situation pertained when the City Centre Plan was prepared and up until 1966 when some 55 acres of docks became surplus to requirements.

The sudden availability of this land posed some serious planning problems. First, there was the question whether the City Centre Plan should be abandoned so that a new strategy could be developed from first principles. This course was dismissed as impractical, since so many decisions based on the plan were already being implemented in the central area, and because there was no certainty about the future development of the site.

The second problem was posed when Harry Hyams' architect, Colonel Seifert, proposed a 10 million square feet office complex on the site, employing 45,000 people and increasing central area employment by 30 per cent, excluding generated secondary employment. The Council, anxious to ensure that this development would bring new work, and not merely drain off development potential from the rest of the central area, obtained an assurance from Mr. Hyams that he intended to lease the accommodation to firms coming from outside the sub-region. But, such an influx of new jobs would result in what could be regarded as an excessively centralised conurbation. Already 27 per cent of the conurbation's retail turnover occurs in the central area together with 23 per cent of the conurbation's job opportunities and to this must be added a university, a polytechnic and a major leading hospital. The effect of further centralisation would be a very limited opportunity for travel to the central area by car, and extreme pressure even on an immediately expanded public transport system. It was also likely to blight the future development prospects of centres in other county boroughs such as Bootle and Birkenhead.

Additionally, in the 55 acre site stood a group of warehouses around a dock, all of which the developer wished to demolish. These were all built by Jesse Hartley in 1845 and occupied 14 acres of the site. At the time of Mr. Hyams' first proposal these warehouses were listed as buildings of architectural and historic importance Grade II and have subsequently been elevated to Grade I. Notwithstanding their considerable architectonic quality, their scale and neglected condition give them a forbidding appearance which deters investors and discourages them from even considering the extremely difficult task of conversion and rehabilitation. However, their architectural quality inspired many architects, artists and conservationists to press for their preservation.

Thus a situation built up in which no one wished to spoil the prospect of attracting 45,000 jobs to an area of chronic unemployment, yet there was real cause for concern about the quality of the urban structure, the fate of other employment and commercial centres and the preservation of part of Merseyside's architectural heritage. None of these matters were likely to outweigh the importance of creating employment but, collectively, they were of sufficient importance to induce the Minister of Housing and Local Government to call in the application. In the course of the ensuing negotiations, the economic climate deteriorated and the developer ultimately lost interest, but it is interesting to note that the stimulus for major change came from the private sector and could have radically changed the conurbation structure. It is equally interesting to note the local authority's readiness to change its plans to exploit this newly found potential resource. In fact, the City Centre Plan was used as a means of encouraging and steering development rather than as a restrictive ordinance.

Public Opinion
There have also been social pressures from various interest groups for more, less and different change. These pressures have resulted in revisions of strategy at city scale, but have tended to be of only tactical significance in the City Centre.

Amongst these social forces particular mention should be made of the local daily press. The *Liverpool Daily Post and Echo* had run a campaign for the rapid development and improvement of the city before either Graeme Shankland or Walter Bor were appointed. As a result, the press have always given very full coverage of planning proposals and of criticisms of planning which has helped to create an informed local public.

Public opinion has, however, expressed itself more specifically through the elected representatives or organised special interest groups. At the political level, planning has of course been criticised for being too much influenced by private enterprise, or too restrictive of that same enterprise, according to the philosophies of different councillors. But, with the exception of general concern about the rate of redevelopment and the difficulties of creating central residential accommodation, there has been a general acceptance of and support for the plan as a whole. In the case of some individual projects, however, there have been strong feelings about high building control and conservation policies.

The subject of aesthetic and historical values is one which has naturally interested the conservation bodies, such as the Merseyside Civic Society, the Victorian Society, the Georgian Group and various district amenity or community groups. It is also a subject which has generated a great deal of heat.

The corporate attitude of the Council is curiously ambivalent. On the one hand it supports, without hesitation, what is probably the finest provincial art gallery, the Royal Liverpool Philharmonic Orchestra and various other artistic enterprises, despite the fact that opinions are sharply divided upon the quality of the achievements in some of these fields. Yet, although the Council has cleaned and redecorated most of its civic buildings, it has shown a reluctance to assist owners to conserve old buildings of merit and an extreme sensitivity to external criticism of the architectural environment.

As a result, even the most well informed and well intentioned utterances of interested societies appear to be resented and seem to increase the Council's determination not to be influenced. Similarly, philanthropic gestures are regarded with some caution and grants or other expenditure to conserve the city's very considerable architectural heritage are limited. This, despite the fact that there is dissatisfaction in the Council about the general appearance of the city and its condition.

The direct and constructive influence of amenity societies upon the City Council has, therefore, not been great, but their influence over local property owners has helped to achieve the conservation of some areas by persuasion.

Adjacent to the Inner Motorway are three residential areas which are all affected by adjacent development projects and all of which contain substantial numbers of local authority walk-up flats. The two areas most radically affected have set up residents' groups, and one of these operates through a local community centre with an extremely energetic leader. Both of these groups have pressed their cases very strongly and have secured some immediate environmental improvements and certain assurances about their future from the Council.

There are, of course, within the City Centre, the offices of the Chamber of Commerce, the Confederation of British Industry and a number of other bodies. The areas of interest of most of these bodies extends over the whole of Merseyside and their activities seldom have a direct bearing on the City Centre development, except where specific comment has been made about the need for more central area car parks and hotels. Several attempts have been made to create a continuing dialogue with business interests in the same way as with local residents' groups. None have met with much success, seemingly because of the difficulty of identifying the area of common interest and the reluctance of commercial organisations to talk about their own futures.

More fruitful have been the collaborative arrangements with highly specialised groups, such as the Liverpool Stores Committee, the Multiple Traders Association and groups of shopkeepers and proprietors in limited areas. In these cases, particular problems of pedestrianisation, changing patterns of trade and the supply of shop accommodation have been dealt with in detail.

Building Technology
The building technology which has caused the greatest degree of concern since central area redevelopment gained some impetus has been the vogue for high buildings.

One of the earliest tall office block proposals was made at an early stage of Graeme Shankland's consultancy by a major business house which sought to rebuild its Victorian offices. The proposed location of the tall block was unfortunate, since it obtruded upon the city's principle banking street, in which nearly all the buildings are nineteenth century four and five storey structures, and at the end of which stands the very handsome eighteenth century Town Hall. The proposal was refused and went to appeal and, although the aesthetic arguments were of great importance, the principal objection was the intensity of the proposed development. The Minister dismissed the appeal and, in so doing, implicitly confirmed that the maximum commercial plot ratio should not exceed 3 : 1. Perhaps more important was the psychological effect of the decision. The banking and insurance organisations which owned and occupied most of the premises in the street apparently recognised that their premises were collectively an urban asset. From then on, nearly all the development proposals in that street have been for re-habilitation or internal modernisation and the owners have had their buildings cleaned.

Elsewhere in the City Centre there has been considerable pressure for high rise office blocks, but most have conformed to the 3 : 1 plot ratio. The City Centre Plan indicated that high buildings would be permissible near the River Mersey, north and south of the existing Pier Head group of buildings. In these areas permissions have been granted, but elsewhere architects representing speculative developers have argued very strongly, but not conclusively, that high rise offices have been the only economic form of development and that the repressive policy of the city is discouraging new development and employment growth. Elected representatives are naturally anxious not to inhibit employment growth, but have generally upheld the high buildings policy. Where high buildings have been refused, low-rise development has usually been proposed and constructed so that, in fact, the city has not suffered by loss of investment.

Although much is said about the advantages of deep office blocks and fully controlled internal environments, very little interest has been shown by developers either in this form of building, or in full air conditioning.

The only substantial deep office block project is being constructed by the Royal Insurance Company, for its own use, and will make a distinguished addition to the riverside frontage. Air conditioning has probably not gained in popularity because of its effect on rental values. The large quantity of old and obsolescent offices in the city have tended to hold rental levels down, and although the Offices, Shops and Railway Premises Act has given a great impetus to rehabilitation and redevelopment, air conditioned offices would not be competitive.

One technical innovation, which may present difficulties in the long run, is the use of large scale oil-fired heating plants. St. John's Precinct, built on the site of the old St. John's Market, heats some 510,000 cubic yards from one set of boilers. Unfortunately, the City Centre is located adjacent to the river and just below a ridge, on which stand the Roman Catholic and Church of England Cathedrals, and the teaching precinct of the University of Liverpool. To prevent boiler gasses from polluting the atmosphere on this ridge a 400 feet high chimney had to be built. The starkness of the flue has been relieved, in this case, by constructing a restaurant on a deck near to the top of this structure, but clearly there is a limit to the number of high level restaurants which would be economically feasible, just as there is a limit to the number of flues which would be visually tolerable. The effects of these restraints seem to result in developers using higher grade oil fuel which does not create the same pollution hazards although in one proposed scheme, the possibility of heating an extremely large volume from one boiler complex, may result in another high flue.

In the main, building technology has failed to keep pace with economic and social evolution. Many buildings are faced with materials which show signs of bad weathering characteristics within a few years of construction, and many new buildings show signs of subsequent modification to overcome the problems of solar gain, heat loss and traffic noise in relation to large glazed areas. It is curious that, despite the existence in the conurbation of a school successfully heated entirely by solar heat, and of an office block heated entirely by its lighting system, little attempt has been made to exploit these successes in the City Centre.

One of the most striking examples of building technology failing to cope with economic restraints has been in the Strand/Paradise Street Scheme. The original sketch proposal was one of the highly imaginative and attractive detailed projects which Graeme Shankland included within the City Centre Plan. The main part comprised a podium, with bus station on the ground level, surmounted by one level of shops and three levels of car parking. Above this, a six storey terrace and five tower blocks of flats and maisonettes were to be constructed. Strenuous efforts were made to realise these proposals in a joint public and private sector venture, but two obstacles were encountered which eventually proved insuperable. The technical problem was that the most suitable column spacing for the different uses differed so widely that the structural costs became prohibitive. The second problem was financial, but equally intractable. At various times central and local government and private enterprise had been willing and able to commit themselves to their share of the total costs, but it proved quite impossible to get all the parties to this point at the same time. When private sector money was plentiful public sector money was scarce and vice versa. In the end, the Council decided that it could not afford to let the matter drag on any longer, and so a new scheme was prepared which contained the same elements but made each a separate ground based structure so that individual elements would have lower structural costs and could start independently of each.other. The new schemes also had the advantage of greater flexibility so that it has subsequently been possible to substitute a complex of Crown and Magistrates' Courts for some of the commercial uses and to introduce a hotel into the recreational element. At the time of writing, one section is completed, one is under construction, one is at the detailed design stage and one (the residential accommodation) still awaits finance.

One aspect of building technology, which seems likely to be of increasing importance, arises from the proposals for the Inner Motorway. The City Council obtained powers from Parliament to acquire a broad swathe of land along the route so that adjoining areas could be redeveloped to take account of the environmental effects of the motorway. Assembly of sites for this purpose is now largely complete and a number of projects are under construction. A variety of design solutions have been adopted but none has yet stood the test of experience.

DEVELOPMENT PLANS, ACTION PLANS AND ACHIEVEMENTS

It was fortunate that, during the time of the preparation of the City Centre Plan, the Ministry of Housing and Local Government and the Ministry of Transport jointly published their "Planning Bulletin on Town Centres" and Walter Bor was serving on the Planning Advisory Group whose recommendations laid the basis for the Town and Country Planning Act, 1968. Consequently, the City Centre Plan was able to embody much of the most recent professional and administrative thought.

Although the City Centre Plan goes into considerable detail, it does seem that it approximates more closely to a district plan, as described in the 1968 Act, than to an action plan. Some areas (including those designated as areas requiring further study), require far more detailed examination, and require precise proposals before development could be implemented. However, experience has shown that action plans are only appropriate where virtually all the development is to be carried out by the local authority. For other areas, planning briefs are prepared which indicate the mandatory requirements and the development potential of the site. If the land is owned by the Corporation, these briefs have been used with very considerable success as the basis for

P

competition between developers. In other cases, the planning department
frequently draws up an agreed brief with a developer's professional
representatives before any design work is carried out, or any planning
application made. In these cases, the briefs have been invaluable in
avoiding subsequent misunderstandings. However, it has been found
that briefs get out of date in the light of changing circumstances. As a
safeguard against this situation, all briefs are published with an expiry
date, after which they may be renewed, revised or withdrawn.

Much of the planning work in the central area does not take the form
of detailed studies of areas. Subjects such as pedestrian flow prediction
and design standards for pedestrian routes go on in parallel, as also does
the examination of trends in office, shopping and other uses. These area
and subject studies are brought together and published annually as the
City Centre Plan Review.

This document is used for a variety of purposes; it makes available to
developers and the public an up-to-date statement of city centre plans
and policies; it makes known matters of importance to the Council, the
relative rates of progress of development and matters requiring examination during the succeeding year; it also acts as a publicity document,
encouraging further development by indicating the development in
hand or completed since the inception of the plan.

Since the Council adopted corporate planning and the programme
planning and budgeting system, the annual review of the plan has
become an important management tool. At a specified stage in the P.P.B.
cycle, the work of the various departments of the Corporation is examined,
against the background of the plan, to measure the achievement of the
departments. At another stage, the budgets of departments are similarly
examined to see that items essential to the plan are included. Clearly
there are conflicts between the priorities of the programme departments
and those of the plan, and when resources are scarce these conflicts are
heightened. It is then the task of the Chief Executive, advised by the
planning officer and the financial controller, to recommend to the Council
ways of resolving these conflicts.

In a management system, where the relevance and effectiveness of
everything is questioned, the utility of the plan itself must come under
review. It is difficult to quantify plan effectiveness, but it is possible to
say that most serious development and improvement proposals which
have been put forward by outside bodies have been in accordance with
or capable of accommodation within the plan. A number of major
projects have only been possible as a result of preparatory work initiated
through the plan and no major project has failed to come to fruition
through planning obstacles. On the contrary, 59 major projects were
completed or commenced between 1964 and 1971.

Opposite: 9. Potential redevelopment areas, showing possible private
or public undertakings.

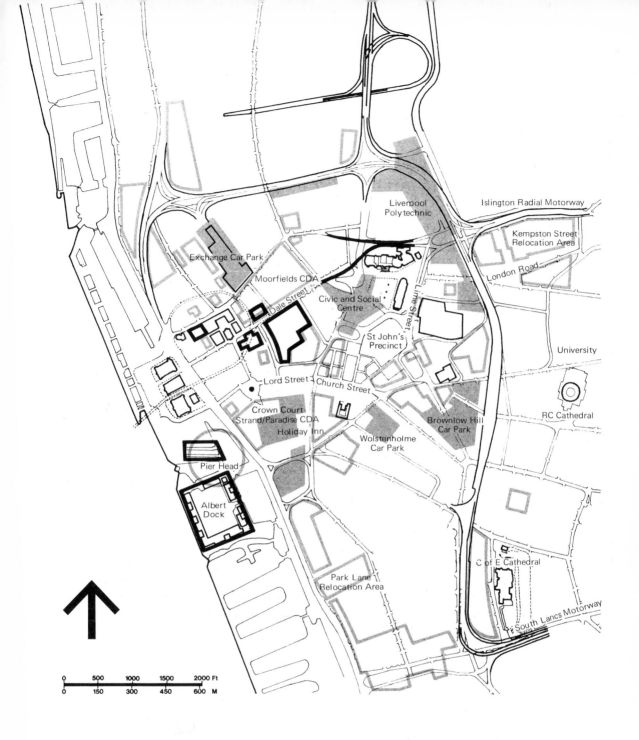

Liverpool
Polytechnic

Islington Radial Motorway

Kempston Street
Relocation Area

Exchange Car Park

London Road

Moorfields CDA

Dale Street

Civic and Social
Centre

Linne Street

University

St John's
Precinct

Lord Street

Church Street

Crown Court
Strand/Paradise CDA
Holiday Inn

RC Cathedral

Brownlow Hill
Car Park

Wolstenholme
Car Park

Pier Head

Albert
Dock

C of E Cathedral

Park Lane
Relocation Area

South Lancs Motorway

| 0 | 500 | 1000 | 1500 | 2000 Ft |
| 0 | 150 | 300 | 450 | 600 M |

Probable Corporation Development

Areas with Private Development and Public/Private
Partnership Development Potential.

Areas with Potential for Comprehensive Rehabilitation

Areas with Development and Rehabilitation Potential

THE FUTURE

The future of Liverpool's City Centre seems to depend largely on finance. Not so much upon the total sum available (although this is important), but upon the manner of its distribution.

In the past few years government financial systems have operated against the interests of the centres of conurbations. The authorities for these areas have often had to cope with central area projects where land and buildings are enormously expensive and with the replacement of the bulk of the conurbations obsolete housing. At the same time, the peripheral authorities have tended to have less expensive problems to solve, and more prosperous residents to pay for the solutions. It seems that local government reorganisation should help to iron out these inequalities and to make the redevelopment of inner and central areas a financially realistic proposition.

Of similar importance is the growing readiness of the Department of the Environment to make funds available for the development of public transport. The disproportionately large investment in highways has done much to undermine the strength of the central area and this should, and could, now be reversed.

The government's interest in attempting to overcome the problems of inner areas through urban aid, education priority areas, derelict land rehabilitation and community development programmes should help to overcome the atmosphere of neglect and depression which surrounds the central area.

All these trends suggest that the central area will, at least, hold its own as a regional centre, in a region where new growth points are being established, but there remains a critical and somewhat philosophical question: the central area has prospered as a centre where people could find variety and quality. But Merseyside's population is changing. The wealthy are fewer and the less wealthy white collar workers are relatively less prosperous. But some of the blue collar workers now enjoy increased spending power and there is no reason to suppose that these new spenders will perpetuate the old style consumer preferences. Furthermore, since these spenders will not come to the City Centre for work, the City Centre may have to change radically to meet the new demands or diminish in importance. It is for this reason, above all else, that the monitoring of the whole sub region is critical for the survival of the centre. To date the central area has held its own in pulling power, but the significance of quality and variety has diminished. Is this change in the qualitative nature of the centre the seed of decay, or the seed of regeneration?

6
Newcastle upon Tyne

INTRODUCTION

Newcastle upon Tyne is the regional capital of North-east England and the centre and focal point of the Tyneside Conurbation which has a total population of approximately one million. The city occupies about one fifth of the land area of Tyneside, and houses about a quarter of the urban population, but the central area provides the major social, economic, cultural and administrative activities for the wider region. The basis of central redevelopment lies in the strengthening and enhancing of the city's position as the regional capital, with special emphasis on its function for shopping, commerce, higher education, libraries and art galleries, entertainment and administration. The impetus for the remodelling of the City Centre has emerged from the historic nature of the city and its growth which led to a situation in which, by the second half of the twentieth century, a large part of the centre was ripe for development. In the 1960s the opportunity arose to conceive the replanning of the City Centre as a whole.

HISTORICAL BACKGROUND

Newcastle dates back to Roman times, and successive historic periods have all left their mark on the growth and form of the city. But whilst history provided a rich heritage it contributed many problems which made the large scale remodelling of the City Centre an urgent necessity.

A Roman station was established in Newcastle on the line of Hadrian's Wall guarding the easternmost bridge over the Tyne. The bridge fell into ruin after the Romans left, but was reconstructed in Norman times when a castle was built to defend it. Around the castle the town developed, and soon became important as a port and market centre as well as a rallying point for warfare against the Scots. As the port trade expanded, first in wool, then superseded by coal, the town expanded up the formidable riverside slopes; steep narrow streets and alleys led to the upper parts of the town in which the main markets were located. At the turn of the eighteenth century, Newcastle was still largely a medieval town centring upon the commercial hub of the Quayside area.

The pre-eminence of the later upper part of the town can be traced back to the work of a group of architects including John Dobson the builder, Richard Grainger and the Town Clerk, John Clayton, whose development of the Grey Street and Grainger Street area in the 1830s was probably the largest and most coherent example of town planning in Britain since Edinburgh New Town. The classical curve of Grey Street is one of the outstanding examples of street architecture in Britain.

The coming of the railway in the 1840s, with the distinctive High Level Bridge spanning the Tyne and the brutal insertion of the main line to Edinburgh across the old town, created a physical barrier between the old riverside area and the newly created upper area of the city. The Central Station became a focal point and the Quayside area suffered a relative decline in status.

By the end of the nineteenth century most of the central area was largely in its present form. Mosley and Collingwood Streets formed the centre of the office quarter. Grainger Street became the principal shopping street, and shops also extended along other thoroughfares such as Westgate Road, Clayton and Newgate Streets, Blackett and New Bridge Streets, Pilgrim and Northumberland Streets, all of which became tram routes.

The only major alteration to the physical pattern of the city between the First World War and the 1960s was the building of the Tyne Bridge, completed in 1928. This caused a new orientation of traffic at a time when traffic was increasing everywhere, and probably encouraged the development of Northumberland Street. Hitherto, this street had been of much less importance than Grainger Street as a shopping street, and substantial pre-war rebuilding did not take place much above its southern extremity. In the inter-war years, however, most of the retail chain firms who were expanding nationally did so in Northumberland Street rather than in Grainger Street, and the former is now one of the highest value provincial shopping streets in the country.

In 1960, before the present plan was conceived, the City Centre reflected therefore not only the work of Dobson and Grainger but also the medieval pattern. The majority of buildings were erected over a century ago, with the exception of the office development in Collingwood Street and buildings in Northumberland Street which were erected after 1920.

The age, structure and form of the central area of Newcastle indicated quite clearly the need for two parallel policies. First, redevelopment of the outworn areas as a large scale undertaking, to be carried into effect in a relatively short period, the age of the centre having created conditions for wholesale redevelopment which would permit the building of a virtually new centre in a short period. And secondly, vigorous conservation of the magnificent classical stone buildings of the Victorian city and the medieval elements which survived in the lower city.

Tyneside, which had been one of the great centres of industrial prosperity during the nineteenth and early twentieth century, began to decline after the First World War and apart from a major burst of economic activity between 1939 and 1945 the sub-region, along with the rest of North-east England, suffered economic contraction coupled with out-migration as a result of its heavy dependence on ship building and repairing, heavy metal industries and particularly coal mining. As a consequence of this, and to some degree due to distance from the national centres of major activity, pressures for central area renewal which built up in the South-east and Midlands in the 1950s did not begin to affect Newcastle until the end of that decade. In the 30 years prior to 1960 very little new development had occurred. This factor together with a late entry into the field of central renewal had positive advantages; the city was able to benefit considerably from other cities' experiences and an opportunity existed for large scale comprehensive redevelopment.

INFLUENCES FOR CHANGE

A low level of economic activity together with a cloth cap image and a less than average level of car ownership gave the city an investment rating rather less than the more prosperous Midlands and the South-east during the late 1940s and early 1950s. Newcastle surprisingly suffered very little war damage, but in common with all centres of nineteenth-century industrial activity had a large housing stock in need of replacement, and initial efforts were concentrated in this field.

As the pressure from commercial interests began to mount in the late 1950s and traffic congestion began to be felt in the City Centre the Council advanced two schemes from pre-war plans to relieve pressures. Both were subject to a good deal of professional and academic criticism and both were rejected by Government. The Council, which had seemed dedicated to policies of no change, now began to face the developing situation. The momentum for change grew rapidly after 1958 when Labour took control of the Council under the leadership of Councillor T. Dan Smith, a politician with a vision of the sort of city he wanted and a clear understanding of the relationship between political and physical objectives. Councillor Smith was concerned to establish an effective administrative platform and resolved to promote the planning service to a main line local government function. At this stage the service was provided by four professionals and six supporting staff under the City Engineer.

When Percy Parr retired as City Engineer in 1960 he was succeeded by Derek Bradshaw and Wilfred Burns became the first City Planning

Officer. The work of these two men was to have a considerable impact on the city.

The Labour-led Council was determined to achieve major redevelopment proposals by direct action, on the grounds that the entire benefit of public action should be to the public. Although the Conservatives believed that redevelopment should be secured by encouraging private initiative, there had been no division on party lines as to the nature of the City Plan or the form that redevelopment proposals might take. Political control of the Council remained with the Labour Party until 1967 when power was gained by the Conservatives and at this point there was some concern amongst the professionals that the new Council might not be anxious to pursue the planning objectives of its predecessor. The oft-repeated assertion that planning policy in the City Centre is truly bi-partisan has been put to the test and proven, but major building schemes have been developed in the last four years on a partnership basis with private enterprise.

A major restructuring of Council committees was carried out in 1968 which provided a much improved working base. Alderman Arthur Grey, who had led the Conservative Party in opposition and was the planning spokesman, became Leader of Council in 1967 and Chairman of Planning Committee. When a Management Committee was set up in the following year he was appointed Chairman of that body. Alderman Grey retired from business in 1968 and devoted his abundant energy and long day to serving the city and the North-east Region, exemplifying the new style executive council leader, demanding a great deal from his officers but dedicated to securing the rapid implementation of the City Plan.

ORGANISATIONAL ARRANGEMENTS FOR URBAN RENEWAL

The word "renewal" in the above heading was chosen quite deliberately to describe Newcastle's policies. Following a long period when local government organisation was much the same in all large cities, the last few years have seen major changes taking place in such a way that there are almost as many systems as there are authorities.

The Maud Report (1967) was influential in changing local government management, but the earlier emergence of planning as a first line activity influenced the situation considerably. Effective planning departments have a way of filling vacuums and this can be illustrated by what happened in the field of housing revitalisation in Newcastle. In 1962 officers and

Opposite:
Top: 1. Central Area, c 1878, showing the Medieval centre near the river and Victorian new centre to the north west.

Bottom: 2. Grey Street, part of the Victorian new centre showing the cleaning and restoration of facades.

political leaders identified the need for a much more comprehensive approach to house improvement than was permitted by the Housing Act, 1959, and a new policy was promulgated in the Review Town Map. The main area to be used for a revitalisation project had unfortunately to be cleared rather than renewed, after attempts to use the Planning Acts for the renewal scheme proved abortive. It was not until the Housing Act of 1969 that the legislative basis for such proposals got on to the statute book.

In Newcastle today a very positive programme of revitalisation of older housing is being pursued by an agency team consisting of members of all the departments involved. The team is under the control of a senior planner responsible to the City Planning Officer. The Planning Department is, in this particular field, responsible at one end of the scale for policy formulation and at the other for putting it into effect, but this is not advocated as a general principle. Executive action in the field of renewal is often a task for other agencies, but when the planner is initiating policy he must often be prepared to take such action himself. The approach can be summarised in a sentence—the Department is in business to build a city. This is reflected in the structure of the Department; about two thirds of the professional staff is fully involved in work connected with on-going developments as members of inter-professional teams which are established at appropriate levels to deal with all major work areas or topics.

A great deal of progress has been made in the field of corporate activity in the last five years. This stemmed from the development of the first five year capital programme which was derived directly from the Development Plan Review. The corporate approach started with a weekly Chief Officers' meeting to review the redevelopment programme and was developed by Frank Harris, who was appointed in August 1965 as the first Principal City Officer with the task of exercising an overall co-ordinating function in respect of all Corporation departments. In 1969 when Frank Harris returned to industry he was succeeded by Frank Ireland, the City Treasurer. At that stage the Council took the view that the task of management co-ordination and executive leadership was of such a wide and involved nature as to warrant the establishment of an Officer Management Group to advise the Management Committee in respect of important policy matters, and to guide the overall executive activity of the Council's departments, particularly in respect of the capital programme. This Officer Management Group is chaired by the Principal City Officer. The other members are the City Engineer and the City Planning Officer. The composition of this team reflects the nature of the City's forward programme, and though it is the ultimate body for executive action it works in close co-operation with all chief and senior officers. Recent changes in organisational methods have not been radical but I believe that a new corporate approach involving all departments is emerging as individual sectoral goals and objectives within the authority are reconciled. It has for some time been the hope and intention of the Department that the first structure plan for the City should in part form a community plan embracing physical structure, social plan, leisure activity plan and economic plan. But the growing movement towards corporate management will be frustrated in the city regions by the imposition of the proposed two tier system of local government which confuses the clarity of thought and expression in the Redcliffe-Maud Report (1969) in support of unitary authorities.

Two further organisation factors merit attention. The first occurred in the early 1960s when the Council, setting its sights high, invited Sir Robert Matthew, Sir Basil Spence and Professor Arne Jacobsen to design three major building projects that it intended to commission directly. The second factor arose as a result of the establishment of the Tyne/Wear Land Use/Transportation Study 1968/71, which brought City Centre policies under close review. The central plan was based on a high level of public transport and this became a vital element in the consultant's brief. Rapid transit proposals have now been approved by Parliament and programmed for the late 70s; thus a high level public transport service is assured with underground stations in the City Centre at Haymarket, Grey's Monument and Central Station.

Tyneside has a Passenger Transport Authority and it will be responsible for this development. A decision to proceed with the underground railway will involve a review of certain aspects of the plan. The proposal is strongly supported by the planners and the engineers, as its development would ensure a high level of public transport service to the city core.

INVOLVEMENT WITH THE PUBLIC

Everyone professionally involved in the field of urban renewal has been deeply concerned for over a decade about relationships with the public, none more so than the planner. Those of us who have served a long apprenticeship at public meetings are well aware of the need to bridge the gap between them and us. But it is not public participation in planning alone that is the core subject—people are concerned about the whole field of urban management. Planning officers in any city find it difficult to develop an argument in support of even a medium term plan; people living in twilight areas cannot be expected to concern themselves about

Overleaf:
Left: 3. Air view of city centre in 1968, showing 1, University; 2, Polytechnic; 3, Civic Centre; 4, Eldon Square; 5, Swan House and Pilgrim Street intersection; 6, All Saints.

Right: 4. Motorway proposals. The numbers have the same references as in the air view opposite.

a brave new world ten years away. Their concern is about tonight and tomorrow morning and perhaps, with a little luck, next year. This concern about the way urban affairs are managed, of which planning is a part, involves the whole of the local authority team, and whilst the town planner will usually be at the forefront in discussion with public groups, he must have the support of his colleagues and his members. Conflicts within an authority must be resolved and a corporate view presented.

In Newcastle great efforts were made to ensure that the Development Plan Review was a corporate proposal, and in the early 1960s a wide ranging series of public meetings were held in an attempt to get the main objectives across before the Plan was submitted. Reactions were, however, limited to a few who were directly affected.

In the field of local planning there was more success, but that is a subject for another book. Public and professional reaction to plans invariably developed too late, often after planning orders had been confirmed and physical and financial commitments made.

The process of urban redevelopment is so complex, the time scale so long and many of the issues so involved, that it is extremely difficult for political leaders and chief officers to keep a changing Council of eighty members fully briefed, let alone lift the public debate higher than that involving the fate of an individual building or a local open space. Even so the possibility of ensuring that such a limited debate takes place in an overall context is quite low.

My conclusion is that participation at the strategic level of planning is barely emergent. If it is to emerge it will call for a great deal of professional skill and time and also considerable responsibility. The onus is on elected leaders and chief officers to provide the proper opportunities, but public responsibility is vital. Local organisations and particularly professional societies must accept responsibility. Too often views are based on little information and too much emotion. Urban renewal must involve the public in the widest way, but sectoral interest must realise that the city planner is more concerned with the community at large and cannot necessarily accede to special pressures.

INDUSTRIAL AND COMMERCIAL ACTIVITIES

The Tyne/Wear area, now a metropolitan county under Local Government reorganisation, has until now been administered in planning by seven separate planning authorities, each with declining populations, increasing unemployment problems and declining rateable value in real terms. In addition Northumberland County Council is promoting two new towns at Killingworth and Cramlington, and a government sponsored new town is being developed at Washington. Although all the authorities

Opposite:
5. Policy Map showing major land uses and the transport and pedestrian network.

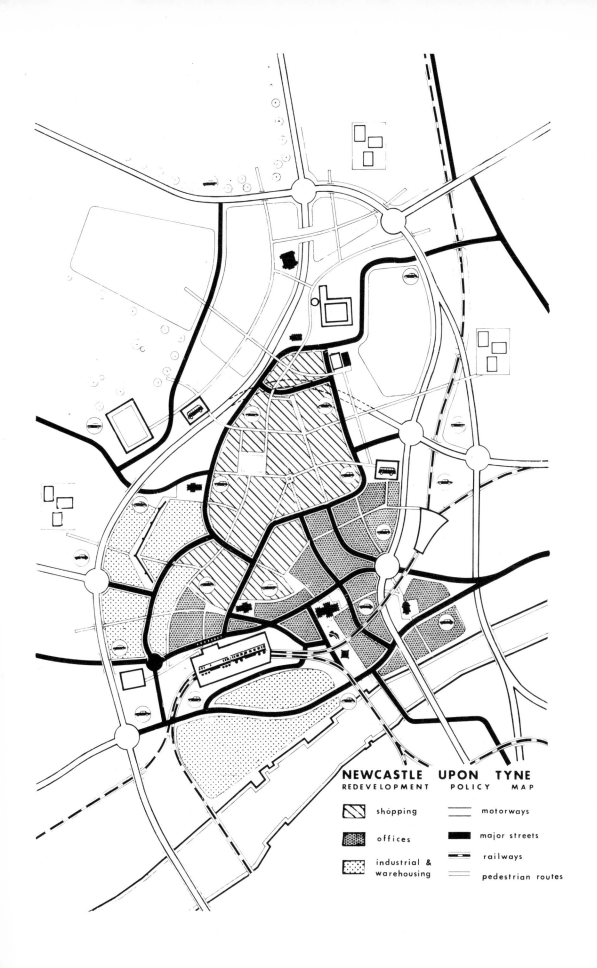

NEWCASTLE UPON TYNE
REDEVELOPMENT POLICY MAP

shopping   motorways

offices   major streets

industrial &   railways
warehousing   pedestrian routes

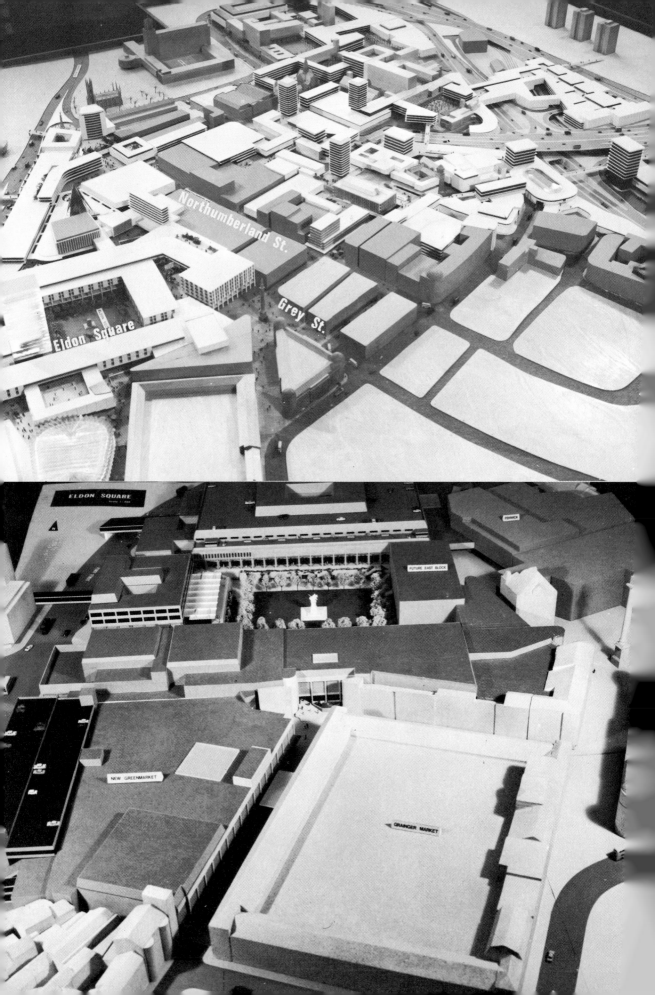

Northumberland St.

Grey St.

Eldon Square

ELDON SQUARE

FENWICK

FUTURE EAST BLOCK

NEW GREENMARKET

GRAINGER MARKET

combine together in a number of regional organisations, in the last resort they are in competition for the limited amount of growth that is available, notwithstanding that in any area of low growth it is important to secure the maximum benefit from all available developments.

This overall situation has enabled the area to offer a wide range of opportunities to incoming industry and to industry seeking relocation from the urban core; it has also encouraged the development of a number of new district shopping centres and given the opportunity for some fairly large scale office decentralisation to take place.

In respect of industry and warehousing, central Newcastle has benefited in that such uses affected by major proposals at the Centre have had a wide choice for relocation. A number of large office headquarter establishments have, however, moved out of the Centre to cheap sites unrelated to existing or proposed rapid transit lines.

A major use that moved from the City Centre to the benefit of its operators and the city generally was the wholesale fruit and vegetable market, which not only created large scale congestion at the morning peak hour but had a deadening effect throughout the rest of the day. The transfer of the market to a new site in Gateshead was an essential first step to securing a key site for the extension of the primary shopping area.

One of the forces for change already identified was pressure from the large multiples for more space in the primary shopping position, and though the preparation of the central area plan enabled many developments to proceed, the fact that the greater part of the need is not met is clear from the evidence that the major shopping scheme to be built between 1972/6 is largely pre-let. Even so, substantial changes are occurring in retailing; as more well-equipped centres are developed in the outer areas, and as areas on the periphery of the central area are redeveloped at lower densities, trading falls off, particularly in areas like Westgate Road where the number of vacant premises is increasing annually.

A matter of concern in all cities is the decline of the individual trader and particularly the specialist shop. The owners can rarely afford the high rents charged for new development, although special measures have been taken to provide small units at lower rentals in the major scheme. Further deliberate steps are being taken in the conservation areas to maintain the supply of small units and to improve very considerably

Opposite:
Top: 6. Central Area Model, Northern Section, showing the early Eldon Square redevelopment scheme with hotel. The square marks the approximate northern limit of the Victorian new centre. Northumberland Street is the main post-Victorian shopping development. New development is shown in white.

Bottom: 7. Eldon Square Redevelopment Scheme 1972.

their environment and trading position.

Despite the large number of diverse authorities administering the urban area, the planners have established a common view with regard to the large scale out-of-town shopping centre on a green field site. These developments are being resisted in view of the effect they would have on established or planned district centres and on the existing small town centres, and though large scale operations have been developed at Killingworth and are in prospect in Washington, they are conceived as part of the town centre operation.

THE PRINCIPLES OF THE PLAN

The preparation of the City Plan has been described by Wilfred Burns, the City's first Planning Officer, in his book *Newcastle: A Study in Re-development at Newcastle upon Tyne* (1967). The role of the Department is one of total involvement, from the first concept to the laying of the last brick, a Department dedicated to the corporate concept and believing that in our city we are really achieving the city's renewal objectives through close professional and political unity.

A clear distinction between Newcastle and many contemporary cities must be drawn. The city—indeed Tyneside, because the latter is the true city—is in fact an area striving, along with the whole of North-east England, to establish a new economic base. It is an area in contraction, an area with an immense backlog of urban renewal calling for vast expenditure if it is going to maintain its position in competition with the more prosperous areas of the country. This influenced the principles upon which the Central Area Plan is based. These principles are:

> The regeneration and revitalisation of the riverside area by injecting new commercial life into the area and alleviating the visual blight and decay. The strong geographical features of the river should be used to their maximum advantage.
>
> The enhancement of the special character of the central area by a twofold approach to conservation of the best parts and the re-development of the northern part of the shopping centre, contrasting but integrated with the historic parts.
>
> A more rational arrangement of public buildings, and the integration of the higher education establishments into the City Centre.
>
> The expansion and improvement of the layout of the shopping area.
>
> The separation of shopping, offices and other uses to allow the centre to function effectively.
>
> The provision of a first-class public transport system, new roads and parking areas designed to achieve a traffic balance.
>
> The separation of pedestrian and moving vehicles with a two tier pedestrian and vehicular circulation system when possible.
>
> The provision of residential accommodation in the City Centre

for those who wish to live there.

The underlying approach is a deep belief in the future of the city as a growing and living force—a belief that the city is an immensely important expression of human life and achievement.

DIFFERENT PERSPECTIVES—LOCAL CASE STUDIES

The Motorways

The motorway system is considered to be an integral part of the central redevelopment. Where the motorway can make a major contribution to the enhancement of an area the City Engineer has designed it as a major element of traffic architecture. Where the motorway is unlikely to play a positive role, it will be integrated with appropriate development so that it does not have a direct impact on people using the City Centre. The approach has therefore not been to impose a motorway on the city but to design and build a whole new area with the motorway forming an important and integral part.

The precise location of the motorways close to the Centre has been widely criticised, but there are two basic controlling factors, the location of the Tyne Bridges and the fact that the destination for over 95 per cent of traffic entering Tyneside from the south is central Newcastle and Gateshead. The location of these central by-pass distributors close in has the massive benefit of freeing very large areas of the inner city for the pedestrian.

Though I believe that we have achieved an effective integration of the motorway in planning terms on the east side of the Central Area and though the Council has successfully acquired 50.58 hectares to secure its planning and transportation objectives in this sector, the problems of implementing the proposals are phenomenal. Even today few people in major decision-making areas see road development and city reconstruction as one single task.

The air photograph and motorways map show locations where some of the agencies are involved. The Polytechnic development is the concern of the City and a Government Department. The area acquired for University expansion which lies on either side of the motorway and will be linked by cross-motorway structures, is the concern not only of the University but of the University Grants Committee which governs the development programme. The bus station is a matter for the Passenger Transport Authority; British Rail have major land holdings associated with the development and other Government Departments are involved. In addition the City Council is pursuing programmes with private developers. Inevitably the time scale for this major area of reconstruction will be prolonged as resource programmes of these multiple agencies are varied by factors completely outside the City Council's control.

The Planner's role is to determine priorities in terms of the total situation, but inevitably conflict arises where development priorities are conceived in a specialist sense. It is worthwhile examining certain situations highlighted in the preceding paragraphs in relation to the motorway.

University and Polytechnic

A major aspect of central area strategy was to consolidate higher education facilities at the very heart of Tyneside. The University was firmly established, but planned to double its numbers within about ten years. The City Council had developed a major programme for Colleges of Further Education on a 12·95 hectare site in the North East sector of the Central Area. This was formally designated a Polytechnic in 1968 and considerable progress has been made with the development. Both institutions have been designed co-extensively with the Central Motorway East and the development programmes were effectively integrated. Changes in the Department of Education and Science and University Grants Committee priorities have riven the programmes apart, and though the motorway construction started in the Spring of 1972 development of adjoining colleges is clearly some years away. The marked reduction in the University's capital programme creates pressure to invest limited funds in teaching buildings, and so link blocks and bridge units associated with the motorway are imperilled. Who pays the extra costs for these developments for soundproofing, for multi-storey car parks and for student accommodation?

Transport Authorities

British Rail are extensive land owners in central Newcastle and much of this land is redundant to operational requirements. They are inhibited by terms of reference which demand high returns from disposals. Strong pressures are imposed to develop schemes with a high commercial content irrespective of site relationship to existing and proposed city functions. Failure to resist their pressure would result in some sections of the inner city suffering because of the relatively low economic ceiling in terms of total demand for shopping and office space.

The Passenger Transport Authority was created to deal with public transport over the whole of the sub-region by the Transport Act of 1969, and though the provision and development of an attractive facility is vital to the success of the overall plan for the city, this new authority is yet another ad hoc body with a limited objective, for the Authority is charged by statute to produce its own plan for the wider area. The Act makes no provision to secure an effective statutory relationship with structure planning, despite the obvious fundamental relationship.

Shopping Redevelopment

Newcastle's influence as a major shopping centre is considerable and the plan aims to strengthen this. Studies showed that there was a substantial demand for the expansion of shopping facilities in the city. The plan therefore proposed a major expansion of the shopping centre westwards, in a comprehensive scheme based on a newly created pedestrian level, with servicing and transport links at existing ground level. The city set the scene for the development by formulating comprehensive development area (CDA) and concurrent compulsory purchase order (CPO) proposals for an area of 3·64 hectares of predominantly obsolescent development very closely associated with the primary shopping locations. After discussions with a very large number of development companies the Council in 1968 selected Capital and Counties Development Company, and it was decided to carry out the proposals in partnership with them. The company appointed Chapman Taylor & Partners as their architects, and a combined inter-professional team have been engaged on the task of pre-planning over the past few years. This process has now been completed and construction on the site began in January 1973.

The form of the development had been established as a basis for the CDA and the concurrent CPO; a system of pedestrian streets connecting new shopping area—the dominant and most significant non-shopping the primary position in Northumberland Street, via Eldon Square, crossing Blackett Street by bridges and connecting up with the thriving retail market and shopping in Grainger Street. A luxury hotel was to be built on the west side of Eldon Square and provision was made for continuous shopping through the hotel complex at pedestrian level. The Square itself was to be retained as open space. The development company was to be responsible for that part of the development on the north side of the Square and the area south of Blackett Street. The city intended to promote the hotel and its associated development and commissioned Professor Arne Jacobsen as designer.

Capital and Counties, on entering into negotiations with the Corporation, accepted the design principles established by the city and the existing commitment. Initially they commissioned surveys of need and demand, and their advisers carried out extensive surveys and produced a model of demand. This was a much more sophisticated exercise than that done by the Corporation officers, but the conclusions were very similar. An increase in shopping floor space provision of the order of 41,810 square metres was justified.

Discussions had been held with the Multiple Shops Federation prior to the CDA submission and further meetings were held at this stage. The Federation, although agreeing with the Council's intention to create pedestrian-only streets, was very firmly opposed to their being located at other than ground level. It was strongly supported by the company's estates advisers.

The "specialist" view at this stage postulated direct, simple connections to strong, existing shopping positions, with servicing and vehicular access from above. This approach had been carefully examined prior to the CDA submission. In our view it was essential to develop a system that could be achieved on an area-wide basis—only by putting the pedestrians above servicing could phased development incorporating existing shops be achieved. An upper level road system would be very difficult to accomplish on a piecemeal basis, whereas the pedestrian already circulated on several levels in large stores. Pedestrian decks are lighter in both plan and section and offer a psychological advantage compared with a claustrophobic subway system. In addition we were clear that the upper level pedestrian system offered considerably greater civic design advantages.

This fundamental issue took almost eighteen months to resolve. The city had no doubts as to the most effective solution; the development company fully understood and accepted the situation, but the Multiple Shops Federation was not persuaded. Individual members of the Federation, however, became very keen on taking space in the scheme, and in spite of the decision to proceed on the basis of the new pedestrian level the scheme has a very high letting demand.

This stage of the work highlighted the contrast between the "interpretive" perspective of the estates/commercial interests based almost entirely on past experience and precedents and the planning or predictive approach taking all current aspects into account and then looking forward.

Eldon Square and Hotel
The Square is the most vital open space in the city, and the planning aim is to ensure its development as a live core to the shopping area, contrasting dramatically with the environment of the shopping malls, which are to be enclosed and air-conditioned. But paradoxically the inward facing approach of the malls contained the seeds of death for the Square and the city streets embraced by the scheme. The problems have been resolved, but not without difficulty. Commercially the Square was seen as a liability; it forced routes round its perimeter and the route down its west side was seen to be weak in commercial terms. The integration of the Square has been achieved by maintaining an external walkway along its north side, providing effective access and ensuring that there are visual links between the malls and the Square.

It was always the intention to secure a wide variety of uses in the new shopping area—the dominant and most significant non-shopping use was to be an hotel, planned to meet an identified need as the focal point of renewal. The site is one of the best in the city and warranted a first class building which Professor Jacobsen was invited to design. The decision was taken to build a high tower, despite the cost implications, and a very high standard of external finish was to be provided. The Council proposed to finance the development but selected at an early stage a hotelier who would take a long lease of the building. Fortes worked with the Corporation and the architect over a long period but for reasons

Opposite:
Top: 8. The new Civic Centre at the northern edge of the city centre.
Bottom: 9. Swan House, southern gateway to the City. Under Swan House is the reconstructed Royal Arcade shown on page 229.

associated with specifications and costs there were delays in reaching agreement.

The merger of Fortes with Trust Houses increased the delays, and inflation drove building costs ahead at a much higher rate than hotel charges. As a result the very high increased costs due to delays fell into the Council's lap—and as the building was an expensive one initially the projected costs became prohibitive and the scheme was abandoned.

Public reaction was one of satisfaction—"a grandiose scheme"—"an ill-advised scheme of civic grandeur"—but I firmly believe that the Council's approach was a correct one; it was defeated by circumstances and inflation. Experience shows that to aim for the best will produce good results; to aim for the good may result in the mediocre; but to aim for the mediocre will surely produce unsatisfactory results.

The abandoned hotel project was a genuine attempt to match and enhance the city's heritage, and to attract visitors to the city with the aim of increasing spending in the city's shops and increasing investment in the region.

The problems created by the decision to abandon the hotel scheme have been resolved by including the site within the Capital and Counties interest. The tall block concept has been abandoned and Eldon Square will be developed in a more conventional manner. The western shopping mall has been strengthened, and a limited area of office development will be built above the mall to maintain the height lines.

Conservation

Whilst redevelopment of the City Centre attracts most attention, an effective policy of conservation is of equal importance. Redevelopment can be regarded as the active element in the process of urban renewal, and conservation the passive element. This passive element must command a great deal of staff time if the future of the city is to be secured and buildings of irreplaceable value prevented from crumbling away. This is particularly important in the inner core, where the new shopping scheme adjoins the classical nineteenth-century development and a satisfactory fusion of the two is essential.

Much of the character of present-day Newcastle comes from its heritage of old buildings. The City has a rich legacy of medieval assets but many of these in the riverside area have been neglected and the cost of restoration here will be high. However much of the city's character stems from the Dobson/Grainger development which centres upon Grey Street.

The 1963 Development Plan Review anticipated the Civic Amenities Act 1967 by proposing four main preservation areas: the Dobson/Grainger Area; the Cathedral/Castle Area; the St. John's Church Area

Opposite:
10. The Old Town Hall, Cathedral, and Castle. The division between the Medieval and Victorian centres.

and the Guildhall Area. These areas are now covered by the 1967 Act and a Conservation Advisory Committee has been set up to assist the Council.

These moves are generally welcomed by the public, who realise that the planners do actually care about the older buildings, and lead to statements in the local press such as "the planners are human beings after all". In these areas persuasion has been used to secure the cleaning of facades, using small grants in special cases to prime the pump, but much depends upon the willingness of individual owners to face up to civic responsibility and their ability to finance what is often a costly operation. Although the purpose of conservation is to preserve or enhance the character of a particular area, the realisation of this is largely beyond the direct control of the planner unless substantial funds are available.

The pressures which endanger listed buildings arise from two extreme situations. On the one hand, where there is insufficient demand for the building in its present form, the result is often lack of maintenance and subsequent decay. Conversely, where demand for the site is high, the pressure is either to demolish the building and erect a new one to exploit the site potential, or to alter the building radically, thus destroying its historic or architectural value.

New development is not precluded in the conservation areas, but it is essential that schemes should be handled with the utmost sympathy. The case of the Old Town Hall is a good example. This building, although the only listed building in the Bigg Market Conservation Area, is incapable of functioning efficiently because of its complex internal structure, and Listed Building Consent has been obtained to demolish it, replacing it with a new development comparable in scale and quality of design.

There are major problems of building use. A limited number of very special buildings have been acquired by the Council and will be used for special purposes. These include the Castle Keep, the Black Gate, the Blackfriars Monastery and the Keelmen's Hospital, the Town Hall and its towers, All Saints Church and the Theatre Royal. But the cost of restoration is substantial and the number of buildings that can be acquired and adapted for use as museums, galleries and places of assembly is strictly limited in a city where the backlog of structural renewal is enormous. A public dedication to conservation such as appears to exist in Newcastle is not enough unless funds are available, and very few of the city's preservationists are prepared or able to find money. There has been one very notable exception in the case of the Holy Jesus Hospital. This has recently been restored and has begun a new life as a period

Opposite:
11. The reconstructed Royal Arcade. A reproduction of the original Victorian new town arcade which provided a pedestrian link between the Medieval and Victorian centres. The reconstructed Arcade provides a similar link.

museum largely due to the enthusiasm and determination of Arthur Grey, a few chief officers and the generosity of the Joicey Trust. This seventeenth-century almshouse provides a dramatic contrast to the modern office complex that dominates the Pilgrim Street entrance to the city from the Tyne Bridge. The planners' determination to reinforce this element of contrast by preserving the old coaching inn facing Fitzroy Robinson's fine new Bank of England in the same complex has so far met with no success.

The problems of conservation in relation to the redevelopment of the City Centre reflect the classic conflict between sectional interests—the community interest versus the profit motive of the developers. The latter possess the upper hand in that they have the money which could go a long way towards enhancing the older buildings of the city and ensuring that they can be appreciated by future generations. Whilst the preservation of old buildings is an undoubtedly worthy cause, there are other more important and more immediate demands upon local authority finance. Such expenditure, therefore, ranks low on the budgeting priorities and has to rely upon scraps of local government finance, supplemented by central government funds.

The paradox exists that whilst national legislation for the conservation of historic areas is now very strong, the financial arrangements to support this legislation are still dependent upon local policies and priorities. The overall burden of conservation is simply beyond the capacity of local government. In Newcastle the basic objectives of the City Plan, welding together a modern centre with the best of the old city, are difficult to achieve, since the burden of conservation rests entirely on private owners and local authorities, with limited support from the Historic Buildings Council. A grant system equivalent to that operating for losses on general redevelopment is essential. The extension of powers under the 1968 Planning Act simply increases the negative powers of the planning authority; power to serve a repairs notice is one thing, but when it leads inexorably to a purchase notice on the authority by the owner it becomes a deterrent not to the owner but to the local authority.

A realistic grant base together with a flexible approach to building use is essential if conservation of historic cities is to have any meaning.

All Saints Office Precinct

This scheme makes provision for large scale office development in the Quayside area of the city. It provides for a logical expansion of the existing office area and is intended to make a positive contribution to the regional employment problem in that sector of potentially high growth. It is a conservation proposal in the broadest sense aimed at re-energising the derelict riverside area and provides for a linked series of offices, with All Saints Church as the focal point.

The local authority used Planning Act powers to acquire the site and development is being carried out by a private developer in partnership

12. Model of proposed All Saints office development and the Quayside.

with the Council.

The planners were concerned to maintain character and scale, but because of high development costs the developers were constantly concerned to increase floor space provision and only a strong stand by the planners maintained the situation. The scheme highlights the conflicting objectives of private and public interests with the developer holding the trump card in the form of finance, maintaining his option to withdraw if the scheme did not produce the prescribed return.

The first stage, comprising 13,940 square metres, has been completed. Public reaction against the scheme has been strong and the preservationists have reacted violently on the grounds that the scheme "kills" the Church despite the fact that it is focused on the Church.

The Council's reaction has been that the scheme is too expensive, providing insufficient return, and that it would have been better to develop offices on more profitable sites elsewhere.

THE FUTURE

In Newcastle, we firmly believe that the City Centre must continue to be strengthened both as the commercial and the cultural focus of the region. This is a matter of making the most of the urban assets that we already have, because the North East is not a growing region and economic resources for radical changes are scarce. But mainly it is because we believe that the region is of such a size that the benefits of centralisation will outweigh congestion and other costs.

It is likely that the strength of anti-city forces will increase, and if the role of the City Centre is to be maintained it will become increasingly important to relate its function to the wider region and, more particularly, to the whole of the Tyne/Wear area. This will be a matter of increasing concern if the population continues to contract. Whatever the circumstances, it will be imperative in the coming decades to operate a sub-regional investment programme to secure the widest benefit, because the availability of finance is seen as a continuing problem. As housing policies take effect and the inner urban population is thinned out, moving people to the fringe and beyond the administrative boundary, inevitably fewer people will be asked to pay rates for an increasing range of regional facilities in the City Centre. As local government reorganisation does not seem likely to provide an effective rate base for the great cities there is a clear case for a more widely based system.

In the North East region the City will need to continue to give a major lead in the attempt to secure regional resurgence by providing opportunities for the expansion of the service sector work force and by increasing opportunities for the development of specialism in all fields within as attractive an environment as can be afforded.

It becomes increasingly important to avoid the application of standard solutions, particularly in view of the varying situation, size and economic circumstances of our cities. Particular concern is felt about the comparison drawn between London and the provincial capitals. Solutions devised for the national capital city in view of its unique circumstances and size rarely have relevance at provincial level, and yet it is quite remarkable how frequently those involved in advising central government see the need to apply blandly the London approach.

The planner must continue to develop his role in the field of corporate management and be prepared to involve himself deeply in the whole process of urban renewal whilst maintaining his professionalism. Closer integration must be achieved with highway and transportation engineers if effective traffic balance is to be not only achieved in our cities but maintained.

One of the main tasks for the 1970s will be to make the central city environment attractive and stimulating, not only as a market place and work place but as a place to enjoy as an art form in its own right. This has become possible now only because of the groundwork of the 1960s, which has given us new legislative tools for conservation and the creation of pedestrian walkways and precincts, and because of the construction of central motorways and an underground rapid transit system to shield the heart of the city from the effects of the motor vehicle.

Indeed the success of two decades of effort in renewing the City Centre may, given economic viability, be judged by many on the spatial and visual qualities of the new environment alone. Quality of materials and architectural detailing, scale and proportions of buildings and urban spaces, good landscaping and sunlight penetration, paving and street furniture, are all just as important in this context as the dramatic statement of a well placed tower or major work of engineering, or an exciting sculptural feature. The planner in his role of urban designer is the only person in a position to draw together and organise the diverse efforts of many other contributing designers into an attractive, convenient and enjoyable urban environment. To do this successfully is perhaps the greatest challenge of the future decade.

USES (land and floor space, '000 m²)	BIRMINGHAM 1950	1968	COVENTRY 1951	1971	198
Retailing	405	532	}61[1]	109[1]	I
Marketing & Warehousing	467	363			
Offices	539	938	23	102	
Public Buildings & Education	349	411	—	86	
Industry	599	231	—	44[2]	
Transportation Networks	76	252	—	192	
Residential	438	190	576[3]	371[3]	3
Open Spaces	83	74	14	16	
Other uses	158	339	—	—	—
Residential Population	14,333 (1951)	9,980 (1966)	1,870	1,280	—
Working Population	120,940 (1961)	108,570 (1966)	—	21,350	—
Land in Public Ownership (hectares)	—	933 (1971)	—	178	—

All figures relate to central area boundaries defined by each city
[1] Not including warehousing.
[2] Including warehousing.
[3] Numbers of dwellings.

Leicester 64 (land use only)	Liverpool 1961	1971	1981	Newcastle upon Tyne 1949	1963	1981
96	390	437	446	332	348	378
53	874	781	595	356	437	390
74	} 930	1,003	1,256	394	448	634
66				—	487	721
152	846	800	669	222	—	—
343	—	—	—	560	553	724[2]
92	493	430	558	273	235	99
9	84	139	186	202	202	303
36	—	—	—	—	—	—
—	21,489	13,813	12,498	10,363 (1951)	7,031 (1961)	3,870
—	130,000	150,000	158,000	—	—	—
245	202	—	—	168	457	705

235

References

Barlow, Sir M. (1940)   Report of the Royal Commission on the Distribution of the Industrial Population, Cmd. 6153, H.M.S.O.

Board of Trade (1963)   *Census of Distribution and other Services, 1961* (Report), H.M.S.O.

Briggs, A. (1952)   *History of Birmingham*, Oxford University Press.

Buchanan, C. (1963)   *Traffic in Towns* (Report of the Working Group to the Minister of Transport), H.M.S.O.

Burns, W. (1959)   *British Shopping Centres: new trends in layout and distribution*, Leonard Hill.

Burns, W. (1967)   *Newcastle: A study in replanning at Newcastle upon Tyne*, Leonard Hill.

Coventry City Council (1951)   *Coventry. The Development Plan.*

Coventry City Council (1963)   *Coventry City Region.*

Coventry City Council (1966)   *Review of the Development Plan.*

Coventry City Council (1966)   *People and Housing.*

Coventry City Council (1970)   *Traffic and Transport Plans.*

Coventry C.C., Solihull B.C. and Warwickshire C.C. (1971)   *A Strategy for the Sub Region* (Report of the Sub-Regional Planning Study).

Cowan, P. and others (1969)   *The Office: A Facet of Urban Growth*, Heinemann.

Esher, Viscount L. G. B. B.   *York: A Study in Conservation*, H.M.S.O.

Friend, J. K. and Jessop, W. N. (1967)   *Local Government and Strategic Choice*, Tavistock Publications.

Hall, P. (1968) in *Man in the City of the Future*, (Eds. R. Eells and C. Walton) Macmillan.

Hodgkinson, G. (1970)   *Sent to Coventry*, Robert Maxwell.

Jacobs, J. (1962)   *The Death and Life of Great American Cities*, Jonathan Cape.

Johnson-Marshall, P. (1965)   *Rebuilding Cities*, Edinburgh University Press.

Leicester City Council and Leicestershire County Council (1967)   Report and Recommendations of the Leicester and Leicestershire Sub-Regional Planning Study.

Lichfield, N. (1956)   *Economics of Planned Development*, Estates Gazette Ltd.

Liverpool City Council, City Centre Planning Group (1965)   *Liverpool City Centre Plan*.

Liverpool City Council (annually)   *City Centre Plan Review*.

Manchester University, Department of Town and Country Planning (1964)   Report on Regional Shopping Centres in North West England.

Marriot, O. (1967)   *The Property Boom*, Hamish Hamilton (1969 ed., Pan Books).

Merseyside Area Land Use and Transportation Study (1969)   Report by The Traffic Research Corporation to the Steering Committee on Merseyside Traffic and Transport.

Ministry of Town and Country Planning (1947)   *The Redevelopment of Central Areas*, H.M.S.O.

Ministry of Transport (1946)   *The Design and Layout of Roads in Central Areas*, H.M.S.O.

Ministry of Transport (1967)   *Cars for Cities*, H.M.S.O.

Mumford, L. (1964)   *The Highway and the City*, Secker & Warburg.

Newcastle upon Tyne, City and County of (1963)   *Development Plan Review*.

Patterson, A. T. (1954)   *Radical Leicester*, University College, Leicester.

Pevsner, N. and Wedgwood, A. (1966)   *Warwickshire*, the Buildings of England series, Penguin Books.

Planning Advisory Group (1965)   *The Future of Development Plans*, H.M.S.O.

Plowden, W. (1971)   *The motor car and politics 1896–1970*, Bodley Head.

Redcliffe-Maud, J. Lord (1969)   Report of the Royal Commission on Local Government in England, Cmnd 4040, H.M.S.O.

Scott, P. C., Lord Justice (1942)   Report of the Committee on Land Utilisation in Rural Areas, H.M.S.O.

Skeffington, A. M. (1969)   *People and Planning* (Report of the Committee on Public Participation in Planning), H.M.S.O.

Sitte, C. (1889)   *Die Stadt-Bauhach seinen Künstlerischen Grundsatzen*, Vienna.

Smeed, R. J. (1964)   *Road Pricing: the Economic and Technical Possibilities* (Report of a Panel set up by the Ministry of Transport), H.M.S.O.

Smigielski, W. K. (1964)   *Leicester Traffic Plan*, Leicester City Council.

Sutcliffe, A. (1970)   *The Autumn of Central Paris: the defeat of Town Planning, 1850–1970*, Edward Arnold.

Thomas, R. (1968)   *Journey to Work*, PEP Vol. XXXIV, No. 504.

Tyne Wear Plan Committee (1970 and 1972)   *Tyne Wear Plan: Land Use and Transportation Study for Tyneside and Wearside* (Report by Alan M. Vorhees and Associates Ltd. and Colin Buchanan and Partners to the Tyne Wear Plan Committee).

Uthwatt, A. A., Hon. Mr. Justice (1942)   Report of the Expert Committee on Compensation and Betterment. Cmd. 6386, H.M.S.O.

Webber, M. M. et al. (1964)   *Explorations into Urban Structure*, University of Pennsylvania.

West Midlands Regional Study (1971)   *A Developing Strategy for the West Midlands*, West Midland Regional Study, Birmingham.

Notes on Contributors

Francis J. C. Amos, CBE, BSc (Soc), DipArchSP, DipARIBA, PPRTPI
Mr. Amos is qualified in planning, architecture and sociology. He was President of The Royal Town Planning Institute, 1971–2, has been City Planning Officer, Liverpool, since 1966 and has recently been appointed Chief Executive, Birmingham. Has published numerous articles on planning and management (and recently chaired a Group at the Centre for Environmental Studies which led to the publication of a book, *Education for Planning*). Has served on advisory bodies to Government, and previously worked at Harlow New Town, the London County Council and the Ministry of Housing and Local Government; also advisor to the Ethiopian Government.

Neville Borg, DSc, CEng, FICE, FIMunE
Neville Borg was appointed in 1963, after a period as Deputy, to be City Engineer and Planning Officer of Birmingham (the last one, as it turned out). Earlier, he had initiated procedures for the earliest great programme of slum clearance and redevelopment in that city. He has been active in Professional Institutes, and in more recent years in a range of co-operative planning studies and proposals in the West Midlands Region and in the Conurbation.

Kenneth A. Galley, DipTP, FRTPI
Kenneth Galley has worked in Newcastle since 1960, first as Planning Policy Officer and since 1968 as City Planning Officer and a member of the City's officer management team. He previously worked in Sheffield and Doncaster. Is Secretary of the Technical Committee of the North Regional Planning Committee and has served at the Royal Town Planning Institute in various capacities.

Terence Gregory, OBE, FRIBA, FRICS, FRTPI
Terence Gregory was Coventry City Architect and Planning Officer from 1964–1973 and is now Chief Executive and Town Clerk. He has been Chairman of the Professional Services Board, Royal Institute of British Architects, a member of Council, Royal Town Planning Institute and studies advisor, National Economic Development Office, Ministry of Transport and Department of the Environment.

John C. Holliday, BA, FRTPI, FILA
John Holliday is head of the Department of Urban and Regional Planning at Lanchester Polytechnic, Coventry. He received his professional education in the new post war school of undergraduate planners at The University of Newcastle upon Tyne; has worked in planning and landscape design in government and local government in the U.K. and abroad; published various articles and been active in education policy on the Council and committees of The Royal Town Planning Institute.

W. Konrad Smigielski, IngArch, FRTPI
Born in Poland where he took degrees in architecture at Cracow and Warsaw Universities; in 1946 became Professor of Town Planning, Polish University College, London and in 1952, Head of School of Town Planning, Leeds College of Art. In 1962 appointed first City Planning Officer, Leicester, leaving in 1972 to become a planning consultant. Won second prize in an international competition for London roads in 1959.

Index

Page numbers in italics are references to illustrations

Abercrombie, Patrick 7, 8
Amos, Francis J. C. 17, 18, 21
Architecture, values and movements 6, 21

Barlow Report 5, 6, 91
Barratt, Sir Charles 98
Bassett-Green, William 110, 112
Berry, Granville 97
Betterment levy 9
Birmingham 30–77
  Aston Expressway 65–66
  Aston University 61–65
  Bull Ring 16
  car parking 15, 68
  central area functions 41–42, 71–73
    1834 *35*, 41
    1971 *40*
  central area road plan 13, *63*
  city centre, old and new 37–41
  Civic Centre plan 76
  Colmore Row conservation issue 19,
    57–61, *75*
  conurbation 31, 34
  Corporation Street 43, 50, 71
  employment 73
  history and growth 31–41
  industry 36, 39
  inner ring road 13, 14, 18, *32*, 51–57
  investment in central area 71
  land in public ownership 38
  land use statistics 72
  local government and planning function
    42–48, 66–67

Birmingham (cont.)
  New Street Station 16, *47*, 70
  office accommodation 72
  offices in Calthorpe Estate 14, 72
  Paradise Circus 59, *62*, 76
  pedestrians, facilities for 20, 67, 68, 69, 70
  post-war redevelopment *63*
  public opinion on redevelopment 48–50,
    67, 68
  rateable value and ownership 74
  shops and shopping 33, 36, 39, 67, 68,
    70, 71, 72–73
  slum clearance 41, 72
  Smallbrook Ringway 16, *62*
  traffic problems 51, 52, 53, 67, 68, 69,
    73–74
  transportation 38, 39, 52, 67, 68, 73–74
  Victoria Square 60, 61
Birmingham Corporation Act, 1946 55, 58
Bor, Walter 1, 183, 186, 199, 203
Borg, Neville 19
Braddock, Alderman J. 182
Bradshaw, Derek 209–211
Briggs, Asa 2, 42
Bristol 10
Browne, Kenneth 7, 151
Buchanan Report 14, 22, 23
Building
  modern materials and techniques 10, 14,
    27
    road construction 14
  post-war control of 9, 10
Burns, Wilfred 1, 15, 209–211, 220

Cadbury, George 6

Car parking 15

Central areas
  continuing vitality 28–29
  decline in populations 17, 18, 21, 24
  planning problems 3–7, 12
  see also under the names of cities

Central government
  control of planning system 8, 28
  grants and subsidies 16, 19

Chamberlain, Joseph 5, 31, 37, 38, 43
Chamberlain, Neville 51
Chamberlin, Peter 164
City centre, model guide for planners 6–7
Civic Amenities Act, 1967 24, 110, 168,
  227–228
Civic design 13, 14
Civic Trust, formation of 15, 18–19
Clayton, John 208
Clean Air Act, 1956 114
Compensation 5–6, 9
Comprehensive development area 6, 13
Compulsory purchase 8, 16
  powers of local authorities 6
Conservation 14, 18, 21, 22, 24, 26
Control of Office and Industrial Development
  Act, 1965 107
Controls, planning 8, 28
Cotton, Joseph 10, 76
Council houses 8

Coventry 78–134
  Broadgate 86, 87, 112, 131
  car parking 15, 23, 92, 102, 104–105,
    119, 123
  Cathedral 88, 107, *111*, 112, 129
  Civic Centre 87–88, 124, 129
  Corporation Street 82
  "Coventry of Tomorrow" exhibition 88
  Development Plan (1951) 93, 102, *106*,
    118
  Development Plan (1957) *109*
    Review (1972) *115*, 118, 123, *132*
  education buildings 113
  employment 83, 107, 128
  entertainment 102, 105, 113, 131
  financial aspects of redevelopment 94–96,
    108, 120, 123, 127
  Gibson plan (1941) 89–90, *95*, *101*
  grants 91–92
  Hertford Street 89, 104, 112, *119*
  historic buildings 108–110
  history and growth 78–83
  Holy Trinity 110, *111*, 112, 131
  hotel and catering provision 102, 108
  inner ring road 13, 14, 18, 23, 82, 89,
    92, 113, 120, *130*
  industry and commerce 86, 87, 102–108,
    127
  Lady Godiva's statue 112
  Lanchester Polytechnic *111*, 116, 124
  land owned by local authority 93–94, 123
  land uses 86, 89, 93, 107, 127
  Lower Precinct *95*

Coventry (cont.)
  local government and administration
    94–101, 129
  motor industry 80
  new building technology 116–118
  office accommodation 102, 107, 124
  pedestrians, facilities for 20, 87, 88, 89,
    92, 103–104, 124
  population 83, 99
  public interest in redevelopment 87,
    88, 99–101, 110, 118
  rateable value 107
  residential area 113
  route centre 79, *81*
  shops and shopping 87, 94, *95*, 102, 103–
    104, 105, 129, 131
  slum clearance 82
  Smithford Street 87, 89
  Spon Street 19, 108, 110, *111*
  sub-region, role in 98–99, 116, 128
  traffic problems 86, 88, 92, 99, 114, 120,
    133
  Traffic and Transport Plan (1970) 121–123
  Trinity Street 82
  transportation 92, 99, 114–115, 121, 129
  war damage 17, 86, 87, 88
Coventry City Region 99
Cowan, Peter 26
Cullen, Gordon 7

Design and Layout of Roads in Built-up Areas 7,
  11
Design considerations 21, 25
Development plans required by 1947 Act 8,
  12
Dick, Sir William Reid 112
Dobson, John 208

Eccles, Sir David 112
Economic factors 8, 9, 25–26, 27
Education Acts 38
Esher, Lord 25
Exeter 10

Floor space index 10, 12–13
Ford, Ernest 82, 83, 88, 89, 97
Friend, J. K. 15, 98

Gibson, Sir Donald 1, 17, 83, 88, 89, 90, 97
Goodby, Alderman H. E. 53
Gracie, J. J. 64
Grainger, Richard 208
Grey, Alderman Arthur 211, 230

Hall, Peter 26
Halliwell, Alderman 82
Harris, Frank 212
Hartley, Jesse 199
Hender, Derrick 98
Herbert, Sir Alfred 82, 112
Hodgkinson, Alderman George 17, 82, 87,
  96

Housing 8, 22, 24, 25
Housing Acts 5, 196, 212
  1959 212
  1968 196
Housing and Local Government, Ministry
  of 9
Howard, Ebenezer 6
Hull 8
Humphries, H. H. 39, 52
Hunt, Joseph 64
Hyams, H. 198, 199

Iliffe, Lord 90
Industry, relocation away from central areas
  20
Inge, W.P. 58

Jacobs, Jane 22
Jacobsen, Prof. Arne 213, 223, 224
Jessup, W. N. 15, 98
Johnson-Marshall, Percy 17, 88

Kennet, Lord 168
Kingston upon Hull 8

Lancaster, Alderman M. L. 39
Land acquisition and market values 8, 9
  grants for 9
Land uses 12, 14, 20
  changes in location 14, 20
Le Corbusier 6, 7, 10
Legislation, planning and public health 4–5,
  6, 8, 36
Leicester 135–174
  car parking 15, 140, 142, 144, 154, 160
  Castle Gardens 168
  Cathedral precinct 168
  central "areas", defined 152
  central area plan 13
  central ring road 13, 18, 142, 145
  city planning officer, appointment of 13
  Civic Centre 163–166, 167
  civic design, balanced 21
  Clock Tower area 149, 152, 154, 161, 162
  commercial centre 151, 161
  conservation 145, 166–172
  Development Plan (1952) 139
  employment 138
  entertainment 161, 162
  Gallowtree Gate 149, 150, 154
  geographical location 138
  Haymarket scheme 161, 162
  historic buildings 144, 145, 151, 166
  history and growth 144–145
  hotel accommodation 160
  industry 138, 144
  local government and administration
    148–149
  Loseby Lane area 158
  Market Square 16, 19, 149, 152, 154–158,
    159, 170, 173
  Master Plan 151–154

Leicester (cont.)
  New Walk 168, 169, 171–172
  park-and-ride 23, 142, 144
  pedestrian movement 20, 142, 144, 150,
    154, 160, 161
  population 138, 140, 144
  public attitude to redevelopment 135
  St. Nicholas Circle and Newarke 160–161,
    164
  shops and shopping 16, 138, 147, 148,
    158
  Southgate intersection 143
  Town Hall square 145, 149, 152, 167,
    168, 170–171
  traffic 13, 14, 139–144, 154
  transportation 23, 142, 144
Lichfield, Nathaniel 9, 25
Ling, Arthur 1, 18, 97, 104
Liverpool 175–206
  Albert Dock area 198–199
  car parking 15, 186, 191, 194, 196
  central area plan 13, 183, 198, 199
  Chapel Street 184
  city planning officer, appointment of 13,
    183
  Civic and Social Centre 197–198
  commercial activity 175–176, 187–190
  compensation for compulsory purchase
    190, 191
  conservation 19, 200
  Cook Street/North John Street 184
  development plans 203–204
  employment 176, 187, 198, 199
  history and growth 175–181
  housing 176, 180, 195–197
  industry 190
  inner ring road 13, 18, 181, 182, 191,
    194, 200, 203
  land uses 189, 192, 193
  local government and administration
    182–187, 204
  markets 187–188
  Mersey Docks and Harbour Board 177
  Merseyside Area Land Use and
    Transportation Study 186, 191, 194
  office accommodation, high rise 201
  pedestrian movement 20, 184, 195
  Polytechnic 197
  population 176, 177
  port 175, 176, 177, 178, 179, 198–199
  private investment 181, 205
  public interest in redevelopment 199
  St. John's Precinct 16, 185, 202
  shops and shopping 181, 188–190
  technical innovation 201–203
  traffic 180, 181, 186, 191
  underground rail loop 23
  warehouses 198–199
Local Authorities Land Act, 1963 92
Local government
  attitudes of local planning authorities 14
  councillors 21

Local Government (cont.)
 planning departments and officers 8, 17
 reform of, in England and Wales 28
 see also sub-entry "local government, etc."
 under the names of cities
Local Government Act, 1972 8
London property speculators 10

Macmorran, J. L. 55
Manzoni, Sir Herbert J. 1, 5, 17, 39, 52, 76
Marriot, Oliver 10, 16
Matthew, Sir Robert 213
Maud Report 211
Maudsley, J. A. 76
Motor car
 increase in use of 5, 11, 15, 23
 planning for, in cities 11, 12, 14
 taxation of private vehicles, proposals 23
Motorways 11, 65
Mumford, Lewis 11, 28–29, 128, 166
Municipal Corporations Act, 1835 34

Newcastle upon Tyne 207–233
 All Saints office precinct 230–232
 car parking 15
 central area plan 13, 211–212, 220
 city engineer 18–19
 city planning officer, appointment of 13,
  19
 civic design 21
 commercial growth 208
 conservation 227–230
 Development Plan Review 216
 Dobson and Grainger 208
 economic decline 209
 Eldon Square redevelopment 19, *218,*
  223, 224–227
 Grey Street 208, *210*
 historic buildings 227, 228
 history and growth 207–209
 housing 209, 211–212
 industry and commerce 216, 219
 inner ring road 13
 land uses *217*
 local government organisation 209–213
 markets, relocation of 219
 Maud Report (1967) 211
 motorway system 221
 office accommodation 220
 Old Town Hall *226,* 228
 pedestrian movement 20, *217,* 220, 223–
  224
 planning authorities in Tyne/Wear
  216–219
 population 207
 public interest in redevelopment 215–216
 redevelopment schemes 211–212
 riverside area 220, 230–232
 Royal Arcade 18–19
 shops and shopping 208, 219–220,
  222–224

Newcastle upon Tyne (cont.)
 traffic 209, 220, 221
 transportation 213, 220, 221, 222
 Tyne Bridge 208
 Tyneside conurbation 207
 university and polytechnic 221, 222
 Victorian "new town" 17, 18–19, 208,
  210

Offices
 building 10, 15
 different functions 26–27
 problems of forecasting needs 15

Parr, Percy 209
Pedestrian movement, planning for 14
People and Housing (Coventry) 99
Percy Report 64
Pevsner, Sir Nikolaus 112, 128
Planning authorities 15
 establishment of planning departments 8
 relations with private enterprise 15, 16
 stipulations on developers' schemes 16
Plowden Report 23
Plymouth 10
Political attitudes to planning 15, 17, 22
Population decrease in central areas 24
Private investment 6, 10, 11, 15, 16, 20
Property, change in ownership, use and
 construction 17, 20
Public transport 23, 29

Rayman, Nathan 97
Redcliffe-Maud Report 213
Redevelopment of Central Areas, The 6–7, 8
Rehabilitation of old buildings 21, 22
Reith, Lord 91
Richards, Alderman Gilbert 97
Road building 5, 7
 advances in construction technique 14
Robbins Report 64

Sandys, Duncan 18
Scott, Sir Giles Gilbert 2, 112
Scott Report 5
Sefton, Alderman W. H. 182
Seifert, Colonel 198
Shankland, Graeme 1, 182–186, 198, 199,
 201, 202
Sharp, Thomas 7
Sheppard Fidler, A. G. 61, 76
Sheridan-Shedden, J. R. 76
Shop building 5, 10, 11
 hypermarkets and out-of-town centres 22,
  25, 26
 land allocation for 15
 re-investment in central areas 25, 26
Skeffington Report 22
Silk, Councillor J. C. 60
Sitte, Camillo 7
Slum clearance 5, 6, 22, 24
Smeed, R. J. 23

Smigielski, W. Konrad 16, 17, 21, 170
Smith, Councillor T. Dan 209
Social habits, changing 18, 27, 28
Society for the Promotion of Urban Renewal
  15
Spence, Sir Basil 112, 213
Stilgoe, H. E. 51
Stringer, Alderman Sidney 82, 96
Sutcliffe, Anthony 24
Szadurski, Leon 21

Thomas, Ray 73
Tower building, influence of Le Corbusier
  6, 7, 10
Town and Country Planning Acts 5, 20
  1932 86
  1944 5, 41, 66, 91, 92
  1947 5, 6, 7–8, 58, 72, 92, 166
    financial provisions abandoned 9
    floor space index (sch. 3) 10
    grants to local authorities 9
    provision for public inquiry 8
  1959 92
  1962 92
  1968 44, 66, 108, 133, 139, 168, 203, 230
  1971 44

Town and Country Planning, Ministry of 6
Traffic problems 7, 11, 13, 14, 20, 23
Transport Acts
  1968 116
  1969 222
Transport, Ministry of 7, 9, 23
Transportation 22, 29
Trustram Eve, J. D. 158

Uthwatt Report 5–6

Venables, Peter 64

War damage 9, 17, 86, 87, 88
Warwickshire, relation of Coventry to 99
Watkinson, Harold 56
Webber, M. M. 28
West Midlands Planning Authorities
  Conference 99
Wilson, Colin St. John 198
Wiltshire, Sir Frank 54

York, conservation study 25–26